THE BEST OF
MEDICAL HUMOR

THE BEST OF
MEDICAL HUMOR

A collection of articles, essays, poetry, and letters published in the medical literature

COMPILED AND EDITED BY

HOWARD J. BENNETT, M.D.

ASSOCIATE PROFESSOR OF HEALTH CARE SCIENCES AND PEDIATRICS

ASSOCIATE DIRECTOR, PEDIATRIC PRIMARY CARE RESIDENCY PROGRAM

THE GEORGE WASHINGTON UNIVERSITY SCHOOL OF MEDICINE AND HEALTH SCIENCES, WASHINGTON, D.C.

HANLEY & BELFUS, Inc.

Publisher: HANLEY & BELFUS
                    210 S. 13th Street
                    Philadelphia, PA 19107

North American and worldwide sales and distribution:

                    MOSBY-YEAR BOOK, INC.
                    11830 Westline Industrial Drive
                    St. Louis, MO 63146

In Canada: Times Mirror Professional Publishing, Ltd.
                    130 Flaska Drive
                    Markham, Ontario L6G 1B8
                    Canada

The Best of Medical Humor   ISBN 1-56053-003-0

Library of Congress Catalog Card Number 90-85031

Last digit is the print number: 9 8 7 6 5

For my parents,
who taught me to look things up

and

For Jan,
who smiles at me when I do

CONTENTS

MEDICAL SCHOOL

INTERNSHIP & RESIDENCY

ACADEMIA

MEDICAL LANGUAGE

WRITING & PUBLISHING

POETRY

CASE REPORTS

RESEARCH

SURGEONS & OTHER SPECIALISTS

CONTENTS

MENTAL HEALTH HUMOR

INFORMED CONSENT & OTHER COMPLICATIONS OF HEALTH CARE

THE PHYSICIAN AT WORK

ODDS & ENDS

APPENDIX

✻   ✻   ✻

ACKNOWLEDGMENTS

I would like to thank the following people, all of whom gave of their time to help me put this book together.

Richard Riegelman, M.D. who made a number of helpful suggestions and whose optimism convinced me that my efforts would qualify as "scholarly activity."

Anne Linton who helped me sidestep my computer illiteracy by doing all of my on-line searches.

Heather Combs-Potter, Barry Kolodkin, George Paul, and Margaret Bunnell who helped me obtain many of the old books and articles I needed to review.

Cassandra Allen and other staff members at the National Library of Medicine who made certain aspects of my research much easier than they otherwise might have been.

Marguerite Fallucco who found material in the archives of the American Medical Association which was not available in any other library.

Marie Stahl, P.N.P., Michael Ross, M.D., and Ellie Hamburger, M.D. for helping me decide whether to include certain articles when, after the twentieth reading, nothing seemed funny to me anymore.

A special thanks to Judith Ratner, M.D. whose sense of humor and moral support were a source of inspiration throughout the book's long gestation.

And finally, to all of the authors who have written medical humor over the years. Without their efforts, a book of this kind would never have been possible.

INTRODUCTION

I got the idea for this book approximately four years ago. It was a Monday afternoon, and I was sitting in my office after a reasonably productive encounter with my filing system. Having never been schooled in efficient paper management, I usually approach this task like a child eating spinach: there are new piles every few minutes, but nothing disappears. On this particular day, however, things went smoothly. I placed a number of articles from my temporary into my permanent files and then refilled the temporary file with articles that had been blocking sunlight from the southeast corner of my desk.

It was during this last maneuver that I ran into Nancy Caroline and Harold Schwartz's article: "Chicken Soup Rebound and Relapse of Pneumonia: Report of a Case" (see p. 99). I had recently copied the article for one of my medical students and, as usual, had tossed it on my desk instead of placing it back in its folder. I reread the article, now probably for the tenth time, and laughed almost as hard as the first time I had seen it. It was and still is a marvelous parody on the case report.

After I put the article back in its folder, I began wondering how many times I had copied it for students and residents. Although it was always well received, to the best of my recollection no one ever told me they had seen the article before. Was this really true? Was it possible that Mrs. Caroline and I were the only ones handing out copies of her daughter's article? And if that was true, what about other articles that had been published over the years? Was it possible that all medical humor was destined to obscurity?

In order to test my hypothesis, I set up a prospective study that same day. I administered a verbal questionnaire to the junior medical students in my clinic (with a 100% response rate) and found out that none of them had heard of Dr. Caroline's paper. A second study with our attendings revealed that 20% knew of the article, but only one could quote any of the references by heart (Bennett, unpublished disappointment). In both groups, however, over 99% said a collection of medical humor would liven up a doctor's otherwise drab and sagging bookshelves. It was at this point that I decided to search the literature to find out if such a project was feasible.

A book is a large undertaking, however, even one that collects previously published material; therefore, a number of questions needed to be considered before I began:

1. How would I go about researching such an unusual topic? If I did a computer search using words like **humor** and **laughter**, would articles on the vitreous humor and gelastic seizures be cited? (Yes, on both accounts.)

2. Had a fair amount of humor been published in the past or would the manuscript end up being the thinnest volume ever submitted for publication?

3. Would the book encourage more editors to see the value of humor and, as a result, increase the space allotted for such writing? Might such a change in editorial policy jeopardize the future of medical research?

4. Is it possible the book would have a profound effect on the sense of humor of our profession as a whole? If that occurred, would it eliminate stereotypes that have developed over the centuries, thereby leaving nothing to parody from now on?

5. Would the book qualify for Category I CME credit?

6. Is it possible the book would influence the style of medical practice such that doctors might begin charging patients for dispensing humor in the office? Would insurance companies provide appropriate reimbursement for services rendered? And finally, would standards of practice develop such that doctors might open themselves up to possible litigation?

LAWYER: Why do you want to sue Dr. Bennett?

PATIENT: His jokes make me sick.

As you can see, this was tricky stuff. Nevertheless, the idea seemed like a good one, so I went ahead despite the possible consequences for the future.

The research itself turned out to be a lot of fun. I began by searching the "Wit & Humor" heading of *Index Medicus* and then moved on to additional data bases in allied health and nursing, medical history, and others. Despite my attempts at an organized approach, the indexing of medical humor has been uneven; consequently, much of my time was spent paging through non-indexed journals, tracking down references, and following up other leads. After 12 months, I was convinced there was enough quality material to put the collection together. In addition, I was surprised by the diversity of humor that had been published over the years.

Medical humor has appeared in a wide range of journals, from those of international reputation, to smaller specialty journals, to "throwaways." The humor itself has varied from jokes, cartoons, and anecdotes to articles, essays, and poetry. Those areas targeted for humor have varied as well, including medical school and residency, research, medical language, academia, writing and publishing, and clinical practice. Although the authors have primarily been physicians, medical humor has also been written by nurses, PhDs, and occasionally even by lay people.

As the collection grew, I began to notice certain trends in the publication of medical humor. While some journals published humor frequently, others avoided the area completely. Not surprisingly, the more prestigious journals published humor less often and usually accepted material of shorter length. For example, I am only aware of three such publications in *Chest* and while *The New England Journal of Medicine* has published a large number of poems and short pieces, these have generally been restricted to its correspondence section. Longer does not necessarily mean better, however, as some of the funniest pieces I discovered were published in *The New England Journal of Medicine*.

The most conspicuous absence, however, was in the area of mental health. Although my literature search turned up a bevy of articles on the use of humor in psychotherapy, I only uncovered a handful of humorous articles in psychiatric journals and only one of these was selected for the book. To remedy this situation, I have stretched my definition of the term "medical literature" by including articles published in *The Journal of Irreproducible Results* and *The Journal of Polymorphous Perversity* (see appendix). While these are not medical journals per se, they are geared to a professional audience and therefore I decided to bend the rules a little to balance the collection.

The type of humor published has also varied between journals. Cartoons, anecdotes, and articles dealing with clinical practice have appeared most commonly in journals like *Medical Economics*. On the other hand, the bulk of what I call "academic humor" has been published in the major journals and ones geared to students and residents. This trend obviously reflects editorial policy and the perceived interests of the readers.

Humorous medical poetry was the most difficult material to find because it is not well indexed and, as a general rule, turned up irregularly in journals. The one exception to this rule is a column called "The Medical Muse," which was published in *Postgraduate Medicine* from 1951 to 1972. The column appeared in almost every issue over a 20-year period and covered a wide range of topics. Interestingly, the poems were all written by the same person, a professor of English literature named Richard Armour.

Although poor indexing limited my ability to search the literature before 1960, it appears as though time has been an important factor in the publication of medical humor. For example, I found more sexist material in the 1950s and 1960s than recently, which undoubtedly reflects changes in our society as a whole. Also, many journals have changed their focus over the last two decades with regards to what and how much medical humor they publish.

The journal which has shown the greatest change over time is *JAMA*. Except for an occasional letter or essay with a light or satiric touch, *JAMA* has not published much humor in the last 20 years. In the past, things were different. Between 1903 and 1968, the journal ran four separate columns that featured cartoons, jokes, anecdotes, poetry, and satire. The names of these columns were: "Tonics & Sedatives" (1903–1962), "The Bright Side" (1954–1961), "Smile A While" (1961–1968), and "Satire" (1960–1968). While the latter two columns featured medical humor almost exclusively, "Tonics & Sedatives" and "The Bright Side" also presented humor with a more general appeal. Unfortunately, these columns (like many others) were published in the journal's advertising pages. As a result, they have not been preserved in most libraries because advertisements are usually discarded in the process of binding journals. In addition to the four columns just mentioned, from 1964 to 1973 *JAMA* published a special issue each April that was called "The Book Number." Although the regular format was included, the issue featured articles on nontechnical aspects of medicine such as medical history, the illnesses of famous people, and that loosely defined area, "Literature and Medicine." Mixed in with these articles was a small sampling of medical humor and satire.

By the time I finished my research, I surpassed my initial expectations and had reviewed over 800 articles and many more short pieces. I next set about the task of molding this material into shape. Although I enjoy cartoons, jokes, and anecdotes as much as anyone, I decided to exclude these from the book. Not only would it be difficult to adequately search for the best in this genre, but collections of this type have been done before. The one exception I made was to include some pearls by Gary Larson, lest we forget that the medical literature is not the only source of humor poked in our direction.

In terms of style, the main issue I considered was that of humor versus satire. Although what distinguishes these two approaches can become blurred at times, satire more often relies on sarcasm to make its point. I was more interested in humor because of its general appeal and because it is more appropriate for a collection of this sort. In those instances where I did include satire, it was because the authors made their point so deftly and with such charm that they fit in with the rest of the book. Finally, because some humor is best left in the classroom, I made a conscious effort to exclude material that was overtly sexist or offensive in character.

In the final analysis, each selection had to fulfill two requirements. First, it had to say something about medicine, its clients, or its practitioners. And second, it had to make me laugh. Sometimes it was a deep, bellowing laugh like the ones reserved for Mark Twain or Woody Allen. At other times, it was the smile of recognition or a gentle laugh like the ones evoked by E.B. White or Garrison Keiller. Although I rejected a lot of older material, a number of authors have shown how durable an article can be if it is well done. The oldest piece in the book is a letter published in 1884 by none other than William Osler himself—under the pseudonym Egerton Yorrick Davis. Finally, it was not uncommon to find two articles on the same subject and, in such cases, I usually chose the best one. In some instances I kept both because each one addressed the issue from a different point of view.

The book is divided into chapters to provide a framework for the variety of humor published over the years. Some chapters are shorter than others, which reflects the amount of material published in those areas and is not due to any bias on my part. For each selection, the author's name is presented with the title and a full citation is listed on the opening page. Selections that were published in a journal's advertising pages are designated with a capital "A" before the page number (e.g., A148). These references reveal a little bit about the history of medical humor by documenting which journals published what type of material. They also serve as a kind of road map for prospective authors concerning where their material might be accepted for publication. Each chapter concludes with a section called "Additional Readings" that provides annotated references for material not included in the book. Most of these references are for articles that were not quite funny enough to be selected but will be of interest to certain readers. The rest are for books that deal with the subject area of the chapter. The final section of the book is an appendix that contains information on additional books and journals of interest and a list of serious articles on the subject area of "Humor and Medicine."

Some people will undoubtedly read the book and notice the absence of their favorite article. As mentioned before, the research was difficult at times, and it is possible that I overlooked some publications. To any offended readers (or authors) I herewith apologize for my oversight. Please send me your neglected material so I can review it for the next edition.

Having now briefly discussed the history of medical humor and how the book was developed, it seems prudent to ask two final questions: What is the point of putting this collection together, and what are its goals?

First, in this age of increasingly sophisticated health care, it is important for physicians to be able to laugh at themselves and to retain a degree of humility about their profession. Contrary to popular opinion, doctors do have a sense of humor, and many editors have devoted valuable space in their journals to show this. Also, by providing a humorous look at the imperfections and oddities in medicine, the book reveals a human side of the profession that often gets lost in its technical writings.

Second, the book not only preserves the best articles in this area, but also facilitates the use of humor in health care and teaching by pulling them together in one source. As an author of medical humor, I have received many letters telling me that my articles have been used in teaching rounds and case conferences, in journal clubs, and even to help relax prospective residency applicants. In my own practice, I use medical humor in lectures, to encourage the discussion of clinical issues, and to balance the serious material trainees and staff are required to read. Humor can teach, albeit from a different point of view than we are generally used to.

Third, although the book's primary goal is not to teach people to be funny, it may encourage health care workers to see the value of humor in day-to-day practice. Although there are few studies that document the importance of humor in medicine, it is intuitive that such a connection exists.

"Whatever its origins, humor is enjoyable. We delight in those people who can laugh at the incongruities in themselves or in the world around them."

from "Humor and the Surgeon" by R. Dale Liechty, MD
Archives of Surgery 1987; 122:519

By sharing a moment of humorous insight, one can reduce the emotional distance between physician and patient and, in so doing, improve communication and mutual understanding. There are those, of course, who would argue that humor has no place in medicine (or in medical writing). To these individuals I would just say that all humor requires timing and must be used in appropriate circumstances. Like any other drug or intervention, the beneficial effects should be weighed against the risks.

"In the undefined Good Old Days, a quality known as bedside manner was held to be important to the success of the physician. Then, the good doctor was knowing, sensitive, and above all, good-humored . . . Humor, like love is indefinable and yet is found to be important for establishing good relationships with patients, particularly the old and the young."

from "The Sense of Humor—Art & Science" Editorial,
JAMA 1970; 212:1696

So sit back and enjoy the book. Most of us will see ourselves in its pages and hopefully will get a good laugh at who we are and what we do to earn our living every day.

Howard J. Bennett, M.D.

MEDICAL
SCHOOL

As long as there are medical students, there will never be a shortage of medical school humorists. Between the jokes, the stories, and the impersonations, no one is safe from their irreverent eyes. And if that isn't enough, each spring medical students put on their annual follies where they dance, sing, and perform their way into our hearts (or should that be through our hearts?). In one memorable skit from a few years ago, the students at George Washington did a take-off on *The Wizard of Oz*. In their version, however, there was a psychiatrist in search of a heart, an internist in search of courage, and a surgeon in search of a brain. Needless to say, it brought the house down.

Despite all of the creativity that goes into these events, medical students rarely publish humor. Perhaps this is because they are still test-takers instead of paper-writers. Or because the medicinal value of humor is best when performed live instead of through hammering it out on a page. Either way, most of the articles in this chapter were written by physicians. The one exception is the article by Anne Eva Ricks which she published as a fourth year student. This was obviously a telling sign, however, as Dr. Ricks went on to write the successful *Official M.D. Handbook* (see appendix).

Final page of the Medical Boards

The Medical School Interview*

ERIC A. RAVITZ, D.O.

"Why do you want to become a physician, young man?"

"I really want to help people. Ever since I was a child, I can remember wanting to be a doctor. Watching Ben Casey and Dr. Kildare on television confirmed my desires, and no other occupation has ever entered my mind . . . . Well, yes, as a matter of fact, I have applied to dental and podiatry schools and graduate programs in anthropology, genetics, and business administration."

"Would you settle in a rural, underserved area?"

"Oh, yes, definitely. I've always wanted to help people in need in locations where no one else wants to work. I think the lack of medical support, facilities,

*Reprinted with permission from Postgraduate Medicine, ©1985; 78(2):100–102.

and colleagues with whom to exchange views would be especially challenging, and as far as my family goes, well, there was life before shopping malls. Besides, I look forward to the invigorating experience of being on call 24 hours a day, seven days a week. My family won't need me."

"Why did you apply to this school?"

"Don't let my December suntan fool you. Since I was a child, I've dreamed about coming to medical school in the northern Midwest. I've always been fascinated by frigid cold and blowing snow, and I'm anxious to learn what such weather feels like and how the hearty, salt-of-the-earth midwesterner survives. I want to be a part of that culture. I figure that instead of jogging on the beach and plunging into the ocean afterward, I can cross-country ski to school for exercise. By the way, your school has a wonderful reputation in southern California. I understand that the local airline has three nonstop flights daily to Los Angeles . . . ."

And so it goes, another medical school interview successfully completed, another candidate accurately chosen. But what about some of the more pointed questions that might be asked during the interview?

"Do you like girls?"

"Well, ah, yes. I mean no. I mean yes, of course!" (I really blew it now. This trick question was intended to evoke "Hell no, medicine is my one and only love. I live, eat, and breathe medicine. I have no time for girls.")

"Do you like Oklahoma?"

"You bet, sir. Ever since I was a child, I've thought of no other place in which to live and practice medicine. Give me that good red dust any time. I just love Olkahomans too. My granddaddy traveled through Oklahoma one time . . . ."

"No, son, I meant the Sooners football team."

"Ah, well, actually I have been following USC and UCLA for many years. Don't you just love John McKay? . . . I guess I could learn to love the Sooners."

"I have a letter of recommendation here that says you are intelligent and athletic and that you make a good appearance," the interviewer says with a chuckle. "Is that true?"

"Well, I would like to think my reference knows what he is talking about. He is a distinguished, well-known, best-selling novelist."

"Oh really? If he doesn't write for *Sports Illustrated* or the *Wall Street Journal*, I've never heard of him."

Would an interview accomplish more if it went as follows?

"So, while you were out of school you worked as a singing waiter at Luigi's Pizzeria on Fisherman's Wharf. How does that help qualify you to be a physician?"

"Well, sir, I met a lot of people and discovered that I'm a people person. I enjoy people, even with their complaints. (Luigi's pizza wasn't the best.) It was a challenge to put a smile on a customer's face. I think I want to be a gastroenterologist."

"Do you have any other interests or talents?"

"I paint."

"Oh, what? Houses?"

"No sir, oils and watercolors. I've sold some of my work at a hometown gallery, too. As a matter of fact, since I don't have kids, I carry pictures of my paintings in my wallet. Would you like to see them?"

"Sure, son, let's have a look. Hmm, very good. Quite creative. I see that you like Picasso and Matisse. Do you think you can be this creative in your work as a physician?"

"If you folks on the committee are creative enough to give me the chance, I'll sure try."

How to Survive
a Case Presentation*

HOWARD J. BENNETT, M.D.

Since the dawn of modern medical education, nearly two thousand years ago, students[1] of medicine have been faced with the delicate and unenviable task of collecting clinical information and presenting it to their attendings. History records that the first case presentation occurred in the year 174 AD when a 12-year-old intern roused Galen at 2:00 AM with the report of a slothful innkeeper who was choking on the jawbone of an ass. Galen correctly diagnosed an acute phlegmatic incarceration based on the history alone (hence the sanctity of the medical history) and dispatched the lad with the appropriate treatment.[2] Practitioners soon began priding themselves on their ability to arrive at diagnoses by reason alone, without the need of patients.[3] As the knowledge of disease and pathophysiology grew, so did the number of questions one could ask about a patient's case. As noted by Pimph (the **h** is silent) in his treatise on the case presentation, "Whether or not my questions have anything to do with the patient's disease is irrelevant."[4] Pimph's doctrine was quickly adopted by most prestigious medical schools, and the era of rounding on patients was soon at hand.[5]

Thus began the long history of having to contend with finding an appropriate response to the inquiries of overzealous, egotistical, and shortsighted professors. Being pimphed, as it came to be called, was a dreaded fear of all medical students, compelling them to stay up nights studying instead of attending the needs of their spouses. An example of the far-reaching implications of this difficult lifestyle can be found in a famous case of adultery that was widely publicized in the nineteenth century.[6] It was inevitable, however, that this system would eventually break down, and reports began to appear in the medical literature of ommissions and frank fabrications in the presentation of clinical information.[7] These practices went unchecked for years until the publication of Quibble's monumental study on the psychology of case presentations and the institutional

hierarchy established therein (Table 1).[8] As a result of Quibble's work, pimphing became less fashionable, although it is still rumored to be practiced somewhere in New England.

Managing Case Presentations

Managing a case presentation, of course, involves more than just reciting clinical information to your attending. It is an acquired skill, much like salivating to the dinner bell, that is passed on from generation to generation. In order to fully master the case presentation, you must first understand its structure. Fortunately, this topic has recently been reviewed, with particular attention to a new approach developed by Peeve.[9] As noted in Figure 1, Peeve's approach stands head and shoulders above the old system. Once the organization of the case presentation is understood, it is only a matter of

Table 1—Quibble's Classification of Case Presentors

The Medical Student:	Presents too much information, only half of which is relevant, and does not know what any of it means.
The Intern:	Obtains most of the information and probably knows what some of it means, but falls asleep presenting it.
The Resident:	Presents all of the information and knows what most of it means, but prefers arguing about the night call schedule.
The Chief Resident:	Obtains all of the information and knows what all of it means, but is too busy making out schedules to present it.
The Research Professor:	Has forgotten what a case presentation is, but will find a reference on it and get back to you.
The Clinical Professor:	Could obtain all of the information if he wanted to, but prefers to have others do it for him. Yes, he knows what all of it means too.
The Chief of Medicine:	Does not have time for case presentations. He is too busy editing the definitive text on differential diagnosis.

*Reprinted with permission from Chest, ©1985; 88(2):292–294.

Figure 1.   The Organization of Case Presentations*

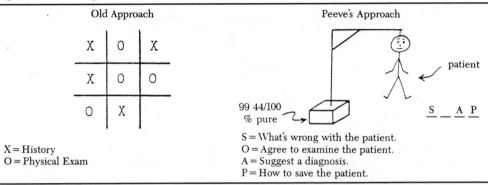

Old Approach	Peeve's Approach

X = History
O = Physical Exam

S = What's wrong with the patient.
O = Agree to examine the patient.
A = Suggest a diagnosis.
P = How to save the patient.

*Note how the O can be used in either approach, but will only solve the clinical problem using the Peeve system.

experience to master its complexities. All students of medicine, however, will occasionally find themselves in a situation where they neglected to obtain all the pertinent information about a case. The key to surviving a case presentation is knowing what to do when you have left something out.

According to Taube, the solution lies with a technique originally used in the field of education (personal communication, 1979).[10] In order to validate Taube's hypothesis, I have spent the last few years collecting information on well over four million case presentations. An initial review of the material suggested that many faltering presentations were, in fact, salvaged by the use of the clinical excuse (Bennett, unpublished doodling). In order to determine which excuses work best, the data was subjected to a detailed computer analysis using high bias tape. The results of this investigation are presented in Table 2.

Table 2—The Utilization of the Clinical Excuse to Save Your Academic Behind—and Future

Clinical Situation	Type of Information Missing from Case	Suggested Response	% Success	Alternative Response	% Success
In bed with your spouse	The case is beside the point; it's your libido that's missing	Initiate Foreplay.	72	Suggest a vacation.	100
Grand rounds	Anything (You're in big trouble)	Faint!	14	Set off your code beeper.	18
Everything else*	History of the present illness	The patient argued that all history, by definition, is in the past.	58	The patient only speaks English.	74
	Past medical history	The patient said he has aphasia.	82	The patient said to get his old chart. (He might as well have aphasia.)	79
	Family history	The patient is adopted.	47	The patient suspects a history of anthrax.	88
	Physical exam	The findings are equivocal; you'll check again after vacation.	38	The area in question is either missing or congenitally absent you're not sure which.	53
	Lab data	The test is only run on the 5th Tuesday of the month.	59	The patient exsanguinated while waiting for the phlebotomy team.	37
	Consultant's report	Rounds went overtime; the patient was transferred to their service.	61	Your pet turtle ate it.	99

*Includes morning rounds, attending rounds, hallway consults, and what to tell the butcher if he asks about his upcoming hernia operation.

Conclusion

The various applications of the clinical excuse have been described in detail. When used as directed, these pearls will prevent undue embarrassment if a case presentation begins to crash. One can also expect a complete remission in the event of pimphing, sneering, eye rolling, frowning, nitpicking, or should the urge to fawn or grovel arise. In closing, the reader is reminded of a well known verse by the late Ogden Cash:

> In this world of patients and places,
> There's no room for those who botch cases.

References

1. Used here in the generic sense, *ie*, a student is someone who knows less than anyone else around him, inanimate objects not included.

2. Galen. The use of an abdominal thrust to relieve acute phlegmatic incarceration: a case report. J Anachronisms 174 AD 20:188.

3. At least without having to see them. I think they still had to pay a consultant's fee or something.

4. Pimph DI. Bearing down on students for the perfect case presentation: a by-product of early toilet training. J Med Dogma 1646; 4:516.

5. Originally described by Grille (a student of Pimph's) as the 'Age of Rounds.' Grille was instrumental in the development of morning rounds, attending rounds, sign-out rounds and, of course, ground round.

6. Shyster B, Goose M. Goldilocks and the three milkmen: a study of legal infidelity. Thyme Magazine, April 4, 1878.

7. Fallopian T. A third trimester pregnancy misdiagnosed as ascites due to the misrepresentation of a patient's sex by an intern. Arch Uterus 1896; 9:326.

8. Quibble D. Who follows the chief into the bathroom? A time-motion study of hospital rounds. Pedestal 1924; 44:128.

9. Peeve L. Three cheers for a new approach to the case presentation. Phosphate Q 1976; 16:123.

10. Taube overheard a third grader tell his teacher that he did not have his English homework because his parakeet had eaten it the night before.

Passing Through Third Year*

A Guide for Wary Travelers

ANNE EVA RICKS

"A third-year medical student is on that part of the totem pole which is imbedded in the ground."

Statement overheard in grand rounds

"What is the difference between a third-year medical student and a piece of dog shit?
    No one intentionally steps on dog shit.
    Correction! No one goes out of his way to step on dog shit."

Graffiti on the medical student locker room wall

With an awareness of statements such as the above, I started third year with some trepidation. The first two years of medical school had been easy in that they were familiar; I'd been taking notes and cramming for exams for 16 years with reasonable success. (I went to a competitive nursery school.)

But third year! Third year is an unknown wilderness about which fantastic reports trickle down to neophyte medical students: horrendous hours, vicious attendings, difficult techniques, chronic stress and anxiety. I had encountered students in the class ahead of me transformed from grubby student-types in blue jeans to grubby doctor-types in white coats, in need of showers and shaves, who would tell tales of eight hours in the O.R. holding a retractor and of being grilled at 6:15 a.m. on the differential diagnosis of hemolytic anemia. I was sure I wouldn't be able to wake up at 6:15, let alone expound coherently.

But on July 1, resplendent in my new white coat and weighted down by enough paraphernalia for a Himalayan expedition, I began my clinical training. Now, a year and a half later I offer the guide to the clinical wards I wish I had had. It is a kind of travel guide-survival manual-encyclopedia-foreign language dictionary. If you are a medical student, use it in or near your third year. If you are a resident, read it so that you might lighten your current burden. I intend to review it when I make my next ascent—to internship.

Starting third year is like going to a foreign country. You don't speak the language, you don't understand the customs, and the natives are not necessarily friendly. As in any foreign land, you must first master the vocabulary. Neither Robbins nor Bailey nor even the venerable Goodman and Gilman will help you. When substantiating a statement, you quote "the literature" or "the green journal," not "the magazines" or "you know, that little green handbook." Under no circumstances do you state, "I don't know where I read it." The more adventurous may state "*New England Journal,* March 24, 1972," but this is advisable in only two circumstances; one, if it really *is NEJM,* March 24, 1972, or two, if you *know* no one has any interest in looking it up. When a topic comes up, you can always say, "I think the [major journal of that specialty] has an article on that," because it usually does and because everyone will be impressed that you are actually reading the journals. If anyone wants more details on it, rather than elaborating, which of course you cannot do (because at most you have read the table of contents), tell him or her that you will bring in the reference tomorrow. And if you can't find the reference, don't worry, no one will likely remember by the next day.

When presenting, the format and the vocabulary are critical. Findings are "pertinent" or they are "noncontributory." Believe me, faces light up when you say the review of systems, occupational history, and past medical history are noncontributory; everyone is rushed and likes to feel confident that you understand what is and isn't important. Of course, your backside is fried if it *is* contributory.

Dress and props are important and should be tailored to the particular specialty. Appropriate props for any medical student include a white coat with at least seven pockets crammed to the top with pens, calculator, index cards, lunch money, stethoscope, ophthalmoscope, reflex hammer, tuning forks, safety pin, *The Washington Manual*, a handbook for the rotation you are on, and a notebook for pearls. Trucking around with the largest textbook put out for that field (anything over 20 lbs.) will intimidate your fellow students, and carrying the latest journal will intimidate your interns (who haven't had time to read anything since they were medical students). Of course, you will use at home whatever concise little handbook is current at the time.

On medicine, wearing almost anything from L.L. Bean but the hiking boots is appropriate; Oxford cloth shirt, knit tie, striped belt, and khaki pants are the uniform. The tie is optional for women. A bow tie is indicated only if: (1) you are either incredibly brilliant and a little strange, or (2) you are the attending who is frequently referred to as "Dr. Smith, the father of his field." Otherwise, you are putting out a lightning rod.

On surgery, scrubs are always appropriate, unless you have an alert infectious disease department. To dress up, you may put on regular trousers or perhaps a white coat. An optimal touch, one to assure everyone that you are not really a medicine intern dressing up in wolf's clothing, is surgical shoe covers with something indescribably foul on them (this can be fallout from the O.R. or just lunch fragments from the VA cafeteria). Track shoes and Job stockings are definite signs that you are a gunner.

On pediatrics, the more outlandish your outfit the better. Colors which test pupillary constriction are popular, especially in combinations. Paraphernalia on your coat is absolutely *de rigueur;* koala bears hugging your stethoscope, buttons promoting fund raising or condemning smoking, and whatever symbols of upcoming holidays that are wearable (skeletons, Easter bunnies, flags) are basics.

On ob/gyn, you can wear anything you want, but avoid being seen carrying *MS Magazine.* A Brooks Brothers suit and a copy of the *Wall Street Journal* (with your broker's phone number scribbled on front) is perfect camouflage for ENT. On anesthesia, adopting a foreign accent might help and *Field and Stream* will assure them that you are "just one of the guys."

Now that you know the language and some of the colorful native costumes, a few cardinal rules to insure your survival are in order.

Remain conscious at all times. Because remaining conscious at all times is difficult unless you have a well-established amphetamine habit, the second best thing is to maintain the appearance of consciousness at all times. In conference, always sit next to the wall, always lean on one elbow, and never put your head down. Avoid sitting next to the attending in conference, as he has probably had seven hours of sleep the night before and will, unlike your colleagues, notice if you snore.

Remain oriented at all times. Your residents will help you with this, orienting you to your location with comments such as "This is the pits," "Compared to this, the Black Hole of Calcutta looks like Club Med," and "No, this isn't Kansas and you aren't Toto—you are a scutpuppy." Your entire team may orient you, as mine once did, with a harmonious and rousing rendition of "Dodedodo dodedodo you are now entering . . . The Toilet Zone!" They will also help orient you to time. Time on medical services is not based on changes in day and night. Everything centers on "Rounds Time," such as in "We have a three blood gases to do and a chest x-ray to find, and it's two hours to rounds."

Keep your thoughts collected. This can be difficult when your mind is blank. However, when the inevitable happens, and you are woke from a deep sleep by the jolting voice of an attending asking, "Dr. Ricks, what is the usual pathogenesis of this encephalopathy," keep calm. Stall for time. Say, "AAAaaaaaaah. . . . wellllll." Don't say "What? Who? Is this a joke?" Rely on the kindness of your residents; if a member of your team is whispering *anything*—from "branched chain amino acids" to "guacamole dip"—repeat it loudly and confidently. Of course, you do have to trust your team.

Avoid maligning the field in which you are rotating. Statements such as "This is the most disgusting thing I have ever seen," or corollaries such as "*Touch* it? Are you joking?" are bound to antagonize your residents and hurt their feelings. Remember, they have chosen, for whatever unfathomable reason, to do this for their whole lives. So don't say it. Of course, you are free to think anything you want.

Be ready for the $64,000 question: What are you going into? Watch out for this. People will ask you for different reasons and have different responses, but remember that this is a foreign place, analogous to prewar Germany, with many fiercely warring provincial duchies, and you are a simple pawn. People leap to all kinds of conclusions about your competence, intelligence, moral character, personality, and avariciousness based on your reply, and you can't even predict which erroneous assumption to which they will leap. However, if you tell the medicine man that you are going into medicine, he will assume that you are an ally and that you are like him. Tell a medicine man you are going into surgery, and you are a willful ignoramus until proven otherwise.

I would tell people what I was going into, but quickly add statements to counteract the reflex prejudice; e.g., to the medicine people, "I'm going into surgery, but I really want to learn medicine and I think it's very important, and, really, I know how to read and I sometimes even *like* to read! Honest!" On psychiatry: "I'm going into surgery but I really do see patients as whole people and I'm not an insensitive oaf. At least not most of the time." What a relief it was to be on surgery. I was delighted when anyone asked me, and always effusive: "Yes, I'm going into surgery! I love this! I want to be just like you!" One woman who is going into psychiatry felt obligated to repeatedly explain that, although her primary interest was the mind, she was interested in all of medicine and wanted to learn as much as she could during her short exposure to the rotations.

Of course, you can be like one scrofulous S.O.B. with whom I worked, who wormed his slimy way through every rotation with brazen flattery, which worked very frequently to smooth his way: from "Why, I think pediatric oncology is without doubt my primary interest," to "I've wanted to be an obstetrician since high school," to "Cardiovascular surgery, just like you, Sir!" I had to up my dose of Compazine when working with him. Although doing this will probably curry the favor of one's attending, you may well become a social pariah. There might, as well, be a few tough ethical questions somewhere down the line.

Probably the easiest thing to do, if you don't want to get involved, is tell everyone you don't know. You may come off as colorless or indecisive, but at least no one will make unwarranted assumptions.

Stay Cheerful. This last rule is probably the most important and the hardest to follow. You really are in a foreign country; remind yourself that you are there by choice. You can always leave, permanently or for a breather. Seek out your fellow students no matter how incompetent, abused, or lost you may feel. Someone else invariably has a story to top yours. No one knows what is going on, and you've got to take your ego off the line. It's hard after decades of academic excellence to feel dumb and foolish every morning, but you can take it.

Even though you have entered a foreign country, you are there to stay.

A Glossary for the Wards

Communication is a major problem for medical students. It's not the writing of the history and physicals nor the deciphering of those ophthalmology consults, nor even understanding the bizarre endocrinology laboratory jargon that's the problem. The real issue is communication between residents and third-year medical students. For instance, most medical students do not understand that when the chief resident in neurosurgery says, "Take those bloods down to lab as soon as possible," he means, "*Run* them down *now.*" Or when the team captain on medicine says to the third-year student, "Do we have an EKG on Mr. Morris?" he means, "Go do an EKG on Mr. Morris, interpret it, and bring it back to me—before attending rounds."

Of course, the average medical student is reasonably bright and will pick up these nuances throughout the third year, with only a few major embarrassing and ego-shattering incidents.

But the following phrases, and their usage may be helpful:

1. "**You have to learn to do this sometime**." This generally refers to a menial piece of scut that is important only in that completion of medical school is predicated on its accomplishment and not because of any intrinsic value; i.e., disimpacting a 101-year-old nursing home resident who has been frozen in a comatose fetal position since the Truman administration, or starting an I.V. in an ex-heroin addict who quit the habit because *he* couldn't find any more veins. But no resident will ever understand that mastery of starting an I.V. in an ex-heroin addict will not help you one bit in your child psychiatry practice in Scarsdale. So just learn to do it.

2. "**Medicine is an art, not a science**." Doubles as a phrase to be used with patients, especially when something has gone wrong, is about to go wrong, or is wrong without medical solution. It is best used with the patient who has just completed the $64,000 work-up for his chronic fatigue, from spinal tap to ultrasound, without arriving at a diagnosis. Also used by out-of-date attendings who haven't kept up their biochemistry and pharmacology and wish to stifle upstart residents who threaten to expose their knowledge deficit.

3. "**All bleeding stops**." Best used by hardened surgical chief resident in dire straits, i.e., when the multiple trauma patient rolls in from St. Elsewhere's with a sucking chest wound and exposed entrails on the E.R. stretcher. Should be said only by surgeon in charge and stated with absolute confidence. It is considered entirely inappropriate for the medical student to say this, or anything, in this situation.

4. "**Everyone has blood**." Most frequent comment made by intern to third-year medical student after unsuccessful attempts at phlebotomy. Statement is generally made in patients' room, where student is surrounded by syringes, 4×4s, tourniquet, wrappers, tubes, lab slips, and at least seven used needles and six blown veins on one irate patient.

5. "**What are you going to specialize in, psychiatry?**" This is a flashing red warning sign if said to a medical student by anyone other than a psychiatrist. If a surgeon says it, he thinks you're nuts, or he caught you actually talking to a patient. If a medicine doctor says it, he thinks you're lazy. If an ob/gyn doctor says it, he simply noticed that you fainted at your first screaming-through-the-E.R.-door-with-a-baby-between-the-legs-and-2,000-cc-blood-loss (mostly on your clothing) delivery.

6. "**No, I'm not a nurse**." Most frequent statement uttered by women residents and medical students. Explaining that you are the Nobel Laureate in endocrinology or the TV repair lady will fall on deaf ears. No matter what you tell the patient hollering "Nurse! Nurse!" at you on rounds, he will then say, "Well, anyway, whatever you are, my bedpan needs emptying." Take it with grace and humor. It will happen often. It will amuse your colleagues and add levity to rounds (which is generally in sore need). It isn't the patients' fault: most people don't realize the number of women in medicine, and 90 percent of the time they're right if they call a woman in white a nurse. Besides, if you get upset every time someone calls you nurse, you're going to need lifelong maintainance cimetidine therapy.

7. "**Maybe it's not too late to go to law school**." Frequently used by students, residents, and attendings alike. Most often heard during disasters and when icky unidentified things are discovered on one's clothing, or in response to any of numbers one to six above. This is never seriously meant and is usually just a wish for a job in which icky unidentified things don't routinely wind up on one's clothes.

8. "**I can't do it. I'm too tired. This is disgusting**." No. No. No. These phrases do not exist for the medical student nor the resident. They are not in your vocabulary. Besides, even if you are really, honestly, too exhausted to do something, they're going to make you do it anyway, be it hold retractors for a renal transplant from 3 a.m. to 7 a.m. or completely work up your seventh E.R. admission with diabetes, renal failure, schizophrenia, and a medical record that comes up Volume 6 of 7 (but 7 is missing). Since you're going to do it anyway, save your energy for the task at hand instead of wasting it on futile protestation.

So on the wards, keep alert for the difference between what is said and what is meant. Sure it's scary to be in the hospitals without any real sense of what you are supposed to be doing or how you should be doing it, but it's not that bad an experience. It'll only hurt a little. Really.

The Student's Dilemma*

HOWARD J. BENNETT, M.D.

The play takes place at 7:30 PM at a Roy Rogers Restaurant. Dennis Miller, a third-year medical student, is hunched over a partially eaten bacon cheeseburger. His face is unshaven, and his eyes look like crushed sardines. Sitting across from Dennis is Dr. Simon, a man in his mid-forties with an open tweed jacket and buttons straining to keep his abdomen out of the coleslaw. Dennis obviously was on call the night before. Dr. Simon, on the other hand, has no excuse for his appearance.

DENNIS: Thanks for inviting me to dinner, Dr. Simon. I really needed to talk to someone.

DR. SIMON: My pleasure Dennis. You certainly sounded distraught on the phone. Tuition problems?

DENNIS: Worse. My fourth-year schedule is due next week, and I still don't know what I want to be when I grow up.

DR. SIMON: Oh, that. All you need to do is set up an appointment with your advisor. He'll straighten things out for you.

DENNIS: You are my advisor, Dr. Simon.

DR. SIMON: Am I really? In that case, Dennis, tell me what's on your mind.

DENNIS: Well, in the first place, it seems like everyone else knows what they want in life but me.

DR. SIMON (lighting his pipe): Uh-huh.

DENNIS: For example, did you always know what you wanted to be?

DR. SIMON: Not until the sixth grade.

DENNIS: You knew you wanted to be a doctor in the sixth grade!

DR. SIMON: Fifth actually. In the sixth grade, I decided on neuropsychiatry as a subspecialty.

DENNIS: Oh great—just what I needed to hear.

DR. SIMON: Sorry, Dennis, but I've always been precocious. Why, I even had my midlife crisis before I was 30.

DENNIS: Then I'm not alone?

DR. SIMON: Of course not.

DENNIS: But what about my classmates? A lot of them seem to know what they want to do.

DR. SIMON: Sure they do. And a lot of them eat sushi, but that doesn't mean it tastes good. You've got to stop comparing yourself with everyone else.

DENNIS: You're right. I know you're right. But tell me, what should I do?

DR. SIMON: First, you should realize that you're probably approaching the decision all wrong.

DENNIS: I am?

DR. SIMON: Well, the mistake most students make is trying to base decisions on their third-year clerkships. That never gets you anywhere.

DENNIS: How so?

DR. SIMON: Most students use what Freud called the laundry-list approach.

DENNIS: You mean making a list of what they do and don't like about the various specialties?

DR. SIMON: Exactly.

DENNIS (reaching into his pocket): I have mine right here.

DR. SIMON: List making may work for buying underwear or getting married, but it's rarely helpful with career counseling.

DENNIS: Maybe not, but what else can I do?

DR. SIMON: You've got to tap into your unconscious.

DENNIS: My what?

DR. SIMON: Your unconscious, Dennis. You know, that little voice that slips out after nights on call or when your blood alcohol level rises above your IQ.

DENNIS: But I thought you were a neuropsychiatrist. Why all this interest in the unconscious?

DR. SIMON: It's just a hobby.

DENNIS: Well, you picked a good night for it. But what does my unconscious have to do with choosing a career?

*Reprinted with permission from Postgraduate Medicine, ©1986; 80(5):266–274.

DR. SIMON: Everything, Dennis. The best way to determine true compatibility is to look for the deeper associations in things. For example, going into surgery just because you like tying knots isn't enough.

DENNIS: But how do I go about tapping into my unconscious?

DR. SIMON: It's quite simple, actually. I'll ask you four questions that relate to some everyday situations. All you have to do is answer with the first thing that comes to mind.

DENNIS: That's all there is to it?

DR. SIMON: That's all. Now, why don't you sit back and relax.

DENNIS (leans back and closes his eyes): Okay, I'm ready.

DR. SIMON: Here's the first question. Tell me, which bodily fluid is least offensive to you?

DENNIS: Hmmm, let me see . . .

DR. SIMON: Quickly now, the first thing that pops into your head.

DENNIS: Urine.

DR. SIMON: Good! That's one for pediatrics.

DENNIS (sitting up in his chair): Peds—are you sure?

DR. SIMON: It's a start, Dennis. We've got more to go.

DENNIS: But peds? I haven't even done my pediatrics rotation yet.

DR. SIMON: You're thinking like a third-year student again.

DENNIS: Okay, okay. But what if I had said blood?

DR. SIMON: Then I would have said surgery.

DENNIS: Sweat?

DR. SIMON: Family practice.

DENNIS: And tears?

DR. SIMON: Psychiatry.

DENNIS: Hmmm. What about Ob/Gyn? What's least offensive to them?

DR. SIMON: No one knows for sure.

DENNIS: And medicine? You didn't give me a choice for medicine.

DR. SIMON: All bodily fluids are offensive to internists.

DENNIS: Well, you're right about that one. And I do like children, but . . .

DR. SIMON: No buts, Dennis. Let's move on to question 2.

DENNIS: If you say so.

DR. SIMON: What card games do you like to play?

DENNIS (sits up in his chair again): Card games! You can't be serious.

DR. SIMON: Dennis, you're going to block your unconscious if you get excited. Now, why don't you sit back and relax.

DENNIS: Okay, I'll try . . . . Well, I do like playing cards with my niece.

DR. SIMON: And what do you and your niece play together?

DENNIS: Go fish.

DR. SIMON: There we go again.

DENNIS: You mean peds?

DR. SIMON: You said it, Dennis. I didn't.

DENNIS: That's true, I did. But I also play bridge with my roommate. Doesn't that count for anything?

DR. SIMON: What does your roommate do?

DENNIS: He's a fourth-year student.

DR. SIMON: And?

DENNIS: And he's going into medicine.

DR. SIMON: I see. Do you like bridge?

DENNIS: Not really.

DR. SIMON: I thought so.

DENNIS: But what about the other specialties? What associations would you draw for them?

DR. SIMON: Good question, Dennis. I'll tell you what. I'll mention the other specialties, and you tell me the connections you would make. After all, you may be an advisor yourself someday.

DENNIS (self-consciously): I'll try.

DR. SIMON: Surgery?

DENNIS: War—at least for general surgeons. Urologists probably play pinochle.

DR. SIMON: Mine certainly does. But let's stay away from subspecialists tonight. Remember, it's only our first session. How about psychiatry?

DENNIS: Crazy eights.

DR. SIMON: Ob/Gyn?

DENNIS: Poker.

DR. SIMON: Family practice?

DENNIS: Solitaire.

DR. SIMON: That's pretty good, Dennis. I think you're getting the hang of it. What's your favorite candy?

DENNIS (leaning forward): Is this part of the session, or do you just want to buy me dessert?

DR. SIMON: You're wavering again.

DENNIS: Candy! What can I possibly learn from candy?

DR. SIMON: Plenty. Now quick, who do you think likes Life Savers the most?

DENNIS: Surgeons?

DR. SIMON: Right! When's the last time you saw a surgeon eat a Butterfinger bar?

DENNIS: Oh no, I can't believe this is happening.

DR. SIMON: Believe it, Dennis.

DENNIS: I know, but . . .

DR. SIMON: But what?

DENNIS: But Dr. Simon, I love Baby Ruth bars. Does that mean . . . ?

DR. SIMON: Yes, Dennis.

DENNIS: And all that time I thought I was eating candy because I liked the way it tasted.

DR. SIMON: Now you know.

DENNIS (looking a little bewildered): It's just . . . all those Baby Ruths I've eaten. Big ones. Small ones. Miniatures on Halloween. (Becoming excited) I love the little ones, Dr. Simon. Do you think I'll end up in neonatology?

DR. SIMON: Perhaps, Dennis. Do you care to make some other predictions?

DENNIS: Okay . . . sure, I'm ready.

DR. SIMON: Psychiatry?

DENNIS: Good & Fruity.

DR. SIMON: Ob/Gyn?

DENNIS: Mounds.

DR. SIMON: Family practice?

DENNIS: Milk Duds.

DR. SIMON: Medicine?

DENNIS: Hmmm, medicine's tough. I never see internists eating candy in the hospital. Wait a second. I've got it—Godiva, right?

DR. SIMON: Perfect!

DENNIS (obviously pleased with himself): This is fun, Dr. Simon. Maybe I should skip residency and go right into medical education.

DR. SIMON: Well, at least wait until tomorrow. We have one question left.

DENNIS: Shoot.

DR. SIMON: If you had to live inside a comic strip, which one would you choose?

DENNIS: Let me think for a second.

DR. SIMON: Not too long, now.

DENNIS: Sure thing, but I already know my answer. I'm just thinking about the other specialties.

DR. SIMON: Okay, Dennis.

DENNIS: I've got it. Go ahead, quiz me.

DR. SIMON: Medicine?

DENNIS: Either *Crock* or *The Lockhorns*.

DR. SIMON: Surgery?

DENNIS: *Prince Valiant.*

DR. SIMON: Psychiatry?

DENNIS: *The Wizard of Id.*

DR. SIMON: Ah, my favorite!

DENNIS: I though so.

DR. SIMON: How about family practice?

DENNIS: *For Better or For Worse.*

DR. SIMON: And Ob/Gyn?

DENNIS: *Grin & Bear It.*

DR. SIMON: Very nice, Dennis. Now tell me, which comic strip would you choose to live in?

DENNIS: The one with my namesake, of course.

DR. SIMON: You mean the little menace?

DENNIS: You bet. He was my role model as a child.

DR. SIMON (laughing): I'm not surprised. Any questions left for me?

DENNIS: Not really. I think I'll go home and have a talk with my roommate, though. I'm dying to find out if he really wants to go into medicine.

DR. SIMON: Let me know how things work out.

DENNIS: Oh, I will. I just hope his advisor will be as good as mine.

DR. SIMON: I'm sure he will be, Dennis—at least the one he's got tonight.

DENNIS: Well, I've got the secret now. If you want things to work out right, just follow what Simon says.

DR. SIMON: It's as simple as that.

Additional Readings

1. Bluestone N: Coffee break. New Physician 1980; 29(10):5,8,12.

2. Bluestone N: Percolation test. New Physician 1980; 29(11):7,10,14.

In this two-part article, we meet Mary Louise, a premed student who suffers from a severe case of medical admissions anxiety. Mary reacts to this stress by adopting the appearance and behavior of a coffee pot.

3. Bluestone N: An empathy test. New Physician 1981; 30(2):7,16.

According to the author, medical students are bewildered individuals who are never sure what they should be doing. For example, "Am I supposed to toss the breast over her shoulder or listen right through it?" She then presents a miniquiz which demonstrates that the rest of us aren't always sure what we should be doing either.

4. Bluestone N: Labor and delivery. New Physician 1982; 31(3):37–38.

Suzy Kew is a third year student at Healthyself Medical School. Despite efforts to orchestrate her pregnancy and delivery with aplomb, Suzy goes into labor one week early. With her entire support system out of town, Suzy is left in the hands of the chairman—Dr. Spike.

5. Smithline F: Up the bronchial tree. Perspect Biol Med 1982; 25(3):436–443.

A fantasy about a medical student named Alice who wanders through the hospital. She meets a number of characters more likely to know the Cheshire Cat than the Chief of Medicine.

INTERNSHIP & RESIDENCY

The main difference between medical school and residency is that with one you pay to become sleep deprived and with the other, someone pays you. There are other advantages to being a resident, however. Now you can really call yourself "Doctor," no one grades you anymore (at least not officially), and you're the one who gets to make out the scut list. But best of all, you can finally say goodbye to all those organ systems that used to make you nauseous. Now, at last, you can concentrate on what you have always wanted to do—like starting IVs at 3 am on pudgy toddlers, disimpacting patients in the emergency room, and obtaining histories from patients whose silences rival those of psychiatrists. As the title of one of the following selections states, "Real Interns Don't Have Time to Eat Quiche."

At Last! Blessed Relief for the Pain and Discomfort of Percentorrhea*

MICHAEL A. LACOMBE, M.D.

House officers bored by endless percentages and professors prone to recite them will benefit alike by committing to memory the indispensable rule presented in this article.

LaCombe's Rule of Percentages (my name is LaCombe) will, when properly applied by house officers, force rounders and attendings to teach rather than perpetuate what Orr calls "shifting dullness." The rule is: *The incidence of anything worthwhile is either 15–25 per cent or 80–90 per cent.*

With this rule in mind, you need only know whether something is common or uncommon in order to affect profound medical knowledge when replying to percentage questions. Thus, you'll force those who want to teach you to deal in pathophysiology rather than percentages, and you may learn something.

Let me illustrate with a clinical example.

ROUNDER: What percentage of patients with Hodgkin's Disease experience pain at the site of active foci following the ingestion of alcohol?

HOUSE OFFICER (thinking to himself): I remember hearing about this once as I was falling asleep in a hematology lecture. . . . He's smiling at me as if I should know, so it can't be too rare. (Aloud, loudly): About 15 per cent to 25 per cent, depending on the study.

ROUNDER: Excellent! Actually, it's 17 per cent. Would you like to become an Associate Professor of Medicine like me?

HOUSE OFFICER: I'm afraid I don't know enough percentages yet, sir.

Now, don't get the idea that the house officer was being dishonest, specious, or glib. He was using LaCombe's Rule as a weapon, fully aware of the tremendous power of the phrase "depending on the study," which can mean anything upward from "I know as many references as you do."

There exist, naturally, exceptions to my rule, and two corollaries must be remembered. The first, called the Scrinch Amendment, refers to that instance when the rounder screws up his face (scrinches) and searches from student to intern to resident before asking for a really bizarre percentage. The corollary: *A scrinch is less than 1 per cent.*

The second, called Dudenhoefer's Corollary after an intern who used it twice, is: *An answer of 50 per cent will suffice for the 40–60 range.* It is to be applied rarely, and only by a master at reading nonchalance in facial expression, verbal nuance, and voice inflection. Why? It takes rare cool for a rounder to ask a percentage question when the answer desired is in the 40–60 realm. Lucky and blessed is the man who once in his lifetime successfully executes Dudenhoefer's Corollary.

With practice, LaCombe's Rule will prove indispensable. Like "The Barnes Manual of Medical Therapeutics," it is an acquaintance that once made will never be shunned.

*Reprinted from Hospital Physician, ©1971; 7(2):102. With permission from Physicians World Communications Group. Edited from the original.

The Intern: A Fantasy*

HAROLD K. GEVER, M.D.

It was another bright, cheerful morning of Internship as I rolled out of bed in my suburban apartment. I had to hurry to make the 9 a.m. commuter train to University Hospital. "Make sure you get home on time today, honey. I hate when you drag yourself in at four in the afternoon," my wife mildly scolded as she warmed the Mercedes to take me to the station.

"Of all the hassles of Internship, this must be the worst," I thought as I fought my way through the end-of-rush-hour crowds to the hospital.

"Good morning, Dr. Gever," spoke the security guard at the entrance, "Shall I tell the telephone operators you're in?"

"Please do, Jenkins. I'm already a little late for attending rounds. It's my first day on the new service, so I better get up there right away. Thanks a lot."

The elevator attendant spotted me from a distance and held the door for me while I was talking to Jenkins. As I walked in, I could tell that some of the other riders didn't appreciate my tardiness, despite my status as Intern. There were several visitor types among the nurses, aides, and respiratory technicians. In the far corner dressed in wrinkled, blood-stained surgical blues, stood a couple of weary looking attendings.

"Bad night on call, doctors?" I asked, trying to be friendly. I always hated to address attendings that way because it seemed so impersonal. Furthermore, I found that attendings always appreciated it when I knew their names; it must give them a feeling of self-esteem to be noticed by an Intern. But these guys were clearly a couple of the many attendings that seem to come and go so randomly at University.

In response to my question, they simply smiled at me servilely and muttered, "Not too bad, sir, just a couple codes and a handful of admissions."

"Well," I chuckled, "could have been worse," as I strolled out of the elevator onto my floor. It always made me feel good to say a few encouraging words to attendings, especially after their nights on call.

I made my way briskly to the back room of the fifth floor to meet with my own new attendings, who no doubt were assembled around the conference table, x-rays already hanging on the viewbox. As I entered, I realized I had forgotten to bring the box of doughnuts I usually offered my attendings. I might have started off on the wrong foot with these sullen fellows, I thought. At University, sometimes the difference between being judged a good Intern and a bad one is in the quality of doughnuts one brings to rounds.

I looked around at my new team. It was a ragged crew, ranging in age anywhere from 28 to 76. Some of them, perhaps, could even remember the Great Medical Economic Revolution when third party payers realized it was cheaper to fund Interns and Residents for services rendered than to pay exorbitant attending rates. Most attendings were forced to either take down the shingle for good or come to subsist in the hospitals. Fortunately, they weren't allowed to unionize. The law was very clear in this regard; regular hospital employees could enter into collective bargaining, not those who merely subsist in the hospital.

My attendings proved to be fairly conversant with the literature. I've always enjoyed being involved with their teaching since it proves to be a mutual learning experience that even the best of Interns can profit from. Right in the middle of my lecture on how to insert IVs, however, the head nurse, Mrs. Phillips, exploded into the room.

"Dr. Gever, I'm so sorry for interrupting, but Mrs. Jones in 21A is short of breath. Can you send one of your attendings to see her?"

"But Mrs. Phillips, this lecture is important. Where are the medical students?"

"Union meetings," she said impatiently.

"Oh, I see. Well then, why don't you, doctor, take a look at her," I said said, pointing to one of the attendings who had just awakened from his nap during my talk.

When the lecture finished, I was still feeling bad about not having brought doughnuts, so I invited my attendings to join me for lunch. The r.s.v.p. was unanimous. It's not often attendings get a chance to eat in the Intern's Dining Room.

I quickly called University Food Services to make a reservation for six at noon. The maitre d' asked me to choose between filet mignon or lobster tail, because with such short notice, only these two items could be properly cooked to order.

Lunch in the Intern's Dining Room was delightful as always. My attendings appeared to be suitably awed. "I'm not impressed by the wine list, though," one of them said boldly. "It's a lot better at City General where my Intern took me when I was doing my surgery rotation there."

Lunch would have passed otherwise uneventfully, if it hadn't been for the obvious gloom of my other colleagues who were flagrantly trying to get drunk on Chateau Lafite Rothschild at the next table. "What's the matter?" I asked, turning my chair in their direction.

"It's time to start looking all over again," one said sorrowfully.

"What do you mean?" I asked. "Leaving University?!"

"We have no choice," he said. "We all just got our letters today from the program director. We're being promoted to Residents.

The whole idea was frightening. Being promoted to Resident meant not only less salary, but longer hours and probationary union privileges. It really left few alternatives. One was to apply for Internship at some other hospital. The best bets were some of the smaller community hospitals that didn't recognize University's Internship as creditable service. But those plums were few and far between and extremely difficult to match into. The only other alternative, of course, was to apply for Internship in some other specialty . . .

Mercilessly, the beeper startled me out of my slumber—a cruel return to the real world. In piercing monotone, it directed me to call my floor to find out about my new admission. As I stumbled to the elevator in the main lobby, the doors shut in my face. It would be another 15 minutes before it would come down again. Too tired to do anything else, I stared at the closed doors, my eyes burning from fatigue. When the doors opened again, I found myself face to face with a well-dressed woman. It was Nurse Phillips.

"Bad night on shift, doctor?" she asked. I nodded in the affirmative. "Here," she said, shoving an opened cardboard box in front of my nose. "Have a doughnut. I don't know why the third party payers keep giving these to us. They know we're all on diets."

From the corner of my eye, I could see Jenkins helping Mrs. Phillips into her Mercedes in front of the hospital. Confidently, she tipped the valet parking attendant and drove off.

"What I wouldn't do to be a Nurse," I heard an older man's voice say wistfully from within the elevator. He looked like an attending.

"I know what you mean," I heard myself say. "Ever since the third parties put Nurses in charge, it's been a thankless job being a physician. Oh well, I'm really just in it to supplement the allowance my wife gives me."

"And I couldn't stand to watch another soap opera," the older man said. "This fills up my day. By the way, when do you go off shift?"

"I'm doing a double today, the night shift and now the day shift. I finish at three," I responded.

"Me too!" he said. "Hey, how about joining me for a beer afterwards. We'll drink to old times."

The Pediatric Internship Screening Test*

HOWARD J. BENNETT, M.D.

Each year, some 16,000 students graduate from medical schools in the United States. Having finished four years of grueling education, these young doctors now begin an experience euphemistically known as "postgraduate training." Unfortunately, residency is to medical school as a blown pupil is to anisocoria.

In the past, residency was seen as a rite of passage, and a "sink or drown" philosophy was adopted at most teaching hospitals. Recently, however, the plight of overworked housestaff has been significantly eased. Today's interns and residents are better paid, have fewer nights on call, and, in most hospitals, are given time off for major illness and death.

In recent years, it has also become well known that development does not end with successful toilet training. In fact, certain aspects of daily living may be viewed as important milestones in adult development: getting married, buying a home, deciding whether or not to circumcise a male infant. In many ways, residency training can also be viewed as a developmental process. Pediatric educators are in an excellent position to study this phenomenon because of their overall interest in the growth of children. This is especially true for program directors who routinely dole out boxes of tissues while taking to tired and grouchy house officers.

The Pediatric Internship Screening Test (PIST) was developed to provide a simple method of testing an intern's adjustment to his or her residency. The PIST focuses on interns for two reasons. First, the internship year requires the skills most like Freud's anal stage and is therefore the easiest to measure and follow. Second, we all know what happens if something goes amiss in that arena.

During the pilot phase of the study, this investigator spent approximately four years wandering the halls of teaching hospitals, talked with hundreds of interns, and underwent analysis in order to relive his own internship experience. The test was then standardized on 1,036 pediatric interns. All subjects volunteered, more or less, for the study, which takes only 15 minutes to complete and thus could not be used as an excuse to refuse an admission or to get out of attending rounds.

In order to avoid type I and type II errors, no effort was made to examine the subjects statistically. It is interesting to note, however, that some subjects had been tested two decades ago in the classic developmental work by Frankenburg and Dodds (The Denver Developmental Screening Test. J Pediatr 1967;71:181). Despite this observation, any similarity between the PIST and the DDST is purely coincidental.

The PIST has been designed so that interns can be tested on a monthly basis from July until the following June. The examiner draws a line through the corresponding month and then administers those items intersected by the line. Footnotes that accompany the form provide additional directions for testing.

How to Score the Test

Each item is scored P for pass, F for fail, or S for asleep. The PIST is then interpreted as normal or abnormal depending on whether the majority of items are passed or failed. An intern is considered questionable if he spent more time sleeping than responding to the examiner.

The PIST is not an intelligence test. It is intended solely to help program directors monitor the progress of the youngest members of their housestaff. The indications for testing include arguing over schedules, failing to change out of scrubs after a night on call, not wanting to come back to work after vacation, and calling home more than once a week. In addition, all interns should be tested between February and March.

When the test is used as directed, interns can be counseled more effectively than in the past. In particular,

*Reprinted with permission from Contemporary Pediatrics, ©1987; 4(5):96–99.

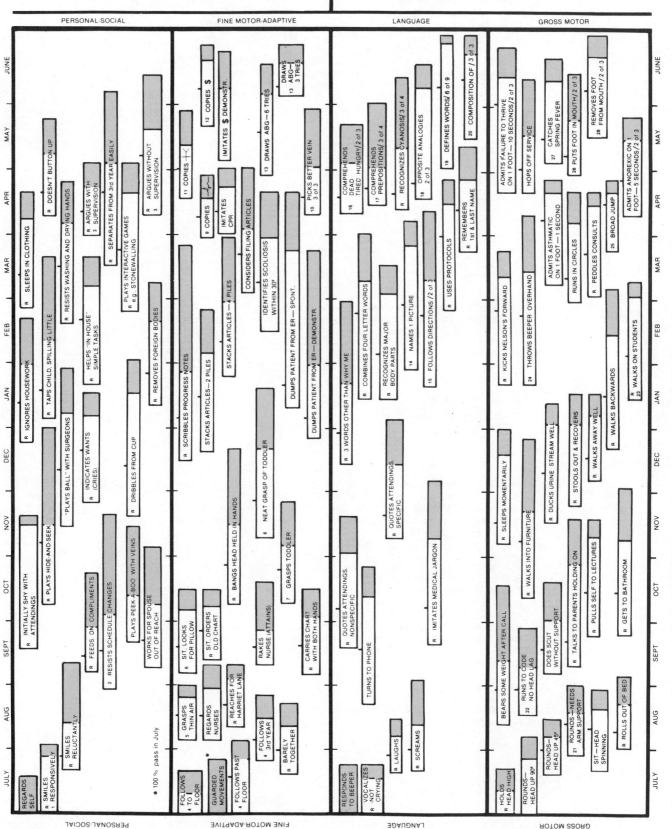

PEDIATRIC INTERNSHIP SCREENING TEST

1. Try to get intern to smile by smiling, waving or offering to take the next admission. Do not touch him.
2. When intern is getting ready to go home, tell him there's been a schedule change and he's on call. Pass if he threatens to quit.
3. Intern does not have to be able to win arguments to pass.
4. Give intern his schedule. Pass if he makes it to the assigned ward.
   (Forgets the next day; follows 3rd year.)
5. Pass if intern tries to bluff when asked questions in attending rounds.
6. Pass if intern looks for a pillow when he sits down to take test.
7. Pass if intern keeps toddler still by holding any part of his body.
8. Pass if intern keeps toddler still by saying it won't hurt, offering a bribe or by sitting on him.

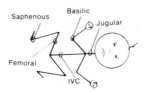

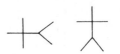

9. Pass normal rhythm. Fail any escape beats or aberrant rhythms.
10. Which vein is better? (Not bigger.) Turn paper upside down and repeat. (3/3 or 5/6)
11. May be oriented in either direction.
12. Have intern copy first. If failed, do not recommend private practice.

13. When scoring, needs ½ cc of blood to pass. Each jab counts as one try.
14. Point to picture and have intern name it. (No credit is given for sounds only.)

15. Tell intern to: Write up student evaluations; prepare a case for grand rounds; finish incomplete medical records. Pass 2 of 3. (Do not help by prodding, growling or withholding paycheck.)
16. Ask intern: What do you do when you are dead?...tired?...hungry? Pass 2 of 3.
17. Tell intern: Write your number on the slip; leave the requisition in the box; lab results will be ready by noon; close the door behind you. Pass 3 of 4.
18. Ask intern: If a horse is big, your salary is? Fire is hot, your sex life is? You are sensitive, chief residents are? Pass 2 of 3.
19. Ask intern: What is a weekend?...a black cloud?...QNS?...a novel?...an LMD?...turfing?...an off service note?...an infiltration?...a slough? Pass 6 of 9.
20. Ask intern: What is an HMO made of?...a PPO made of?...an IPA made of? Pass 3 of 3.
21. During work rounds intern leans on chart rack for support.
22. Intern runs to code. Pass if his head follows.
23. Intern may use third or fourth year students, preferably third year.
24. Intern must throw beeper overhand into the hall or at the chief resident.
25. Intern must perform standing broad jump over nursery flow sheet (36½ inches).
26. When questioned on rounds, intern argues about workup then realizes he knows less than he thought he did.
27. Take intern outside on a sunny day. Pass if he forgets he's on call.
28. Intern stops arguing.

DATE AND BEHAVIORAL OBSERVATIONS (How intern feels at time of test, last meal eaten, recent Fri/Sun call, state of consciousness, etc.):

they can be reassured that they are developing well and should not be overly concerned with their physiologic celibacy. Those with abnormal results on the test might consider switching to a radiology residency or opening a gourmet ice cream parlor. Interns with a questionable PIST can either spend an extra month in the nursery or agree to be retested in four to six weeks, whichever they prefer.

The author is now completing work on a revision to be called the PIST-R, which is designed for use with PL-2 and PL-3 residents. It remains to be seen whether they will take this sitting down.

The following point-counterpoint* was written by two residents and an attending. Although the residents went first, considering all the ribbing that goes on in hospitals, it could just as easily have gone the other way around.—*H.B.*

Real Interns Don't Have Time to Eat Quiche

Real Interns . . .

- don't wake up their residents at night
- don't request cardiology consults
- don't admit patients from the emergency room
- do their own scut work
- change diapers
- treat meningitis as an outpatient disease
- can stay awake during X-ray rounds
- answer equally well whether awake or asleep
- answer questions to which they don't know the answer with "Yawn, I don't know, I was up all night on call"
- can find something to complain about in the morning even if nothing went wrong on call
- circumvent their attendings and do things the right way.

Steven Blatt, M.D. and Rita Ryan, M.D.
(Former Real Interns, now Real Residents)

The Attendings Strike Back

If "Real interns don't have time to eat quiche" (April 1985, p 76), then real attendings don't know what quiche is. The whimsical list submitted by two interns cries out for a rebuttal. Thus, real attendings:

- always sound awake when the intern calls at night
- play tennis with the cardiologist
- admit their patients right to the floor
- find more scutwork for the intern to do
- recommend against the use of diapers
- can cite every article that supports *their* way of treatment
- come late to radiology rounds and insist the films be reviewed from the beginning
- always have one more pearl
- call on the one medical student who can answer the question the intern missed
- tell about the good cases they saw on call during their residency
- call the nurse to circumvent the intern.

Michael Martin, M.D.

*Reprinted with permission from Contemporary Pediatrics, ©1985; 2(4):76 and 1985; 2(8):12.

The Young Boys Network*

NAOMI BLUESTONE, M.D.

"John, dear, you're going to have to do something about little Johnny." The senior resident braced himself. "O.K., what is it now?"

"He's been playing doctor again."

"Oh, no. How many times do I have to tell that kid to keep his hands to himself. If I've said it once, I've said it a hundred times: 'Never Lower Tillie's Pants, Mother Might Come Home.'"

"No, dear, that's not what I meant. I mean he's *really* playing doctor."

The usually cheerful face turned grim. "All right, honey, give me a drink and let's have it." He threw his bag on the table and opened his necktie.

"Well, it was a rainy day and he was feeling ornery, so at first I thought it might work when I heard him say to his little sister that he felt like being a doctor, and that she had to be his nurse since he really didn't trust any of the other little girls in the neighborhood. He promised her a huge salary and lots of time off and even said he'd start a tax-deferred annuity for her. So she called up to the white cape on the corner and asked the little Wilkins girl if she'd come over and play because they needed a patient. Well, the Wilkins's baby sitter was only to glad to dump her, so the next thing I knew the three of them had taken over the game room and were starting to divvy up the roles.

"I must say it started amiably enough. Johnny said he needed some experience cutting, and since he wants to be an orthopedic surgeon, he thought the Wilkins girl should have an open fracture of the femur so that he could reduce it and get some nice mattress sutures into place. But then Martha decided to assert herself and let Johnny know that that didn't suit *her* needs at all. She told him that she'd had all the med-surg nursing she wanted under her belt and she was damned if she was going to give another anesthetic or even start an I.V. again. She said Wilkins needed intensive care and she was just a floor nurse, and besides,

they only had an hour or two until Wilkins had to go home for her nap, and she didn't want to get in over her head. She said she wanted to practice her OB, and that if Wilkins wasn't going to be in the third stage of labor, she wasn't going to play. Then Johnny started yelling that with his luck, Wilkins would probably turn out to be a breech, and how could they possibly get a breech out before naptime?

"Well, just when it looked like they were coming to blows, the little Wilkins girl decided to put her two cents in. She has three older brothers, you know, so she's used to fighting her way through a screaming mob. She told Johnny and Martha that she was damned if she was going to break her leg for them, and that she wasn't going to let them stick her after what they'd done to her veins the last time. She said she was still sick from the *last* time they'd given her anesthesia. You remember how they dropped that wine vinegar on an old sponge and tried to tie it to her nose with her mouth stuffed full of old nylons? Well, they asked her why she was being such an uncooperative patient and advised her that if she didn't stop interfering, they'd send her over to the Johnson boy down on Fifth Street, and between you and me, dear, he really is a butcher.

"So then she got a little meek, and asked them (rather nicely, I thought) if they wouldn't consider letting her be a dotty little old lady who couldn't remember her own name. That way they could just do a brief mental status and then leave her be. She tried to point out that they both would get a chance to study for their exams while she was napping.

"Well, right about then the phone rang, and it was Mrs. Smith across the street. She'd just lost a filling and had to run to the dentist and could I please take the twins for an hour? I had to say yes, because you never know when the favor will be returned. So in they waltz, and both decide that there's a place for them in all of this. Phil decided that he wanted to be the consultant,

*Reprinted with permission from The New Physician, ©1981; 30(6):9–12. Copyright by American Medical Student Association.

which was fine with Johnny because he knew he could count on him for support, through the young boys' network. Rose, on the other hand, decided that what the group needed was a high-powered social worker, someone who could see the reality of placement problems and who knew how dispensable physicians really are. And that's when it all started, dear."

"Oh, God, Alice, are you really sure you want to tell me this? I really had a lousy day. Don't you think you're exaggerating? Give me another drink." He elevated his feet onto the coffee table and rearranged the cushions behind his rhomboid of Michaelis. "I'm ready."

"The twins are generally quite tractable, John. But whenever Phil gets to play consultant, he starts carrying on like Hannibal Homer. He wears his grandfather's pocket watch, and he keeps clearing his throat, and no matter what diagnosis Johnny makes, he always has a better one. He's fond of prefacing everything with, 'As the students at the Mass General feel . . . ' and then he gives some esoteric syndrome that no one ever heard of before.

"Rose, on the other hand, has made a career for herself showing everyone that no one cares about the patient but Rose. She acts as if diagnostic procedures were performed for the sole purpose of delaying or destroying her placement procedures, and no matter what a doctor writes on a chart, she faults the wording, the sentiment, or the timing. I've told her mother she is going to be in a bad way when she reaches middle school, but she feels that Rose was destined to marry young and so none of this has any meaning anyway.

"Well, to make a long story very short, Phil decided that the patient could not have anything but a bad sprain, as much as he knew that his colleague had his heart set on an open, clean break. And Rose decided that placing a crowning multigravida was easier than placing a female organic brain syndrome. The patient decided that she didn't want to be interviewed by either the social worker or the consultant, and that she thought the nurse was being pretty damned callous and clumsy. Martha said that no social worker was going to interfere with her nursing responsibilities, and that since no official consult request form had been filled out by Johnny, Phil had no right opening his mouth and upsetting the apple cart.

"I was just about on my way in to break it up, because I saw Phil pick up a small rock, and he had a pretty ugly look in his astigmatic eye. But then Johnny let loose. Dear, I wish I could have taped it. I mean, he just went berserk. He started screaming that he was the captain of the team. He said that God had given the captaincy of the healing team, and that while he respected the right of every person in the room to have his opinion and his competency, he was damned if he was going to let them take over as if they owned the joint. He told the patient to shut up and that she was going to have whatever disease he thought was in her best interest. He told Martha that he would put her on report with the nursing supervisor if she made one more reference to childbirth. He told Phil that his services were no longer required, nor would they ever be again, since when was the last time he'd referred a patient to *him?* And he told Rose that she was a pain in his gluteus maximus, and why hadn't *she* gone to medical school? Then they all said they were sick of playing doctor, and they were going home."

"How awful for you, honey, how did you handle it?"

"Well, I told Phil and Rose that perhaps it really *was* time that they went home, and that they should try to be forgiving because they had gotten into fights with *their* little playmates, too." "And the Wilkins kid?"

"She's traumatized, dear. She's supposed to go for her pre-school vaccinations soon, and now there's no way her mother will be able to drag her in. I've heard that the Smith girl is a pretty good shrink, though, and they have a good relationship, so maybe she'll work it out. I'm not too worried about Martha. I gave her some milk and cookies, and she just treated it all philosophically and said she really wanted to be an astronaut."

"But what about Johnny?"

"Please talk to him, dear. I sent him up to his room to cool down, but for hours he was just ranting on and on about how he always wanted to be a captain, and medicine just wasn't the tight ship it used to be, and how is he supposed to pass his Boards if he doesn't get the kind of clinical material and professional support he thinks is necessary? He has no insight, I'm afraid. He still can't see why no one wanted to play it his way. He's starting to obsess about what a bad doctor he is, and how his father won't be proud of him. A boy needs his father at a time like this."

"Of course, I'll talk to him honey. It's not so terrible. He just got carried away a little bit. I think it's because he's presenting at Grand Rounds tomorrow. Do you know if he worked up his case?"

Additional Readings

1. Cilley RE: There are many ways to kill a resident: Try house officer's headache or intern's neck. JAMA 1985; 254(14):1905–1906.

As house officers advance in rank, the paraphernalia in their white coats decreases in weight from an average of 2.0 to 1.0 kg. Residency, it would seem, is a pain in the neck both figuratively and literally.

2. Morrell RM: Sequelae to roundsmanship. New Physician 1964; 13(1):A77–79.

The author suggests a number of ways for residents to outmaneuver attendings ("frontrowmen") during Grand Rounds. For example, how to block pearls before, during, or after delivery.

3. Sapira JD: Rules and guidelines for house staff involved in general medical rounds with attending physicians whose own training predated the present era of educational consumerism. South Med J 1981; 74(7):866–67.

A satire which presents 16 tips on how to avoid learning anything during bedside rounds. For example, "Be late for rounds. If this is not possible, be punctual but be in the wrong place."

ACADEMIA

When patients read articles on "How to Choose a Doctor," one of the most common suggestions is to find out whether the physician is affiliated with a medical school. Ostensibly this means the individual will be up on the latest advances and therefore will give better medical care. In reality, of course, being a faculty member means something entirely different. It means having no control over the hiring and firing of employees, having to go to endless meetings and serve on countless committees, remembering to show up for lectures (giving them, not hearing them), worrying about promotion and tenure, having to evaluate students continuously, avoiding the chairman when quarterly reports are due concerning research in progress, and last but not least, having to accept a lower salary for the privilege of putting the word "professor" after your name. Although the following articles do not address all of these issues, they do shed light on some of the oddities in academic medicine. A few should be suitable for your next staff meeting.

Dear _____
(a) Sir   (b) Madam   (c) Dr.*

MELVIN HERSHKOWITZ, M.D.

Last year our 45 house officers asked for 310 recommendation letters for examination eligibility, further training, and medical licensure. What can be done about the need to produce this mass of correspondence, admittedly important for the credentials and welfare of medical students and house officers, but so substantial a drain on the time and energy of department directors and secretaries? While I cogitated over yet another letter to be written about a house officer I don't number among my closest friends, a fantasy brought forth the following:

This letter supports the application of Dr. X for ____ *(a) internship (b) residency (c) license to practice (d) fellowship (e) moonlighter* in your ____ *(a) department (b) emergency room (c) methadone maintenance program (d) ambulatory plastic surgery center (e) skilled nursing home (f) stress testing facility (g) executive health clinic (h) professional standards review organization (i) hospice (j) corporate medical division.*

I have observed Dr. X during his/her ____ *(a) period of training (b) tour of duty (c) educational experience (d) clinical rotation (e) liver rounds* here and have had ____ *(a) abundant (b) sufficient (c) very little (d) hardly any* opportunity to evaluate his/her performance. I can therefore report that Dr. X is ____ *(a) a Nobel Prize contender (b) highly competent (c) average (d) below average (e) hopelessly incompetent* and that his/her fund of knowledge and familiarity with the literature is ____ *(a) encyclopedic (b) average (c) below average (d) abysmal (e) typical for one who cannot read (hearsay).*

His/her clinical judgment is ____ *(a) exceptionally mature (b) satisfactory (c) erratic (d) consistently unreliable.* Dr. X is also ____ *(a) unusually industrious (b) diligent (c) very lazy (d) rarely seen in the hospital* and shows what may be considered ____ *(a) a deep and genuine interest (b) only casual interest (c) a general lack of interest (d) sincere avoidance* in his/her work. In addition, Dr. X's charts and medical records are ____ *(a) well organized, thorough, and legible (b) a bit careless (c) disorganized and illegible (d) chaotic (e) brief and uninformative* because Dr. X's command of the language is ____ *(a) excellent (b) fair (c) poor (d) utterly unintelligible.* Dr. X's personality is ____ *(a) passive and silent (b) outgoing and pleasant (c) nasty and hostile (d) psychotic (e) nonexistent* and his/her moral character is ____ *(a) beyond reproach (b) apparently good (c) flawed and untrustworthy (d) typically political.* We have confirmed this by observing his/her relations with ____ *(a) attending physicians (b) fellow house officers (c) medical students (d) nurses (male and female) (e) technicians (f) hospital administrators (g) patients.*

We may add that Dr. X's participation in teaching activities has been ____ *(a) catalytic and stimulating (b) active (c) minor (d) to attend and sleep (e) to not attend* and his/her response to emergencies is ____ *(a) rapid and*

*Reprinted with permission from The New Physician, ©1981; 30(8): 24–25. Copyright by American Medical Student Association.

efficient (b) slow and uncertain (c) anxious and unpredictable (d) to faint (e) to disappear. When asked to work under stress and with fatigue, Dr. X's response is ____ *(a) to try hard and adjust well (b) to decompensate (c) to request an immediate vacation.*

In view of the above, we recommend Dr. X ____ *(a) with unreserved enthusiasm (b) hesitantly (c) with a heavy heart (d) with fear and foreboding,* and we are certain that he/she will be ____ *(a) an invaluable addition to (b) a valued member of (c) a grave handicap to* the already outstanding program you are supervising.

Yours sincerely,

_____

A Weary Faculty Member

Now that Dr. Hershkowitz has made writing letters of recommendation as easy as popping dinner into the microwave, Barry Kirkpatrick* shows us how to interpret those unwieldy missives known as dean's letters. For those of us who actually have to write (or read) these letters, this piece will have an unmistakable ring of truth beneath the laughter. Dr. Kirkpatrick wrote his letter in response to an editorial that criticized the way students are currently evaluated in U.S. medical schools (Friedman RB: Fantasy land. N Engl J Med 1983; 308(11):651–653).—*H.B.*

What the Dean Really Means

To the Editor: I submit the following guide for interpretation of what the dean really means:

THE DEAN'S LETTER	WHAT THE DEAN REALLY MEANS	THE DEAN'S LETTER	WHAT THE DEAN REALLY MEANS
Sensitive	Cries easily	Grasps new concepts quickly	Basically stupid, but flexible
Very sensitive	Cries on Rounds		
Very cooperative	Easy; will work extra nights	Highly satisfactory	About average
Relatively good	Would not want him for my doctor	Compulsive, goal-oriented drive	Obnoxious, but more so than the self-motivated individual
Sensitive to patients' needs	Steals food from their trays	Recommended to you with confidence	Glad to get him out of our school
Extremely capable	A little better than average		
Well-liked	His mother always spoke well of him	Recommended to you without reservation	Glad to get him out of our school
Extremely conscientious	Probably paranoid	Look forward to watching this individual as he matures in his career	Hope the turkey improves
Assertive	Real S.O.B.		
Self-motivated	Obnoxious		
Outstanding integrity	On parole; is watching every step	Will be an asset to your program	Don't call us, we'll call you
Enthusiastic	Hebephrenic		

Barry V. Kirkpatrick, M.D.
Medical College of Virginia
Richmond, VA

*Reprinted with permission from The New England Journal of Medicine, ©1983; 309(12):735.

The next selection was taken from an essay published in JAMA's weekly column, "A Piece of My Mind." Like the editorial just referred to, Dr. Schneiderman was concerned with the problem of communicating a student's performance in written reports. Though his essay was serious, he ended on a light note by providing the following whimsical adjectives to describe medical students' performance in just "the right word."—*H.B.*

Le Mot Juste*

Performance Percentile	Descriptor
99	Magnificent
98	Superlative
93	Extraordinarily strong
88	Notable
83	Wonderful
80	Terrific, radiant, and humble
78	Accomplished
75	Nonsteroidal anti-inflammatory
70	Well read
65	Capable
60	Intermittent
55	Well above the mean
50	Strong
45	Hearty
40	Friendly
35	Well groomed
30	Attentive and respectful
25	Pleasant
20	Punctual
15	Imminently about to blossom
12	Present and fully continent of all excreta
10	Normocephalic and nonfelonious
8	Claudicative
6	English speaking
5	Ambulatory
3	Respirating and well perfused
1	Charmingly fresh in outlook
0	Eukaryotic and possibly diploid

Henry Schneiderman, MD
Farmington, Conn

*Reprinted from JAMA, ©1988; 259(1):87, with permission from the American Medical Association.

Lectureshipmanship*

IAN ROSE, M.B., B.S., L.R.C.P., M.R.C.S.(Lond.),

During the past decade it has become abundantly clear that teaching is no longer a privilege allowed gifted consultants, but has become a necessity for the survival of any specialist. No longer are the stethoscope and scalpel the mark of his calling; the microphone and the 35-mm. slide have become the symbols of his station in the profession.

It must be clearly understood at the outset that the last thing the lecturer should attempt to do is to communicate. He should sometimes be impressive or mysterious, generally inaudible and unintelligible. It is also necessary for the neophyte specialist to realize that audiovisual aids are available for the purpose of coming between him and his audience.

Lecturer Personalities

As we have indicated in previous papers, it is fundamental for the specialist to select a personality to present to his audience. The following are well-tried lecturer personalities, any one of which can be safely selected and made a life study:

1. The Research Worker Specialist

He is vague, obscure, rather untidy, and generally gets tied up with microphone cords. He delivers the more important parts of his lecture with his back to the microphone. Another useful gambit for him is to turn off all the lights so as better to see a slide on the screen and then not have enough light by which to read his paper.

2. The Successful Administrator Type

He is well-dressed, dynamic, flies in just in time to get to the meeting and flies out as soon as his paper has been delivered. He uses no notes but has a large supply of slides on which his paper has been transcribed. He then reads the paper as it is projected onto the screen.

3. The Older, Father-of-the-Profession Type

This personality can, in many instances, stray far from the general tenets laid down in this article and may in fact make no use of audiovisual aids. He must spend at least 10 of the 15 minutes allocated to his paper on general remarks and *bonhomie*. His opening must always be personal, creating a warm and glowing sense of manly love between him and the younger members of his profession, the audience. One of the most successful openings for this type is to refer in extremely affectionate terms to the joy felt at once again being able to visit this most hospitable, friendly, magnificent, beautiful, exciting town of . . . . (at this point the lecturer should hesitate and consult a small slip of paper in his hand before continuing) of Coleville.

Another effective opening for the father-of-the-profession personality is to refer to some personal tie with the town, such as the fact that the doctor's wife's second cousin Matilda was born there, or was buried there, or married there.

The tie referred to should always be biological (i.e. birth, death or—least effective—marriage). Holidays, fishing trips, minor offences or time spent in the local jail by relatives are not effective in cementing the bond between the lecturer and his audience.

It is noted that according to Dr. Lawrence K. Winkle, the biological incident referred to in this opening should apply to the family of the doctor's wife. In this way warmth is spread, personal familiarity is imparted, and the fact that the doctor's wife needs entertaining during the visit is tactfully established—sometimes known as Larry's Law.

The Construction of a Paper

A. *The audience must have no idea* of the argument of the paper until the last possible moment. Data must be presented in profusion and in a random manner. It is most effective to include a digression into a technique

*Reprinted with permission from The Canadian Medical Association Journal, ©1969; 101(Oct 4):114–116.

of methodology, provided this is not in the direct field of the audience. Thus a biochemical digression is effective for an audience of clinicians, or digression into radiological technique if the audience consists of pathologists.

The conclusion of the paper is the expression of the thesis. When properly executed this can be a complete surprise to the audience.

B. *Delivery should be inaudible and monotonous.* If the lecturer makes the error of being understood, the audience will conclude that he is more of an actor than a specialist. The more unintelligible he is, the more his reputation will be enhanced.

Inaudibility is usually not difficult to achieve. Fixed microphones can be avoided easily. When one is slung around the neck it is a little more difficult, but by trial and error it is usually possible to find an angle for the head where the microphone will not pick up the voice. If all else fails, it can be surreptitiously slipped inside the shirt during a moment in the dark.

Occasionally one may find a very irritating and persistent chairman who is always interfering and resetting the microphone. These officious people can usually be discouraged by twisting them up in the microphone cord. If all else fails, a sharp kick in the shins during the showing of a slide will gracefully take him out of circulation while he receives first-aid in the next room.

Basic Audiovisual Technique

Great use can be made of the mechanisms for the projection of slides to discompose the audience. A simple device is to punctuate the paper by continually having the lights turned on and off for each slide. This is not only a good way to keep an audience awake but may bring out the occasional latent epileptic.

Another useful gambit is to have the electric pointer fail during the showing of a very full and complex statistical slide. If the pointer is attached to an electrical cord, a sharp tug to unplug it should do the trick. Battery-powered pointers can be scuttled easily by a sharp downward blow on the lectern.

The use of multiple sizes in slides can lead to a lot of humour at the expense of the projector operator. A little indirect humour subtly introduced in this way can be most helpful.

It is probably unnecessary to deal extensively with the various manipulations of the sound systems. We are sure that the fertile mind of the student will have little problem here. However, we would be remiss not to point out the benefits of feedback. In spite of the most modern equipment, with a little resetting of the controls in the wings during the previous paper, some very interesting wailing effects are within the compass of any reasonably industrious lecturer.

Content

This is the area where the harvest can be reaped. In both audio and visual fields the cardinal rule is "complexity." Never use a simple sentence when a complex one will do; insert parentheses liberally. Winterbottom Throgmorton was a master of parenthetical complexity. He once achieved the distinction of a parenthesis within a parenthesis within a parenthesis. It is, unfortunately, impossible to quote this classic here as it belongs to an age more bountifully endowed with newsprint and is longer than the whole of this article. We will, however, send interested readers a reprint of the Throgmorton Parenthesis on special request (accompanied by 50 cents for postage).

The preparation of sufficiently complex slides to mystify the audience can take a long time. To simplify this for the lecturer we can make available, for a small fee, statistical blanks as shown in Fig. 1. It should be noted that these figures are available typed with a special typewriter using extra small print. The lecturer can thus purchase these, fill in the appropriate explanations at the top of the column with such statements as "age," "ionized Ca," "percentage fat," "tweedledee coefficient," etc., etc.

Fig. 2 shows an example of one of our graph overlays. The symbols are printed on Cellophane and can be affixed to any desired graph paper. It is then a simple matter to fill in the abscissae and ordinate units with appropriate figures and a minimum of delay.

Fig. 3 illustrates another of our series.

=	=	=	=
6278	1354.4	7693.3	9756
1222	1122.3	7669	8564
6665.1	6754	7788	9992.1
2435	6574	8884	5777
6758	8877	5543	3465
7986	5566	4444.1	3245
3334	7658	9870	0078
1112.1	2435	8970	6705
2435	7865	9988.3	6574
8675	7689	9999	7675
1111	6754.1	7564	5555
8866	5564	4539	5764
2444	8888	6745	7385
7777	2435	6457	7854.6
7850	7865	8866	4556.8
8978	7856	6456.2	7775
8764	2222	5541.6	6752

FIG. 1.

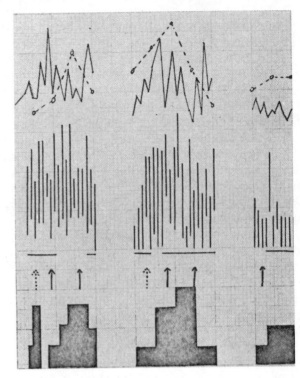

FIG. 3.

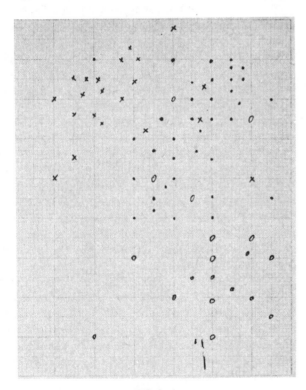

FIG. 2.

General Rules

1. A lecture may amuse but must never communicate.

2. Never use a simple sentence when a complex one will do.

3. The content of the lecture should be obscure and unintelligible.

4. The lecturer must be inaudible.

5. Slides must be complex and made in the smallest possible print.

6. Statistics must be used to obscure facts—not elucidate them.

The Art of Pimping*

FREDERICK L. BRANCATI, M.D.

It's hard work becoming a revered attending physician in a university hospital. The task daunts the newly appointed junior attending as he strides down the corridor of his first ward with his first team. Oh, he's made some changes in anticipation of his new position. He's wearing a long coat now, an all-cotton coat with razor-sharp creases and knit buttons. The stained, shrunken polyester white pants and tennis shoes have given way to gray, light wool slacks with a cuff and polished loafers. Framed certificates bear testimony to his intelligence and determination. He should be ready to take the helm of his ward team, but he's not. Something's missing, something important, something closer to art than to science. When physicians talk about the "art of medicine" they usually mean healing, or coping with uncertainty, or calculating their federal income taxes. But there's one art this new attending needs to learn before all others: the art of pimping.

Pimping occurs whenever an attending poses a series of very difficult questions to an intern or student. The earliest reference to pimping is attributed to Harvey in London in 1628. He laments his students' lack of enthusiasm for learning the circulation of the blood: "They know nothing of Natural Philosophy, these pinheads. Drunkards, sloths, their bellies filled with Mead and Ale. O that I might see them pimped!"

In 1889, Koch recorded a series of "Pümpfrage" or "pimp questions" he would later use on his rounds in Heidelberg. Unpublished notes made by Abraham Flexner on his visit to Johns Hopkins in 1916 yield the first American reference: "Rounded with Osler today. Riddles house officers with questions. Like a Gatling gun. Welch says students call it 'pimping.' Delightful."

On the surface, the aim of pimping appears to be Socratic instruction. The deeper motivation, however, is political. Proper pimping inculcates the intern with profound and abiding respect for his attending physician while ridding the intern of needless self-esteem. Furthermore, after being pimped, he is drained of the desire to ask new questions—questions that his attending may be unable to answer. In the heat of the pimp, the young intern is hammered and wrought into the framework of the ward team. Pimping welds the hierarchy of academics in place, so the edifice of medicine may be erected securely, generation upon generation. Of course, being hammered, wrought, and welded may, at times, be somewhat unpleasant for the intern. Still, he enjoys the attention and comes to equate his initial anguish with the aches and pains an athlete suffers during a period of intense conditioning.

Despite its long history and crucial importance in training, pimping as a medical art has received little attention from the educational establishment. A recent survey reveals that fewer than 1 in 20 attending physicians have had any formal training in pimping. In most American medical schools, pimping is covered haphazardly during the third-year medical clerkship or is relegated to a fourth-year elective. In a 1985 poll, over 95% of program directors admitted that the pimping skills of their trainees were "seriously inadequate." It comes as no surprise, then, that the newly appointed attending must teach himself how to pimp. It is to this most junior of attendings, therefore, that I offer the following brief guide to the art of pimping.

Pimp questions should come in rapid succession and should be essentially unanswerable. They may be grouped into five categories.

1. **Arcane points of history**. These facts are not taught in medical school and are irrelevant to patient care—perfect for pimping. For example, who performed the first lumbar puncture? Or, how was syphilis named?

2. **Teleology and metaphysics**. These questions lie outside the realm of conventional scientific inquiry and have traditionally been addressed only by medieval philosophers and the editors of the *National Enquirer*. For instance, why are some organs paired?

3. **Exceedingly broad questions**. For example, what role do prostaglandins play in homeostasis? Or, what is the differential diagnosis of a fever of unknown origin? Even if the intern begins making good points, after 4 or

*Reprinted from JAMA, ©1989; 262(1):89–90, with permission from the American Medical Association.

5 minutes he can be cut off and criticized for missing points he was about to mention. These questions are ideally posed in the final minutes of rounds while the team is charging down a noisy stairwell.

4. Eponyms. These questions are favored by many old-timers who have assiduously avoided learning any new developments in medicine since the germ theory. For instance, where does one find the semilunar space of Traube? Or, whose name is given to the dancing uvula of aortic regurgitation?

5. Technical points of laboratory research. Even when general medical practice has become a dim and distant memory, the attending physician-investigator still knows the details of his research inside and out. For instance, how active are leukocyte-activated killer cells with or without interleukin 2 against sarcoma in the mouse model? Or, what base sequence does the restriction endonuclease *Eco*RI recognize?

Such pimping should do for the third-year student what the Senate hearings did for Robert Bork. The intern, in contrast, is a seasoned veteran and not so easily rattled. Years of relentless pimping have taught him two defenses: the dodge and the bluff.

Dodging avoids the question, wasting time as well as a valuable pimp question. The two most common forms of dodging are (1) to answer the question with a question and (2) to answer a different question. For example, the intern is asked to explain the pathophysiology of thrombosis secondary to the lupus anticoagulant. He first recites the clotting cascade, then recalls the details of a lupus case he admitted last month, and closes by asking whether pulse-dose steroids are indicated for lupus nephritis. The experienced attending immediately diagnoses this outpouring as a dodge, grabs the intern by the scruff of the neck, and rubs his nose back in the original pimp.

A bluff, unfortunately, is much more damaging than a dodge. Allowed to stand, a bluff promulgates a lie while undermining the academic hierarchy by suggesting that the intern has nothing more to learn from his attending. Bluffs weaken the very fabric of American medicine, threatening our livelihood and our way of life. Like outlaws in a Clint Eastwood movie, bluffs must be shot on sight—no due process, no Miranda Act, no starry-eyed liberal notions of openness or dialogue—just righteous retribution.

Bluffs fall into three readily discernible categories:

1. Hand waving. These bluffs are stock phrases that refer to hot topics in biomedicine without supplying detail or explanation. For example, "It's a membrane transport phenomenon" or "The effect is mediated by prostaglandins." In many institutions, they may evolve directly from the replies of Grand Rounds speakers to questions from the audience.

2. Feigned erudition. The intern's answer, though without substance, suggests an intimate understanding of the literature and a cautiousness born of experience. "Hmmm . . . to my knowledge, that question has not been examined in a prospective controlled fashion" is a common form. Frequently, the bluff is accompanied by three automatisms: clearing of the throat, rapid fluttering of the eyelids and tongue, and chewing on the temples of the eyeglasses. This triad, when full-blown, will make the intern bear a sudden resemblance to William Buckley and is virtually pathognomonic.

3. Higher authority. The intern attributes his answer to the teaching of a particular superior. When the answer is refuted, the blame of ignorance comes to rest on the higher authority, not on the obedient, accepting intern. The strength of the bluff depends on just whom is quoted. An intern quoting a junior resident about pathophysiology is every bit as cogent as Colonel Qaddafi quoting Ayatollah Khomeini about international law. An intern from an Ivy League medical school quoting the "training" he received on his medical clerkship goes over like Dan Quayle explaining the Bill of Rights at an ACLU convention. The shrewd intern, however, will quote his Chairman of medicine or at least a division chief, pushing the nontenured attending to the brink of political calamity. Did the chairman actually say *that?* The attending is powerless to refute the statement until he is certain.

Indeed, a good bluff is hard to handle. Sometimes the intern's bluff sounds better to the ward team than the attending's correct answer. Sometimes it sounds better to the attending himself. Ultimately, the cunning intern is best discouraged from bluffing by aversive training. Specifically, each time he bluffs successfully, the attending should counter by inducing Sudden Intern Disgrace (SID). SID is induced in two ways:

1. Question the intern's ability to take a history. This technique depends on the phenomenon of historical drift. That is, a patient's story will reliably undergo a significant change in the 8- or 16-hour interval between admission and attending rounds. The attending need only go to the bedside and ask the same questions the intern did the night before. Now the entire case is seen in a light different than that cast by the intern's assessment. Yesterday's right upper quadrant cramping becomes right-sided pleuritic chest pain. Yesterday's ill-defined midepigastric "burning" becomes crushing substernal heaviness radiating to the arm and jaw. Suddenly, the intern is disgraced. He will never bluff again.

2. Question the intern's compulsiveness. In less rigorous programs, this is easy. Did the intern examine the peripheral blood smear and the urine sediment himself? If the intern does routinely examine body fluids, a more methodical approach is required. In this case, results of the following tests, procedures, and examinations may be requested in rapid succession: Hemoccult slide test, urine electrolytes, bedside cold agglutinins and serum viscosity, slit-lamp examination, Schiøtz's tonometry, Gram's stain of the buffy coat, transtracheal aspiration, anoscopy, rigid sigmoidoscopy, and indirect laryngoscopy. Once the attending discovers a test or examination left unperformed, he asks the intern why this obviously crucial point was neglected. (The tension may be heightened at this point by frequent use of the word "cavalier.") The intern's response will generally revolve around time

constraints and priorities in diagnostic evaluation. The attending's rejoinder: did the intern eat, sleep, or void last night? The scrupulous intern at once infers that he has placed his own needs before the needs of his patient. Suddenly, he is disgraced. He will never bluff again.

Clearly, pimping—good pimping—is an art. There are styles, approaches, and a few loose rules to guide the novice, but pimping is learned in practice, not theory. Despite its long and glorious history, pimping is in danger of becoming a lost art. Increased specialization, the rise of the HMO, and DRG-based financing are probably to blame, as they are for most problems. The burgeoning budget deficit, the changing demographic profile of the United States, the Carter Administration, inefficiency at the Pentagon, and intense competition from Japan have each played a role, though less directly. Against this mighty array of historical forces stands the beleaguered junior attending armed only with training, wit, and the determination to pimp. It won't be easy to turn back the clock and restore the art of pimping to its former grandeur. I only hope my guide will help.

The following article was published in 1902 in the *Fort Wayne Medical Journal*. Although it would be unlikely to find such a disparate group of physicians at the same meeting today (grand rounds and the hospital cafeteria notwithstanding), the theme of this parody has aged quite well.—*H.B.*

Report of a Meeting of a Modern Medical Society*

F. E. BUNTS, M.D.

FIRST SURGEON (DR. JONES): I am pleased to bring before the members of this society a report of an extremely interesting case of rupture of the liver. The patient was accidentally kicked over a fence by a mule and landed with his right side on a pig's head. No symptoms developed for twenty-four hours. When the family became alarmed at the absence of symptoms, I was called in to see the case and at once diagnosed a

rupture of the liver. The signs were somewhat obscure, but an operation made thirty-six hours hence proved the accuracy of my observations. The liver and portal vein were carefully sutured and the abdominal wound was closed with four rows of sutures—catgut, silk, silkworm gut, and silver wire, respectively. The patient made an uneventful recovery and returned to his occupation as a mule driver nine days after surgery. In

*Reprinted from the Fort Wayne Medical Journal, ©1902; 22:288–290. Edited from the original.

conclusion, I would say that the chief points of interest in this case are the accuracy of the diagnosis and the excellent results following a most hazardous and desperate operation.

CHAIRMAN: This most interesting paper by Dr. Jones is now open for discussion.

OPHTHALMOLOGIST: I am sure we are all very much indebted to Dr. Jones for his most valuable contribution to surgical knowledge. In fact, it reminds me of a case I was called in to see about a well known man who ruptured his eyeball while attempting to watch a troupe of ballet girls all at once. In this case I made a careful examination and found marked evidence of blepharospasm, a choked disc, and external strabismus. The treatment consisted of prompt removal of the eye. The cure was immediate and uneventful, and the patient has never again attended a ballet performance. In conclusion, I again congratulate the author for his paper.

GYNECOLOGIST: The subject under discussion is somewhat out of my line of work; however, its brilliant result reminds me of a case of endometritis fungoides complicating a Bartholin's cyst in a 96-year-old patient. In this case I removed the uterus and appendages per vagina after excision of the cyst. The patient made an uneventful recovery, has since remarried, and now feels as young as she did seventy years ago. I would like to thank Dr. Jones for the opportunity his paper has given me to present this case.

OTOLARYNGOLOGIST: I cannot allow this opportunity to pass without referring to a case which Dr. Jones' valuable paper has brought to mind. Some years ago, a patient of mine snuffed a bean up her nose. A careful inquiry at the time failed to reveal the bean, but yesterday (two years from the date of the first examination), there appeared an unmistakable bean-sprout extending from the anterior nares. I at once diagnosed a sprouting bean and removed it under cocaine anesthesia. No untoward effect was produced and the patient made an uneventful recovery. I congratulate Dr. Jones for his most excellent paper.

NEUROLOGIST: Rupture of the liver should remind all of us that sudden jars may also cause rupture of the cerebral sinuses or hemorrhage into the spinal canal. In a case similar to the one by Dr. Jones, motor paralysis was present from the moment a patient sustained the shock of receiving a doctor's bill. I made the diagnosis without any difficulty. Fortunately, the patient recovered in time to make the races the very next day. Again, I wish to congratulate Dr. Jones on his very elaborate and painstaking paper.

SECOND SURGEON: I can endorse everything that Dr. Jones has said and appreciate fully the value of his paper. I wish to take exception, however, with his means of diagnosis and to say that from the symptoms related in the history, there could not possibly have been a rupture of the liver. Nor could he, in my estimation, have sewn up the portal vein without seriously interfering with the functions of the liver and bringing on an attack of the piles. In all cases of this kind, I have made it a point to also dissect out very carefully the pile-bearing area. In conclusion, Mr. Chairman, I would say that I hope no one will think from my remarks that I differ in any essentials from the practice of my distinguished confrere.

CHAIRMAN: As there is no further discussion about this paper, I would say that we are all very pleased by the elaborate and carefully prepared discussion which it has called forth. Dr. Jones will now close the meeting.

DR. JONES: The field of surgery has been so fully covered this evening that I feel it is impossible for me to add anything to that which has already been said.

The Fine Art
of Disappearing From Meetings*

HAROLD J. ELLNER, M.D.

As my hospital-staff presidency neared its end, my awareness of the expertise of some of the medical staff in prematurely departing from meetings had finally crystallized. During ascendancy to this position, I could not fully appreciate the extent of this ingenuity. As secretary, I was too busy trying to record the minutes. As vice-president, I had an understudy's engrossment in the president's predicaments and could observe little else. But after the torch was passed and, upright, I faced my seated colleagues at staff meetings, I had a talent scout's view of this venerable art form.

The Telephone Gambit: This classic maneuver deserves mention as the forerunner of all the innovative techniques that follow. The phone calls begin shortly into the meeting, each one summoning a specific physician to a brief but earnest conversation. The callee strides out purposefully, not to return. Practitioners of this method have usually scheduled the call themselves or, serendipitously receiving any call whatever, hit upon it as a cause to leave. The same doctors seem to get called at roughly the same time during each meeting. In fact, one of our former members was called away regularly by his wife for 17 years in this manner.

The Page: A variation of the Telephone Gambit, this method requires an intrahospital page to extricate the doctor from a staff meeting. It is more difficult to orchestrate than the Telephone Gambit, but fortunately often occurs by chance. A good relationship with the page operator doesn't hurt, however. The adaptable staff member, once out, does not return.

The Indignation Ploy: This method requires a certain amount of boldness to succeed. The staff member professes his displeasure soon after the meeting begins. He advises the president that he expected to use his valuable time to transact certain hospital business (whatever is not on the agenda). He then strides off— to the cocktail lounge.

The Fidgetary Finesse: In this maneuver, escape velocity is gradually achieved by the more timid members in attendance. It starts when one of them begins to get restless. Next, the doctor makes the first of many trips to the coffee urn (the one near the door). A final effort propels him through the portal when escape velocity is reached. As the year progresses, the staff member usually gains confidence and requires fewer trips for coffee. He may eventually omit the formality of stopping at the urn altogether.

The Direct Approach: With this method, the doctor stands, glances at his watch (optional), purposefully adjusts his head slightly downward, and exits.

The Intermission Exit: For those too reticent to use the Direct Approach, it helps to remain until halftime and to exercise a modicum of timing. A clear advantage of this technique is that it is compensated by refreshments, conversation, and fellowship. After these have all been enjoyed, but before the first sign of the recall to order, one oozes out a nearby door.

Early Surgery: This is a special situation that requires a breakfast meeting to work. The surgical schedule is traditionally set back to allow the staff to meet. The practitioner of this maneuver claims to have gotten a complicated patient on his service at an inconveniently late night hour. The doctor schedules emergency morning surgery from his bed. He then comes to the meeting, has a leisurely breakfast, preempts the scheduled cases, and does his "emergency."

The foregoing summarizes only the basics in a field where there is great opportunity for those with talent and imagination. Doubtless, much has been omitted. Each practitioner has his own style, and methods must be studied in order to determine which ones will best serve an individual's needs.

*Reprinted from JAMA, ©1982; 247(4):508, with permission from the American Medical Association. Edited from the original.

Additional Readings

1. Bluestone N: Signing out. Resid Staff Physician 1986; 32(10):85–88.

After 18 years of service to Farethewell Hospital and the Healthyself Medical School, the Chief of Surgery gets a letter telling him he is subject to mandatory retirement soon after his 62nd birthday. The letter details the protocol he must follow, including such items as being sure all of his library fines are paid in full.

2. Copple PJ: Conferencemanship. New Physician 1961; 10(5):A80–81.

The author presents 15 tips for organizing and running a case conference. For example, "Schedule the conference for those hours when people are at their best, such as 8 am Monday, 1 pm any other day, 4:30 pm Friday, or 11 am Saturday."

3. Coulter DL: The academic oedipal crisis. J Polymorphous Perversity 1987; 4(2):17–19.

This article examines a developmental milestone not mentioned in most standard psych textbooks: the need of assistant professors to kill their department chairmen.

4. Eisman B, Thompson JC: The visiting professor. N Engl J Med 1977; 296(15):845-850.

A satirical essay on the visiting professorship. It includes a universal form letter that is complete with blank spaces for the visiting professor's name, the choice of lecture topics, and dates, etc.

5. Markivee CR: Rating of speaker performance. AJR 1985; 144(4):864–865.

The author presents a system for rating medical speakers. Points are added or subtracted depending on ones proficiency or ineptness in several areas: the use of a microphone and light pointer, the quality and quantity of medical slides, etc.

6. Pauker SP: Grand rounds whiplash. N Engl J Med 1970; 283(11):600.

The author suggests the use of Thomas collars to prevent complications that might occur when tired house officers attend grand rounds.

7. Smith RP: Conference coma. Obstet Gynecol 1983; 61(5):647–648.

A formula for figuring out how much sleep you can expect during a conference. It takes into account the number of slides to be shown, the distance the speaker had to travel, and other variables.

MEDICAL
LANGUAGE

When medical students begin their education, they have no idea that half of medicine is learning the language. Within days, however, they discover that an armpit is no longer an armpit but really an axilla and that the belly button, that long contemplated dimple in our midriff, is now called an umbilicus. Then, after a two year crash course that teaches them the nouns, verbs, and adjectives in medicine, they hit the wards to learn the grammar. Patients, they find, are not merely taken care of, but "followed," "digitalized," and "covered with antibiotics." In addition, they learn that a major goal in medicine is to cram as much as possible about a patient's life onto a 3 × 5 card. The jargon, the initials, and the other conventions are only a means to that end. The selections that follow take a humorous look at this area by showing some of the ways that medicine dislocates how we speak and write.

A Lesson
In Medical Lingoistics*

JUSTIN DORGELOH, M.D.

Scene: A classroom filled with eager medical students. As the curtain rises, Dr. Jaargon, Professor of Medical Lingoistics, enters.

DR. JAARGON: Good morning, students. Today we'll review some of the terms you will be required to use as doctors. First, what must patients do before they die?

CLASS *(in unison)*: Go downhill.

STUDENT: Or pursue a downhill course.

DR. J.: Very good. Now, to demonstrate diagnostic acumen, what must one have?

CLASS: A high index of suspicion.

DR. J.: Right again. Normal lungs are always—

STUDENT: Clear.

DR. J.: And a flat abdomen is—

STUDENT: Scaphoid.

DR. J.: And a pharynx is—

STUDENT: Clear or injected.

DR. J.: To look up published medical articles we—

STUDENT: Review the literature!

Dr. J.: *What* literature?

CLASS: *The* literature!

Dr. J.: Excellent. Now tell me what is wrong with the following statement: "There is no history of rheumatic fever, malaria, or syphilis."

STUDENT: A patient must always *deny* syphilis.

DR. J.: Correct. Now, I overheard one of you saying yesterday that the treatment given one of our hospital patients was "ineffective." The required phrasing is, "The patient responded poorly to treatment." Please note the subtle shift in responsibility. That brings us to a related subject. What may a drug manifest?

CLASS: (No answer)

DR. J.: Side effects. Not drawbacks or poisonous properties (heaven forbid!), but *side effects.* Now to go on. Feeding a patient is—

CLASS: Alimentation.

DR. J.: And how about intravenous feeding?

STUDENT: Parenteral alimentation.

DR. J.: And a patient excreting less or more nitrogen than he absorbs is in—

STUDENT: Nitrogen imbalance.

DR. J.: No! The patient is always in *balance.* Positive balance or negative balance, but never. imbalance. Remember that. Here's another question: Available remedies form a doctor's—

STUDENT: Therapeutic armamentarium.

DR. J.: Right. Now, diseases of which we don't know the cause—

CLASS: Diseases of obscure etiology.

DR. J.: And such a disease may be called—

STUDENT: Idiopathic.

DR. J.: Or?

STUDENT: Cryptogenic.

DR. J.: Or?

STUDENT: Agnogenic.

DR. J.: Ah! *There's* a word to inspire respect in the listener. And casual reference to such items as polyploidy, hamartomas, the Kell factor, and the chi square formula can be similarly effective . . . A disease capable of causing varied signs and/or symptoms is invariably known as—

STUDENT: A disease of protean manifestations.

DR. J.: And a congenital or familial disease of metabolism is—

STUDENT: An inborn error of metabolism.

DR. J.: Right. Now, to proceed: An antibiotic affecting a variety of bacteria is a—

STUDENT: Versatile antibiotic.

DR. J.: No.

STUDENT: Broad-action antibiotic.

DR. J.: No, but you're closer. The proper term is broad-*spectrum* antibiotic. One might think that iridescent, multicolored, or rainbow would do, but they won't. It must always be *broad-spectrum* . . . Now, class, a serum which will affect a variety of bacteria is a—

STUDENT *(confidently)*: Broad-spectrum serum.

---

*Reprinted with permission from Medical Economics, ©1954; 31(Jan):189–193. Copyright by Medical Economics Company, Inc., Oradell, NJ 07649.

DR. J.: No. You have fallen into my trap. It is a *polyvalent* serum. At this point a few more warnings may be in order. You can proctoscope, cystoscope, or bronchoscope a patient, but you cannot *stethoscope* him. For that matter, you cannot sphygmomanometer him, either. The internist is clearly at a disadvantage in this regard but has retaliated by adopting *digitalize* before that term could be claimed by the proctologist.

STUDENT (breaking in): Pardon me, sir, but how did we do in our written examination?

DR. J.: Let's see. You were asked to rephrase, in a form suitable for medical publication, the statement: "The patient's nose was large and red." Mr. Jones' composition was the best. His translation is as follows, and I quote: "The case presented an erythematous blush of the nasal region, superimposed upon a process which had induced changes associated with a size at or just beyond the upper limit of the range generally considered the physiologic norm." Congratulations, Mr. Jones. You can really roll those syllables around.

(Here the curtain falls momentarily to indicate a short recess. As it rises again, Dr. Sinktest, a pathologist, enters.)

DR. J.: Students, I have asked Dr. Sinktest to address you on Pathological Lingoistics. Dr. Sinktest, will you say something?

DR. SINKTEST (startled): The body is that of a well-developed, well-nourished—

DR. J.: No, no, Dr. Sinktest. That's a microphone, not a dictaphone. Suppose, instead, you answer questions. What do you call a lump in the body?

DR. S. (promptly): A tumor mass, of course.

DR. J. (to the class): Dr. Sinktest is an expert in tautology.*

DR. S. (defensively): There might be some doubt about a tumor, or a mass, but with a tumor mass you've got something.

DR. J.: And a tumor mass always shows something on—

DR. S.: Cut section. Sometimes the clinicians claim I forget to section the tumor masses. *Cut* section emphasizes the matter. "Cut section slicing" might convince those bums even better—

Dr. J.: Thank you, thank you very much, Dr. Sinktest! . . . Class dismissed.

CURTAIN

---

*The needless repetition of an idea, statement, or word.

Notes From a Medical Lexicographer's Waste Basket*

H. S. GRANNATT

A-bor'-tion: 1. The quantity usually served to one person; as, "Give me abortion of potatoes." 2. A serving of beetflavored soap; as, "All I had for lunch was abortion a couple of bagels."

A-or'-ta: Proper or required behavior; as, "If there's nothing more to drink maybe aorta go home."

Ap'-ne-a: Form of greeting to one whose arrival has been unduly delayed; as, "We was wondering what apnea."

Bi'-gem'-in-y: Auxiliary intensive; derived from a phonetically disguised invocation of the Deity, used mainly for emphasis; as, "You'll pay this bill, bigeminy, or else."

Cau'-ter-ize: To have become the object of observation by a third party; as, "He kept looking at her until he finally cauterize."

Cer'-e-bra'-tion: A joyous ritual (Japanese); as "In Tokyo, when cherry brossoms broom, we have big cerebration."

Co-ry'-za: Manifestation of emotional disturbance; as, "Everytime I hafta go out on a night call, she sits down and coryza eyes out."

Dig'-i-tal'-is: Introductory phrase of inquiry as to information conveyed from the second person; as, "If we weren't supposed to know about it, why digitalis?"

En'-e-ma: One who is unfriendly; an antagonist; as, "A guy like that is his own worst enema."

E-phed'-rine: The use of plumage as adornment, especially when named for an Italian paste; as, "Stuck ephedrine his hat and called it macaroni."

Hem'-or-rhoid: Transportation afforded a third person; as, "He didn't have his car so I offered hemorrhoid."

He-red'-i-ty: Located in the present time; as, "We're heredity and gone tomorrow."

Myx'-e-de'-ma: Transitive verb, past tense, for having combined fluids for the ingestion of the third person; as, "I knowed he was thirsty, so I myxedema martini."

Par'-o-ti'-tis: Costume worn on the lower half of the body by an acrobat or trapeze performer as, "Before you go out there on the stage you'd better put on a parotitis."

Scir'-rhus: Comment on unrestrained speech or behavior; as, "What are you trying to do, scirrhus to death?"

Su'-pi-nate: Departure from the usual dietary practice at the beginning of a meal; as, "I passed up the supinate the salad."

Tris-'mus: The festival of the nativity; yuletide.

U'-ri-nal'-y-sis: Relating to the environment of the second person with respect to the lodgings of a specified third person; as, "I'm in Mary's room and urinalysis."

Ur'-ti-car'-i-a: Indicative of a desire to be manually transported by a third person; as, "The only reason that kid is screaming at her mother is that she wants urticaria."

Xiph'-o-cos'tal: An estimate of value; as, "It ain't pretty but it looks as xiphocostal lot of money."

Zo'-na ra'-di-at-a: Relating to the probable cause of thermally induced olfaction; as, "It smells in here like somebody left a can of sardines zona radiata."

*Reprinted from JAMA, ©1961; 176(8):A236 and 178(3):A246, with permission from the American Medical Association. Edited from the original.

Milkman's Syndrome?
You Mean Dr. Milkman*

JUSTIN DORGELOH, M.D.

Eponyms are as spicy to medical parlance as sand traps to a golf course and often just as deadly. To be sure, few doctors now expect a speedy Quick test; and none but a layman would choose the Drinker apparatus for a tipsy brother-in-law. Such transparent traps are obviously for mere duffers. So let's shift our attention to veritable quicksands that threaten even the low-handicap physician.

Lest the reader not realize the magnitude of the problem from the start, I submit three examples for immediate consideration: (1) Head's zones can be mapped out over most of the body, not just the head. (2) Frog, rat and rabbit tests notwithstanding, Magpie's test (for salts of mercury) requires no magpies, and the Eagle test (for syphilis) uses no eagles. (3) Patella's disease (pyloric stenosis in TB patients) was named by or for a Dr. Vincenzo Patella, who perhaps refrained from ever mentioning patellas on principle.

On the other hand, it's entirely possible to play around a verbal sand trap that doesn't exist. When word of the rice diet was first whispered about in hospital corridors, I lightly assumed that, whatever the diet was, it must be the brainchild of some Dr. Rice. Dr. Augustus Rice somehow came to mind (though I have never heard of anybody named Augustus Rice). It was finally pointed out to me, gently, that the rice diet is simply a diet of rice.

Possibly I muffed this one because Patella's disease had tattooed my diencephalon, because I'd learned that the quite sippable Sippy diet was named after Dr. Sippy and because at an early age I had to be set straight on the Diet of Worms.

I soon afterward sliced into a medical sand trap that *did* exist. One memorable morning, our hospital radiologist pointed to some X-ray portraits of bone streaks and murmured, "Milkman's syndrome." I still remember the scene vividly, for a respectful hush immediately settled upon the little group of doctors present. (More enigmatic than the face behind a poker hand is the cautious physician face to face with a challenging eponym.) Unable to fathom whether "Milkman's syndrome" was an everyday term among my strangely silent colleagues, I happily remembered an autopsy I hadn't finished and propelled myself to the hospital morgue.

During the following weeks, I turned over the "Milkman" question at length, usually while trying to fall asleep at night and invariably when no medical dictionary was closer than two miles. First off, was "Milkman's syndrome" just a hoax, an offhand fabrication tossed out as a bait by our fun-loving radiologist? Hardly, since the maneuver would have been a dangerous one for any job-loving radiologist beset by creditors.

Next came the inevitable question: Does it refer to a doctor named Milkman? As far as recent experience went, Patella's disease and the rice diet pointed in opposite directions. The streaks of calcium (or lack of calcium) in the bones irresistibly suggested a relationship to milk—and hence to milkmen (who, for all I know, wouldn't be caught dead with a glass of milk). Consideration of the many bona fide occupational diseases—such as woolsorters' disease, pearlworkers' disease, shuttlemakers' disease and brass-founders' ague—finally lulled me into thinking of Milkman's syndrome as vibrational lines of stress in the bones of milkmen (a natural result of incessantly rattling milk bottles to arouse sleepy-headed customers in the wee hours of the morning).

Then one day I happened across M.S. (Milkman's syndrome) in my medical dictionary. I discovered that the bone lesions bear no more relationship to milkmen than Baker's cyst to the bread industry. It so happens that the syndrome *does* bear a relationship to the late Dr. Louis Arthur Milkman of Scranton, Pa.

At this juncture, I would gladly have ascribed the "coin lesions" of chest-film X-rays to anybody named

*Reprinted with permission from Medical Economics, ©1966; 43(Oct 31):190–197. Copyright by Medical Economics Company, Inc., Oradell, NJ 07649.

Dr. Coin. But the common-noun nature of the term was explained to me straight off. The chest surgeons' unquestioning acceptance of this potential slur is a source of wonderment to me, for it is only a matter of time before some non-chest surgeon snidely paraphrases mass-survey coin lesions as "pennies from heaven." Forsooth, the "coins" of today are but the "balls" of yesteryear: cannon balls, tennis balls, Ping-Pong balls. (Of course, "Ping-Pong ball" became obsolete as a figure of speech after medical science succeeded in stuffing *real* Ping-Pong balls into human chest cages. Medicine's is a dynamic, ever-changing tongue.)

Austin Flint and Graham Steell murmurs are patently named after human beings.* The irony here is that each first name sounds like a last name; and I tend to think of the murmurs as Austin "flint" and Graham "steel" (especially since the minerals tie in well with a water-hammer pulse).

The double-name nomenclature finally sows the seeds of its own destruction by way of the hyphen. Unfortunately, the human ear cannot distinguish a silent hyphen from a slight impediment of speech. For example: Paul-Bunnell could well be Paul Q. Bunnell, if he (or they) were not as a matter of fact two men tied together by infectious mononucleosis and a hyphen. On the other hand, "Graham Steell" *sounds* hyphenated and could be misinterpreted as indicating Dr. Graham and Dr. Steell. Even the *printed* hyphen is not foolproof. Pel-Ebstein and Smith-Petersen add up to three people, and you've got one name left over.

Another tidbit for the troubled mind is the matter of multiple references. Klebs-Löffler bacillus cannot cause Löffler's syndrome, and any conjunction of Addison's disease and addisonian anemia is sheer coincidence. Nothnagel's syndrome, seated in the brain, is definitely unrelated to Nothnagel's bodies, encamped in the feces. Speaking of bodies, did you ever contemplate a Wolffian body catching up with a Jolly body? They would probably end up in Room 606 of Charcot's joint.

Possibly the worst all-round troublemaker in medical terminology is the name Weber. It pops up in such unrelated maladies as Weber's disease, Sturge-Weber syndrome, Weber-Christian disease and Rendu-Osler-Weber disease. It also lends itself to Weber's law, Weber's paradox, Weber's corpuscles, Weber's glands, Weber's organ, Weber's point, von Weber's triangle and Weber's douche. Furthermore, there are three distinct Weber's tests, by either two or three Webers.

As a matter of fact, *seven* Webers are entangled in the 15 items listed above: Theodor, Moritz Ignatz, Ernst Heinrich, Eduard Wilhelm, Sir Hermann, Friedrich Eugen and Frederick Parkes. Incidentally, "Weber" is pronounced differently, depending on which Weber you're talking about (assuming that you know).

The name of Friedrich Daniel von Recklinghausen was destined to link two totally unrelated diseases,† but it is doubtful that he or anyone else foresaw how this bit of whimsy would eventually lead to utter confusion. To start slowly, Recklinghausen's neurofibromatosis is, of course, no more related to Recklinghausen's osteitis fibrosa cystica (hyperparathyroidism) than hallux valgus is to athlete's foot. But someone dubbed Recklinghausen's bone disease "osteitis fibrosa cystica generalisata" (so that it could more easily be confused with the totally unrelated osteitis fibrosa cystica disseminata).

Now hold tight: Word has got around that osteitis fibrosa cystica disseminata (*not* to be confused with osteitis fibrosa cystica generalisata, or Recklinghausen's disease) is very possibly a manifestation of neurofibromatosis (the other Recklinghausen's disease).

The Weber-Nothnagel-von Recklinghausen class of sand traps should clearly be retained for divertissement in medical conversations. Just say, "Are you referring to *Sir Hermann* Weber?" and you'll probably have your adversary over a barrel.

However, the proper noun-common noun trap is another matter entirely. A short perusal of any metropolitan telephone directory will show what this class of eponym can lead to. Future medical students may well have to cope with the Pickle diet, the Doolittle treatment, Longenecker's palpitation, the Gorey operation, the Flatt-Foote syndrome or the Loos-Love curet.

I say it's high time hazards like these were ruled off the fairway.

---

*However, the genus and species of a proper name cannot be assumed in all instances. For example, the three strains of poliomyelitis virus are named after a human patient, an American city and an ape named Brunhilde.

†There is also a third Recklinghausen's disease: neoplastic arthritis deformans. For the sake of clarity, this entity will not be introduced into the text.

Crisis in Oncology—Acute Vowel Obstruction (with Apologies to Oncologists Everywhere)*

ROBERT McMILLAN, M.D.
ROBERT L. LONGMIRE, M.D.

Initially, it seemed like an isolated incident involving an un-co-operative patient—a nonconformist; however, the subsequent reverberations were soon to rock the foundations of organized oncology, the National Cancer Institute (NCI), the Federal Drug Administration (FDA), Congress and even the oval office. The first problem developed when a patient was referred by her private physician to the large cancer center, the Northnortheast Oncology Attack Unit (NOAU). After complete evaluation, the diagnosis of carcinoma of the solar plexus was made; extensive metastases to bone, liver and lungs were documented. Clearly, chemotherapy was indicated, and she was assigned to the newest Northnortheast solar Plexus Cancer Study Group protocol comparing the response of this neoplasm to three different drug combinations: two previously successful and commonly used combinations—WHAMMO and SOCKO[†] and their most recently devised protocol—MZRXCL.[‡] When the patient was randomized and informed that she might receive MZRXCL, she said, "Doctor, in all due respect, how can an intelligent person like yourself expect me to receive a group of drugs called MZRXCL? Now, WHAMMO and SOCKO have a dynamic anti-cancer ring to them but I could never have faith in a drug combination called MZRXCL."

This isolated incident was at first a source of luncheon joviality at the dining room at NOAU and was even used as an anecdote in the president's opening address at the next regional cancer meeting. However, over the ensuing weeks, more and more patients with solar-plexus cancer refused randomization into the MZRXCL protocol, each objecting to the distinct lack of anti-cancer "punch" to the name. Gradually, the comparative study was breaking down since the NOAU statisticians only allowed 50 percent of the patients in each group to be unevaluable. Simultaneously, other groups throughout the country were experiencing the same reaction—clearly, something had to be done. One suggestion was to substitute generic names for brand names or vice versa. Unfortunately, this attempt resulted in RZMLPY, which was equally unacceptable to the patients.

The NCI was notified of the developing crisis, and an emergency meeting was called. The problem was obvious—the chemotherapeutic agents in MZRXCL (or RZMLPY) had all been recently assigned FDA numbers, after one year's evaluation in Europe or Japan and 15 additional years' evaluation in this country, and for some reason had all received names beginning with consonants. By this time, several congressmen had been notified by patients and family members that several patients with solar-plexus cancer had been subjected to unfair randomization. Since this treatment clearly constituted prejudice against a minority group, in direct conflict with the Constitution, immediate action was needed. A congressional hearing was called. Owing to the sensitive nature of the topic, coverage by the media was limited to prime-time television monitoring, which was carried by all major networks and beamed by satellite to the other continents (excluding Antarctica).

*Reprinted with permission from The New England Journal of Medicine, ©1976; 294(23):1288–1289.
†Kuror KNCR: The effect of WHAMMO and SOCKO on solar plexus malignancy. Bull NOAU 6:14–467, 1974.
‡A combination of Maximycin (20 mg/M²), Zongotessin (2 µg/M²), and Removzit (4 mg/M²) on days 1 and 7; Xelon (2 units/M²/day), Cylax 45 mg/M²/day and Lassu (4 IU/M²/D) on days 1–14.

Several prominent oncologists were interrogated. After a lengthy preamble by each, on the 18 neoplasms now curable as a result of the new cancer program, they were asked to limit their comments to the subject at hand, solar plexus cancer and protocol MZRXCL (or RZMLPY). It was the opinion of all that the absence of vowels at the beginning of the drug names was the central issue, and since drug companies name their drugs, it was obviously their responsibility.

The presidents of the involved drug companies were called on the stand, and each professed innocence since owing to the secrecy necessary during drug research, there was no way of knowing the names chosen by other competing companies. A prominent senator reasoned, at great length, that an easy solution was simply to change the names of some of the involved drugs. A resounding "Not so fast, Senator" was heard throughout the room, and 365 million homes around the world. The chairman of the New Drug Name Approval Section of the FDA slowly rose and after a meaningful pause informed the congressional committee that the names of therapeutic agents could not be changed willy-nilly and, if changed, would require complete re-evaluation of the involved agent, including extensive phase 1 and 2 studies. A hush was noted in the room, and a drug company president had to be forcibly restrained from jumping through a nearby open window; two others fainted. On the following day the stock of all companies fell 60 per cent.

Letters to congressmen poured in. Not only were their constituents concerned about the medical crisis but they had also missed four months of prime-time television. A special bill was prepared, acted on by both houses of Congress and signed immediately by the President. Two of the drug names were changed—Zongotessin to Ingotessin and Xelon to Alon. This change resulted in the protocol—MIRACL, which would be, of course, acceptable to everyone. Patients with solar-plexus cancer again entered the protocol studies and, happily, solar-plexus cancer became the 19th neoplasm cured by chemotherapy. When the cure of this tumor became apparent, the data were assembled and immediately presented to a prestigious medical body, the science editors, so that the information could be rapidly disseminated by the most appropriate vehicle, the newspapers and weekly magazines. Publication in the medical journals followed six months later. Fortunately for the practicing physicians, they were briefed about these new findings by their patients, who had by this time accumulated a plethora of newspaper clippings on the subject. This alertness afforded their physicians the opportunity to be aware of the findings and also to file these clippings for future reference until such time as the information was published in the medical literature.

This crisis, although alarming, shows how smoothly the American health bureaucracies can work together, if appropriately stimulated, and also proves the old adage, "in times of crisis, there is often nothing as satisfying as a good vowel movement."

Translating Medical Idiom[1]

To the Editor: The following translation guide may be helpful to medical students struggling through the foreign verbiage of the medical language while attempting to assimilate new skills and knowledge.

IDIOMS OFTEN USED AT MEDICAL GRAND ROUNDS

IDIOM	MEANING
"In my experience . . . ."	I have seen ONE such patient.
"In my series . . . ."	I have seen TWO such patients.
"In case, after Case, after CASE . . . ."	I have seen THREE such patients.
"I haven't had a whole lot of experience with this . . . ."	Well, ah, actually, ah, never seen one before.

We sincerely hope this short guide will bring insight to the neophyte and shorten the process of developing seasoned physicians.

James Dolezal, M.D.
James Plamondon, M.D.

Iowa City, IA

That's Funny—Something Is Gained in the Translation[2]

L. A. HEALEY, M.D.

At international medical meetings where papers are presented in several different languages, simultaneous translation enables the audience to understand the speakers. Yet it hasn't been widely recognized that translation can also offer much in local meetings where it's assumed that everyone speaks the same language. Here's a list of statements commonly heard at the latter sort of meeting. Following each, in parentheses, I've given the actual meaning. Take this with you to the next meeting you attend and see if it doesn't add quite a bit to your comprehension of the presentations.

I do not have to relate in detail for this audience the history of this condition. *(I didn't look it up in the literature.)*

For purposes of the present discussion, let us assume that . . . *(This is the key to my argument but I can't quite prove it.)*

This slide depicts the results of a representative study in one dog. *(This is the only one that came out right.)*

Careful clinical observations show . . . *(If I'd had controls, I'd be presenting this at the A.M.A. clinical convention.)*

Omphalograms were not performed at this time. *(I forgot to do that.)*

Probst reports a recurrence rate of 20 per cent, but in our experience, this has not been the case. *(Neither of my patients had one.)*

Time does not permit us to describe fully the enzymatic pathways that are involved in this type of reaction. *(I never was very good in biochemistry.)*

That's a good question. *(I don't know.)*

Please repeat the question. *(I don't know that either.)*

That's a very interesting question. (*That* I know.)

The cases are potentially complicated, and consultation with a specialist should be obtained early. *(I need referrals.)*

For the most part, such cases are readily managed by the primary physician. *(I have a busy practice, thank you.)*

[1] Reprinted with permission from The New England Journal of Medicine, ©1976; 295(3):176.

[2] Reprinted with permission from Medical Economics, ©1971; 48(Aug 30):137. Copyright by Medical Economics Company, Inc., Oradell, NJ 07649.

During my research, I ran into a number of authors who poked fun at medicine's obsession with initials. The following letters, published 20 years apart, say it best.—*H.B.*

Sorry
(<u>S</u>o <u>O</u>ur <u>R</u>iddles <u>R</u>ile <u>Y</u>ou)[1]

To the Editor: After glancing through the June 12 issue of the *Journal* I wonder about my ability to keep up with the language—let alone the pace—of modern medicine. I think I can follow the role of EBV in PTM—not to mention CMV. But when one does a CF for CMV does one require C$\bar{1}$, C' or merely C2? Perhaps my comments are NA—but even though I can tell DNA from RNA I am floored by MTX, dU, HTdR and CGD. I thought (see above) that I knew what "CF" meant, but I'm wrong—it's "citrovorum factor"! If this keeps up I'll be DOA before they can get me to the EW.

Chestnut Hill, MA

Geoffrey Edsall, M.D.

Abbreviations
in the Medical Literature[2]

To the Editor: There is a recent trend (RT) in the medical literature (ML) to abbreviate previously unabbreviated phrases for the sake of efficiency (PUPSAE). Although it makes good sense (GS), the frequency with which it is used can tax the inexperienced reader (IR). Sometimes repetition can actually be beneficial (RCABB) by allowing the reader to retain words he does not constantly have to refer back to (WOHCREBT).

I would like to suggest to the Editor (ED), that for the IR who doesn't wish to have PUPSAE, he have the GS to change the ML so that RCABB and he can eliminate WOHCREBT.

Steven G. Mann, M.D.
Santa Cruz Radiation Oncology
Medical Group

Santa Cruz, CA

ED's reply: We agree with Dr. Mann, but protest our innocence (POI). We do not ordinarily abbreviate PUPSAE because we also believe RCABB and we know that the IR needs WOHCREBT. But it makes GS to allow some previously abbreviated phrases (PAPS) when they are in widespread use (WU), and we occasionally even allow abbreviation of PUPSAE when repeatedly spelling them out would be unusually cumbersome (STOWBUC). We admit, however, that WU of PAPS and PUPS in the ML, even when STOWBUC, often raises the IR's and the ED's BP and HR.

[1] Reprinted with permission from The New England Journal of Medicine, ©1969; 281(4):223.
[2] Reprinted with permission from The New England Journal of Medicine, ©1989; 320(17):1152.

Additional Readings

1. Brickner WM: Acute anatomy. Amer J Surg 1921; 35(3):67.

This article satirizes some recent abuses of medical language—recent that is for 1921! It seems we are not the first generation of physicians that has had to contend with muddled terminology.

2. Christy NP: English is our second language. N Engl J Med 1979; 300(17):979–981.

In this amusing satire, the author takes a scalpel to Medspeak—that inbred and sometimes pretentious language of the hospital. Among other things, he scoffs at the use of big words (symptomatology, armamentarium) when small ones would do and the use of verbal screens to dodge questions on rounds: "Was the man anemia PTA?" Answer: "Not really."

3. Freedman, Bernard J: Just a Word, Doctor. New York, Oxford Medical Publications, 1987.

A collection of witty essays on the origins of medical words and usages. The essays were originally published in the British Medical Journal between 1977 and 1986.

4. Gaño SN: Deficiencies in the English medical vocabulary. Leech 1960; 5(1):52–53. (Note: This article is also reprinted in JAMA 1964; 188(3):278.)

The author describes some amusing inadequacies of language as it applies to clinical practice. For example, when getting a history on a patient with dyspnea, wouldn't it be more concise to ask, "Does she dysp?" Or, if a patient is having ventricular extrasystoles, can it be said that he is "extrasystolizing?"

5. Robb J: Medspeak made simplifax. Br Med J 1981; 283(Dec 19–26):1683–1684.

This is another article that takes some pot shots at Medspeak. The essay has fewer barbs than Dr. Christy's, but is just as amusing. For example, "One often sees on a haematology report 'essentially normal film'—a type of Haemspeak. Does this mean that the film is 'perfectly normal,' or 'more or less normal?'" The author concludes that it doesn't matter what we say to each other as long as we "layspeak" to the patient.

WRITING & PUBLISHING

Physicians write a lot, some because they like to and others because they have to. While the former are certainly in a better position than the latter, I suspect they exist in smaller numbers. In fact, as one of my old professors used to say, "The only thing doctors do more than write is procrastinate about writing." Despite all the fuss, the articles still manage to get written, and the medical literature is healthy, if not somewhat corpulent, as a result.

During my research, I found a number of articles that took a swipe at the process of writing and publishing. I also ran into a few with amusing titles. The award for the funniest title goes to an article published in 1881 by Dr. Rufus Griswold (Clin News 1881; 2(15):199–200). Although the article itself is not that funny, the title is perfect: "Medico-Literary Tenesmus."

The next three selections were published in the *British Medical Journal* under the caption, "Zany Lessons for Academics." The author, who has two other articles in the book, would make a great advisor.—*H.B.*

How to Create a Data Base*

BERRIL YUSHOMERSKI YANKELOWITZ, M.D.

Inasmuch as I have achieved international notoriety in umbilical research, I will use my own example to show how serendipity and a little imagination can lead one to great discovery and intellectual progress through the steps of analysis, perturbing the system, and correlation and generalisation.

One day I was sitting on a veranda overlooking a southern California beach and accidentally spilt my coffee. The coffee was quite warm and some of it landed directly in the navel of a rather obese bikinied lady sunning herself on the sand below. She sat up and abruptly assaulted me with a few choice words, but calmed down when I assured her of the unintentional nature of the mishap. That evening, I reflected on the event and noted serendipitously that, even from the distance of my observation, the coffee did not go straight to the bottom of the navel but was partly restrained by the swirls and folds. Great scientific discoveries are regarded by many as accidents that are observed by the prepared mind; consequently, I conceived of the great untapped area of umbilical science, based on my brief experience on the beach.

I next set out to see what would happen if I repeated the experiment intentionally and observed the large variety of umbilical fluid retention patterns for which I am now accorded scientific recognition. I used only coffee at first, but dropped tea, Coca Cola, Seven-Up, and a variety of fruit juices into the navels of various bathers under different weather conditions.

Nevertheless, recognising the limitations of such simple observations, it was then that I decided to take the project to the laboratory to begin a real analytical phase of umbilical research. This began with simple things like measuring the diameter, depth, and clockwise or counter-clockwise swirling of volunteers' navels. By this time, I had a grant to pursue animal studies, and

we began to look at rat and dog navels. Umbilical proteins were extracted; at first we used polyacrilinide gel electrophoresis and isoelectric focusing to find out what was there. We then did our now famous separation of the proteins, pulse labelled with tritiated glycine, by curved gradient ultracentrifugation and sephadex columns. We analysed the components with spectrography, electron spin resonance, nuclear magnetic resonance, amino-acid analysis, gas-liquid chromatography, and circular dicroism. In fact, this is how we got our first 250 publications, as each of these tests warranted an article or two.

Initially, there seemed to be a striking difference between dog and rat umbilical proteins; it was at that point that Peter Flurd, my research fellow, came up with the notion that the results might be the result of contamination by navel lint. We developed the now widely used procedure to measure differences in navel-lint precursor pool size, and eventually we were able to show that this accounted for the difference in dog and rat proteins. Later, we repeated all these experiments on human navels.

By this time we were up to 500 publications, and felt we had definitively analysed the normal navel. It now remained to see what happened if we *perturbed* the navel. Again using volunteers, we "tickled" our system with coffee to determine the importance of my original observation. We were now prepared to use all the aforementioned techniques. One of my technicians was relaxing with his shirt off and having a beer; he poured some beer into his navel and we analysed his navel protein, and proceeded to perturb our system with hot chocolate, Tiger Balm, and a variety of fine oriental teas.

With the production of 200 more publications, we then got our grant to look at umbilical proteins in

*Reprinted with permission from the British Medical Journal, ©1979; 2(Sept 8):596.

cancer patients and found se ral unique proteins which we feel are induced by various forms of environmental carcinogens and may well cause carcinomas in man. This is still under study.

The next step, of course, is *correlation*—we compared things such as navel depth versus umbilical protein dicroism, normal dog navel lint with human cancer navel lint, and so on. This brought us up to 1000 papers and we felt it was time to see whether our techniques could be applied to other investigations. Our navel lint extraction procedure proved valuable in extracting protein from horses with hangnail, rhesus monkeys with acne, and lymphocyte cultures. Having written 2000 publications, we are now meeting our responsibilities as scientists to the general community and are actively publishing work about the relevance of our results to scientific intellectual progress, peer review, the two-party system, and the urban poor.

I was humbly thankful for the recent award of the Nobel Prize, which implies that we have found the definitive truth about navels and that there is no further need for anyone to think about them again—after all, if progress stops, we must have found final truth.

In summary, the young investigator need only follow my example with the basic principles of careful observation, analysis, perturbation, correlation, and generalisation, and he also will become famous and stop progress in science by getting everyone to agree that he has found the ultimate truth.

How to Create
a Long CV from a Single Data Base*

BERRIL YUSHOMERSKI YANKELOWITZ, M.D.

In this day when fame and academic promotion depend on the dry weight of a curriculum vitae rather than its content, it is important to get as much out of a piece of work as one can. This lesson shows the principle of amplification to achieve success.

(1) It is usually wise to have a data base to start with.

(2) Never write one paper when you can write two—that is, split your data base. Each split will hereafter be referred to as a "study." In addition to local publications, publish each study in at least three foreign journals.

(3) Change the title and submit each study to another journal.

(4) Change the arrangement of the listing of the authors and resubmit the study to another journal.

(5) Change 3–5 words in each paragraph and resubmit paper to yet another journal.

(6) Add a data point, and submit to original journal as a follow-up.

(7) Repeat steps (3)–(5) with new data point.

(8) Add a second new data point and repeat steps (3)–(7) twice more.

(9) Write a paper entitled: "Final Results of (list your study here)." This paper should look a lot like your last follow-up study.

(10) Repeat steps (3)–(5).

(11) Write review article about study.

(12) Repeat steps (3)–(5).

(13) Write a book chapter entitled (name your study here).

(14) Repeat as often as you are requested to write book chapter.

(15) Write an article called, "An historical perspective of (list your study here)."

(16) Repeat steps (3)–(5).

You should now have at least 24 papers, four book chapters, four review articles, and four historical perspectives for a total of 36 listings on your CV. With 10 data bases this represents 360 listings, minimum.

If you also buy stock in a paper company, you'll not only be promoted, you'll be rich—so good luck and happy writing.

*Reprinted with permission from the British Medical Journal, ©1979; 2(Nov 3):1139.

How to Write Nifty Titles for Your Papers*

BERRILL YUSHOMERSKI YANKELOWITZ, M.D.

General Principles

(a) When you are up for promotion, the committee will most likely not read anything you have written, but trust in the judgment of the journals to decide on the quality of your articles. This is especially true if your titles are so esoteric that the promotions committee would not dare even to peek at the text.

(b) Titles should "sound" like original contributions.

(c) Titles should be esoteric (see (a) above).

(d) If your study is not particularly good, make the title catchy or timely to help get it accepted.

(e) If your study is decidedly dull, use the longest possible title you can invent.

When to Write Titles

(a) If you have not thought of a project, and a title comes to mind, use it and work a paper around it.

(b) Titles are best written with a proper brandy and a cigar after dinner. Titles written on an empty stomach are likely to be dull and witless.

(c) Some great titles have been done while sitting at stool. This is an excellent and productive time to engage in title creation.

Examples of Titles for Your First Papers

(a) "A patient with pimples and coronary occlusion—case report of a new association."

(b) "The association of pimples and coronary occlusion—a case report."

(c) "Concurrence of coronary occlusion and pimples in a patient—a new observation."

Examples of Titles for Follow-up Papers

(a) "Two patients with pimples and coronary occlusion."

(b) "A second case of pimples in coronary occlusion and review of the literature."

(c) "Pimples and coronary occlusion—a historical perspective."

Catch Words and Phrases to Make Your Study Sound "Sound"

(a) Starting phrases—try to use statistical terms: "A randomised trial of . . ."; "Multiple linear regression analysis of . . ."; "The frequency of the occurrence of . . ."; "The rarity of the occurrence of . . ."; "The association of . . ."; "The correlation of. . . ."

(b) Phrases to make you sound honest and reliable (insert whatever you like in the blank spaces): "The failure of _____ to influence _____"; "_____, an important negative study"; "The unreliability of _____ in assessing _____"; "The implausibility of _____ in understanding _____"; "The total and utter ineptness of _____ to comprehend _____."

(c) Phrases to make you sound innovative: "The omega factor, a critical new parametric enfoeffment in examining the (*choose a body organ*)" (the omega factor can be anything you like); "Creating life, starting with one and two carbon compounds and rare earths—a progress report"; "The pathophysiologic relationship between pimples and coronary occlusion—a hypothesis."

(d) Phrases to make you sound timely: "The relationship of the omega factor to *urban health* care"; "The *labour party* and the omega factor"; "*Medically underserved* patients with pimples and coronary

*Reprinted with permission from the British Medical Journal, ©1980; 1(Jan 12):96.

occlusion"; "*Peer review* in assessing the quality of care of patients with pimples, with *special emphasis on the subpopulation* with coronary occlusion." (The length of this alone is catchy; do not mind the content. Note how length hides dullness.)

(e) Ending phrases you can use (insert your study in the blank spaces): "_____, an essential tool in evaluating _____"; "_____, a preliminary report"; "_____, a randomised double-blind prospective scientifically investigative trial"; "_____, statistical analysis and consideration for the future"; "_____,

a negative study"; "_____, a hypothesis"; "_____ in urban society"; "_____ in the medically underserved"; "_____ in New York City between 1921 and 1922."

(f) Middle phrases you can use: "_____ in a population with _____"; "_____ in a family with _____"; "_____ in the senile great aunt of a patient with _____."

These title suggestions should get you off to a proper start. Happy writing, and enjoy the promotion.

Parse Analysis: A New Method for the Evaluation of Investigators' Bibliographies*

PAUL J. DAVIS, M.D. 0.92
ROBERT I. GREGERMAN, M.D. 0.08

During the past five years our laboratory has been concerned with the development of a quantitative system for describing the relative contributions of authors to multiple-author manuscripts. The concept that has evolved is termed "parse analysis" and has been logically broadened to include the measurement of manuscript quality. This report reviews the basic principles of parse analysis and describes their recent application to the evaluation of scientific careers. We emphasize the point that the principles outlined here are the product of cooperative efforts of a host of scientists—many of them from abroad and elsewhere—working in our laboratory. Without the imagination and insight of these investigators, the concept of parse could not have been formalized. The work was facilitated by the availability of an IBM 360/50 computer.

The system of parse analysis was created to meet the following specific needs: evaluation of relative contributions of authors to papers with more than one author; determination of the order of authors listed on title pages of manuscripts; weighting of the degree of difficulty of the scientific problem under investigation in a given manuscript; quantitative evaluation of the quality of execution of the study described; and indication to prospective employers of the net worth of a set of publications to which a prospective investigator has contributed.

The first principle of parse is the assignment of decimal fractions to each author of a given paper to indicate contribution to overall effort. These fractions in all cases follow each author's name, as in the example, "'Beta-adrenergic Blockade,' by R. L. Fernley 0.24, P. L. Pritchard-Grant 0.08, T. Bates 0.36 and R. G. Ferguson 0.27."

This is not a particularly good example because the sum of the decimal fractions is only 0.95, a parse analysis finding indicating that the work is incomplete

*Reprinted with permission from The New England Journal of Medicine, ©1969; 281(18):989–990.

or is significant only at the 5 per cent level, or includes work (about 0.05 worth) performed by a visiting investigator no longer affiliated with the laboratory. However, the basic idea is clear. In this particular example, the blame for the work must be fairly evenly apportioned among Fernley, Bates and Ferguson. Pritchard-Grant was probably the senior author* of the paper, in the light of his negligible contribution. This distribution of decimal fractions devolves as a unique responsibility upon the authors, themselves, and can, conceivably, result in serious delays in the submission of manuscripts. Occasionally, manuscripts might not even be submitted for publication because of the authors' inability to agree upon a parsing; when this happens the literature has most probably been done a service. An alternative solution is the submission of decimal assignments agreed to by a majority of the authors but not unanimously approved. In these cases the decimal fraction that is contested is followed by the notation, U.P. ("Under Protest"), as in the example, "R. G. Ferguson 0.27 U.P." In no case should the sum of the fractions be greater than 1.00. The independent studies of F. R. C. Johnstone,[1] of Vancouver, have recently been pointed out to us, and readers may note certain similarities that are gratifying in the development of his work and the first principle of parse analysis.

The second principle of parse is the determination of the order of authors on a manuscript according to the method of Pecks.[†] Experience has shown that the following factors may be considered in determining author order: number of papers previously published by each of the collaborators (the so-called reciprocal factor of Pecks); responsibility for the basic concept of the work; responsibility for the actual work done; duration of stay of each of the collaborators in the senior author's laboratory (the so-called tenacity factor of Pecks); and alphabetization of collaborators' last or first names. Tables of natural Pecks factors are available from our laboratory, if not from Pecks himself. In general, we point out that high Pecks scores are the reward of the devoted, underpublished collaborator but seldom influence author sequence on manuscripts.

The splendid work of Harriet A. Zuckerman[2] can hardly be overlooked in this context and should be of interest to scientists and others.

The third and fourth principles of parse are designed to provide casual readers with easy methods of evaluating at a glance both the difficulty of the subject matter attacked by investigators and the quality of the attack made on the problem. For example, in the study of "Beta-adrenergic Blockade" by Fernley et al., it is obvious that everyone nowadays is working on beta-adrenergic blockade, and the degree of difficulty of the subject is only about 1.6 out of a possible 3.0. Careful reading of the paper by Fernley, however, indicates that whereas the subject matter was rather easy, the design of the experiment was complex, ingenious, novel and yet somehow carried out within the guidelines set by the Declaration of Helsinki. The execution of the study therefore rates a 2.3 out of a possible 3.0. We will not go into the interesting derivation of such scoring at this time. The product of the degree of difficulty and the execution is called by convention the "parse product." In this case it is $(1.6)(2.3)$, or 3.68. The parse product divided by the parse potential—a perfect score of 9.0—represents the "parse index" (usually expressed $\times 100$), in this case 40.8. Since the overwhelming majority of papers in the literature parse index at slightly better than 10.5, the paper by Fernley et al. can be seen at a glance by the casual reader to be a very good paper indeed. The parse index is assigned by journal referees and is usually printed immediately after the title of the paper, as in the example, "'Beta-adrenergic Blockade 40.8,' by R. L. Fernley 0.24, etc."

The final virtue of parse analysis is its uncanny and inherent capacity to sum up an investigator's career in one or two easily manipulated numbers that obviate job interviews and the reviewing of a great many dull bibliographies. These numbers may be the basis for the tendering of academic offers. This penultimate parse is called "career parse." Like many of the other principles elaborated by the 360/50, the career parse is composed of two factors and their product. The

---

*Two definitions in absolute terms of "senior author" are current: where no collaborator has an office, the author with fewest desks in his laboratory is senior; where several collaborators have offices the collaborator whose office is farthest from the laboratory is senior.

†P. L. Pecks, a former collaborator in our laboratory who is remembered primarily for his cream-cheese sandwiches and shrill countertenor.

factors are the *sum* of decimal fractions of relative contributions to all papers on which the author's name appears and the *mean* parse index of all the papers to which he contributed. The product (career parse) has been determined by R. L. Fernley, who has kindly lent his bibliography to our laboratory. Fernley, who is now engaged in the private practice of medicine in upstate New York, is one of the authors of the well known paper on beta-adrenergic blockade, and his career decimal-fraction sum—obtained from a series of twelve papers published between 1955 and 1964—was 1.76, which is not much of a sum. However, because during that period Fernley worked on a number of extremely complex, ingenious and novel projects, his mean paper parse index was a whopping 43.7. It takes only a parsing knowledge of mathematics to see that Fernley acquired a career parse of 76.91. This was not enough, we are sorry to report, to acquire tenure at any of the seven institutions at which he worked. He also barely passed his State Board Examination.

Conclusions

Responsibly applied, parse principles have immense potential for defining academic success in easy-to-understand, mathematical terms. At present in our laboratory we are investigating parse at both the theoretical and practical levels. These investigations include the building of a multicompartment, journal-specific mathematical model to describe the kinetics of parse indexing,* and a parse-or-fail system for computer matching of academic positions and prospects on a countrywide basis (National Data Bank for Career Parses or NDBCP).

References

1. Johnstone FRC: The true publication index. A measure of scientific endeavor. JAMA 202: adv p 371, Nov 20, 1967.
2. Zukerman HA: Patterns of name ordering among authors of scientific papers: a study of social symbolism and its ambiguity. Amer J Sociol 74:276, 1968.

---

*So far, and this is tentative, it looks like 11 compartments will do it (unpublished observations).

Letters in Response to Parse Analysis*

As with all ground breaking articles, the one by Davis and Gregerman generated a flurry of responses by readers of *The New England Journal of Medicine*. The three that follow were the most illuminating.—*H.B.*

To the Editor: Both pithy and poignant, the "Parse Analysis" paper by Davis and Gregerman (October 30, 1969) prompts profuse permutations—and perturbations. When its theoretic construct is amalgamated to Parkinson's Law and Peter's Principle—plus the pragmatic parameters of successful grant getting—a breakthrough is obvious. At last a mechanism is beginning to emerge by which we can "PPBS" a necessary faculty structure to staff those "new, imaginative, innovative, and unique" conglomerates called medical schools without having to consider either potential student bodies or their possible needs. Long, long overdue!

But could the authors provide one point of clarification? Among a random sample of our faculty, repeated attempts to get appropriate "parse inputs" allocated to a stratified sample of multiple-authored papers led only to uniform "Under Protests" (U.P.) designations—even among our multiple disciplinary teams. With appointments and promotions encounters just around the corner, we need help in adjudicating this dilemma. We have considered the faculty-committee approach—but what with their extensive travel commitments, meetings are hard to arrange. We have discussed seeking student involvement—but students reject our requirement of not assigning any negative "parse numbers." We have even resorted to trying out the dean's office—but are told that such people have long since ceased reading any professional publications, and not simply their mail. And we hesitate to seek out any reader opinion because, frankly, readers are so hard to come by. Where, sir, can we turn?

William O. Robertson, M.D.
University of Washington
School of Medicine

Seattle, Wash

To the Editor: The recent significant (p less than 0.05) contribution of the pediatric gerontologists David and Gregerman (New Eng J Med 281:989–990, 1969) regarding "Parse Analysis" has prompted me to submit the following preliminary report of a new method of hospital staph evaluation. The New Math will be utilized to develop a formula to express the Medical Achievement and Development (MAD) index of each staph member. Since we are dealing with integral physicians, only integral numbers, multiples of integral numbers or fractions thereof will be used. The formula will assign equal weight to CC units (Clinical Care), TS units (Teaching Skill) and BS units (Basic Science). In appropriate cases a Reality Adjustment Technique Slope factor (RATS) will be applied, to be identified by the subscript RATS.

Determination of MAD index: CC = S + E + X where

S (Skill) = number of occasions staph member has been one up on house staph.

$$E \text{ (Economics)} = \frac{\text{Income}}{30,000} \div 5 \text{ RATS}$$

(Note: money is a dirty word)

X (Xyst) = DRF (Dining Room Factor) Number of lunches in staph dining room per week divided by 5 with a special credit of one eunuch per dinner at hospital per week.

TS (This is complicated but has been simplified so that)

$$TS = WV + \frac{OPD}{100} \text{ RATS where WV (Ward Visit)}$$

has been given an arbitrary value of 5 and OPD = number of hours per week in outpatient department.

BS (This is simple) BS = PAP (papers already published) Therefore:

$$MAD = \frac{S + E + X}{3 + RATS} + WV + \frac{OPD}{100} + PAP$$

If the result is not an integral number, do not pass Go. Do not collect $200.

Waban, MA   H. Walter Jones, Jr., M.D.

*Reprinted with permission of The New England Journal of Medicine, ©1970; 282(3):170–171.

The highly theoretical "Parse Analysis: A new method for the evaluation of investigators' bibliographies" must be considered a major contribution, though several key factors that are surely of use in deriving a suitable parse potential were not mentioned.

Is the parse potential inversely or directly proportional to number of authors involved, especially when over 10? Do isolated case reports, such as "Proofreader's Prostatitis" (New England Journal of Medicine 280:1130, 1969), which has important medicolegal significance, score higher or lower than original research reports— "Production and Excretion of Hydrogen Gas in Man" (New England Journal of Medicine 281:122–127, 1969)?

Finally, how can the confused reader evaluate articles written by authors in private capacities, without official support or endorsement by the appropriate governmental agency. Should the parse potential in such a case by multiplied or divided by 5?

The area of research Davis (0.92) and Gregerman (0.08) have thrown open is a vast one, and further studies will be anxiously awaited. The results will provide us all with a powerful tool with which to dig through the rich lode of medical literature, which enlarges from moment to moment.

James A. Angevine, M.D., 1.0
Associate Pathologist
St. Mary's Hospital

Madison, WI

The Editorial Ordeal of Dr. Job Plodd*

ALVAN G. FORAKER, M.D.
A. E. ANDERSON, JR., M.D.

> Podunk General Hospital
> Podunk, Missabama
>
> January 2, 1975
>
> Fritz Dingleburr, M.D.
> Editor
> Northeast Journal of Medicine
> Northeast City
>
> Dear Doctor Dingleburr:
>
> Please consider the enclosed manuscript for publication.
>
> Sincerely,
>
> Job Plodd, M.D.
> Pathologist

*Reprinted from Pathology Annual, ©1976; 11:189–199, with permission from Appleton & Lange, Inc.

Northeast Journal of Medicine
Northeast City

March 17, 1975

Job Plodd, M.D.
Pathologist
Podunk General Hospital
Podunk, Missabama

Dear Doctor Plodd:

The Editorial Board has voted not to accept the paper by B. Button, M.D., and yourself, entitled, "Omphalosarcoma: A Clinical and Histochemical Review." This nonacceptance does not imply major criticism, since the Journal receives thousands of manuscripts each year, and can publish less than one percent of these. For your interest, there is enclosed one reviewer's comment. We do not, however, suggest that you return this manuscript to us after revision, since the decision of our Editorial Board is final.

Sincerely,

Fritz Dingleburr, M.D.
Editor

(Anonymous Reviewer's Comment)

February 16, 1975

I do not recommend acceptance of the paper by Plodd and Button. They have reviewed 37 cases of omphalosarcoma from their hospital and have applied certain basic histochemical tests. The work is adequate, on a low-level scientific and intellectual plane, but not inspiring. It is not believed likely to appeal to the majority of readers of the *Northeast Journal*. In addition, the horrible misuse of the subjunctive mode renders this opus unattractive, although doubtless this conforms to the linguistic practices among the denizens of Missabama.

Memorandum

March 19, 1975

To: B. Button, M.D., Attending Omphalologist
From: J. Plodd, M.D., Pathologist

This rejection was anticipated. I'll redraft this manuscript, trying to be more correct in use of the subjunctive mode, whatever that is. Then we'll try the next journal on our list.

J. Plodd, M.D.

Podunk General Hospital
Podunk, Missabama

April 16, 1975

Esau Terrick, M.D.
Editor
Journal of Investigative Biomolecular Omphalology
Department of Bio-Omphalology
Metrocolossal University Medical Center
Metrocolossal City

Dear Professor Terrick:

Please consider the enclosed manuscript for publication.

Sincerely,

Job Plodd, M.D.
Pathologist

Department of Bio-Omphalology
Metrocolossal University Medical Center
Metrocolossal City

June 28, 1975

Job Plodd, M.D.
Podunk General Hospital
Podunk, Missabama

Dear Doctor Plodd:

I regret to inform you that our editorial advisors are uniformly opposed to acceptance of your manuscript, which is returned herewith with one typical reviewer's comment. Please be assured we are always willing to consider investigative papers which conform to our scientific and intellectual criteria.

Sincerely,

Esau Terrick, M.D.
Editor and Research Professor

May 6, 1975

The returned paper by Plodd and Button is indeed plodding and should be pigeon-holed if not button-holed. The histochemical techniques are simplistic and obsolete. Pookashonase localizations are not well defined, and the pH of the incubating solution should be expressed to the third decimal point. The general tenor of this opus minissimus suggests a high school science student's project. They applied the ancient chi square test to their data, rather than the more modern zeta-beta techniques. There may be a place for studies on human omphalosarcoma, but not in the *Journal of Investigative Biomolecular Omphalology*. Studies of this type should be considered only if currently accepted scientific technics are applied, such as four-dimensional interference-ferrito-electron microscopy, allied to immunophoreto-globulinic delineation of regressase in relation to omphalines.

Memorandum

July 1, 1975

To: B. Button, M.D.
From: J. Plodd, M.D.

There is not much we can do about these scathing criticisms, but I will redo the manuscript to emphasize general pathology and try it on one of my own trade journals.

J. Plodd, M.D.

Podunk General Hospital
Podunk, Missabama

August 4, 1975

Strikk Lee Beynall, M.D., Ph.D.
Editor
Annals of Omphalic Pathology
Burgeon University
Burgeon City

Dear Doctor Beynall:

Please consider the enclosed manuscript for publication.

Sincerely,

Job Plodd, M.D.
Pathologist

Department of Pathology
Burgeon University
Burgeon City

October 15, 1975

Job Plodd, M.D.
Podunk General Hospital
Podunk, Missabama

Dear Doctor Plodd:

Our Editorial Board has recommended rejection of your manuscript, which is returned herewith. A reviewer's comment is enclosed.

Sincerely,

Strikk Lee Beynall, M.D., Ph.D.
Professor and Chairman
Editor
Annals of Omphalic Pathology

(Anonymous Reviewer's Comment)

September 30, 1975

This puerile piece is far, far below the standards of the *Annals.* It is rather illegitimate, to speak kindly, being too surgical for a pathology journal, and not good enough for us, although it might be accepted in a journal of *clinical* surgery. The anatomic pathology descriptions are inadequate. There are entirely too many old fashioned H & E photomicrographs, and absolutely *no*, repeat *no* electron microscopic illustrations. Fancy that in 1975! Virchow might have written this piece, although he would have done it better. In my view, physicians from Podunk should treat their patients, count their money, check their cotton fields and oil wells, and not try to be scientists. This just wastes the time of serious investigators who have to read such stuff.

Memorandum

November 3, 1975

To: J. Plodd, M.D.
From: B. Button, M.D.

I've had it up to here with these "longhairs." I'm gonna rewrite, emphasize the surgical side, and send it to my old chief. He'll help me out.

B. Button, M.D.

Podunk General Hospital
Podunk, Missabama

November 22, 1975

Watt A. Greatfella, M.D.
Editor, Surgical Omphalology Journal
Professor and Chairman
Department of Surgical Omphalology
Metrocolossal University Medical Center
Metrocolossal City

Dear Doctor Greatfella:

I'm sure you remember me as your good resident in 1949–1952. As I told you in the bar at the clinical meeting in Las Vegas, I'm doing some research on omphalosarcoma, aided by our pathologist, Plodd. Here is our latest work, "Surgical Aspects of Omphalosarcoma, with Histochemical Notes." I hope you can find room for this in the Journal.

I hope also you will accept my long-standing invitation to come down for the pheasant shooting next February. You'll get a full bag.

Your loyal resident,

B. Button, M.D.
Chief
Service of Omphalology

Department of Surgical Omphalology
Metrocolossal University
Metrocolossal City

December 23, 1975

B. Button, M.D.
Podunk General Hospital
Podunk, Missabama

Dear Button:

Your Christmas present is enclosed—your manuscript back. Sorry, your surgical technics are obsolete. You're not using the new Greatfella retroverse inverse procedure for radical omphalectomy. I was developing this during your time here, and I expect all my men to follow my teachings. Your man Plodd's stuff on histochemistry (whatever that is) and pathology adds little to the presentation.

Sorry, I can't make it for the pheasant this coming February, since I'm scheduled to do an omphalectomy on some fellow named Mow in Communist China at that time. Keep up the good work, Button, and use the Greatfella omphalectomy—it's the greatest!

Your friend,

Watt A. Greatfella, M.D.
Professor and Chairman

Memorandum

January 7, 1976

To: J. Plodd, M.D.
From: B. Button, M.D.

There's just one shot left in my locker. This guy will take anything—believe me—anything.

B. Button, M.D.

Podunk General Hospital
Podunk, Missabama

January 11, 1976

Boyy Biggvoyce, M.D.
Editor
Missabama State Medical Society Journal
Chief, Service of General Practice
Gladesdale Community Hospital
Gladesdale, Missabama

Boyy, you old son-of-a-gun:

How're ya, Boyy. Here's a real scientific piece for your monthly rag, and we're doing you a large favor. This is good surgical stuff, with strong clinical flavoring, and a seasoning of science added by my path man, Job Plodd. Don't say I never did anything for you.

When we get together at the spring meeting in Vapid City, I'll show you some great pictures and tell you about sailfishing off the coast of Latinonia. I'm telling the IRS I went to a meeting. The fish were great.

Your old drinking buddy,

Bill B.

Gladesdale Community Hospital
Gladesdale, Missabama

March 13, 1976

B. Button, M.D.
Podunk General Hospital
Podunk, Missabama

Dear Bill:

Here is your piece back. It's way too scientific for us Missabamian medicos. I can't understand a lot of that guff, and those microscopic pictures by Job Plodd are real yawn producers. Everybody knows you're the greatest belly button cutter outer in the state anyway, and you don't need to blow your horn with us. Why don't you try this mass of mush on some egghead publication like the *Northeast Journal?* It should be just their cup of tea.

Why don't you write a piece for us about your sailfishing trip to Latinonia, with some good big fish pictures? The readers of my monthly blast would really go for this.

Sorry, I just don't see you and Job as scientists. Come back to earth, along with the rest of us Missabamians.

Your good friend,

Boyy Biggvoyce, M.D.

Memorandum

March 29, 1976

To: J. Plodd, M.D.
From: B. Button, M.D.

I give up. Cut this piece up into paper dolls, stuff it in File X—do what you wish. I'm going to give up research and concentrate on writing fishing stories for doctors—as my hobby.

B. Button, M.D.

Podunk General Hospital
Podunk, Missabama

April 18, 1976

M. Y. Opick, Ph.D.
Editor
Western Missabama Quarterly Journal of Science
Assistant Professor of Biology
Podunk Junior College
Podunk, Missabama

Dear Milt:

Please consider the enclosed manuscript for publication.

Your friend,

J. Plodd, M.D.

Podunk Junior College
Podunk, Missabama

April 26, 1976

Job Plodd, M.D.
Director of Laboratories
Podunk General Hospital
Podunk, Missabama

Dear Doctor Plodd:

I am delighted to accept the excellent article, "Omphalosarcoma: A Clinical and Histochemical Review," by Dr. Button and yourself for publication in *Western Missabama Quarterly Journal of Science*. It is good to have such a fine paper on human problems. As you know most of our publications are by junior college and high school biology teachers, such as classifying the snakes in Chattahoochie Creek.

You will be expected to pay publication costs of $75 per page, and to purchase 500 reprints for about $275. We appreciate your maintaining your sustaining membership in our Science Teachers Association at $100 per year, and your continuing support of science education in Western Missabama. Your paper will probably appear in our Winter, 1977 issue.

Thank you for allowing your outstanding research paper to appear in our journal.

Respectfully,

M. Y. Opick, Ph.D.
Editor
Western Missabama Quarterly Journal of Science

The following selection was compiled from three separate articles published in the *Southern Medical Journal* by Dr. Fred and Ms. Robie. While the book was in press, the authors came out with a fourth addition to the literature: "Dizzy Medical Writing: Report on Recent Relapses" (South Med J 1989; 82(7):897–899).—*H.B.*

Dizzy Medical Writing*

HERBERT L. FRED, M.D.
PATRICIA ROBIE

After completing his glorious pitching career, Dizzy Dean became a popular baseball announcer. In response to a listener who accused him of not knowing the King's English, Dizzy said, "Old Diz knows the King's English. And not only that. I also know the Queen is English."

Old Diz may have known the King's English, but you couldn't prove it by how he spoke. Similarly, many physicians and scientists may know the King's English, but you couldn't prove it by how they write. We decided, therefore, to present the 1983 "Dizzy Awards" for outstandingly dizzy medical writing. Only recent articles in prominent American medical journals were eligible (references available upon request).

The winners are:

The Postponed Because of Wet Grounds Award

"The presence of a bladder tumor in our patient, and in previous reports, demonstrates again . . ."

—We are saddened to learn that the medical literature, in addition to its many other ailments, now has bladder tumors.

The Cases at the Bat Award (three-way tie)

"Eight other cases obtained from liver biopsies referred from other hospitals were also reviewed . . ."

—Did you hear about the alcoholic whose liver biopsy revealed a case of Scotch?

and

"Cases also smoked significantly more cigarettes than controls . . ."

—Our cases smoke only when the record room is on fire.

and

"The cases, who were 20 to 49 years old at the time of diagnosis . . ."

—Our 20- to 49-year-old cases are either in cobwebs or on microfilm.

The Out in Left Field Award

"Alpha factor analysis has been shown to yield a lower bound estimate to the number of factors and allow psychometric interference to a universe of variables."

—Take me to your leader.

The Touch Every Base Award

"Alternatively, and in our view, far more likely, it is possible that if edema forms during the obstruction, it may be roentgenologically masked, perhaps by increases in lung volume."

—Would you care to qualify that statement?

The Knot-Hole Award

". . . subsequent reports suggest that colonoscopy can recognize angiodysplasia."

—But only after they've known each other for a long time.

*Reprinted with permission from the Southern Medical Journal, ©1983; 76(9):1165–1166; 1984; 77(6):755–756; and 1985; 78(12): 1498–1501.

The Placed on the Disabled List Award

"The author experienced severe pulmonary edema after standard CPR in 20 of 71 patients who suffered sudden, unexpected cardiac arrest and regained heart function by CPR."

—Presumably, the author's severe pulmonary edema resolved.

The Blooper Award

"Usually (although invariably) HS is associated with venous insufficiency of the lower extremities."

—Huh?

The No Hitter Award

"The results demonstrated the absence of clinical evidence in all cases."

—As Shakespeare might have said, "nothing ado about nothing."

The Balk Award

"However, in the absence of a thyroid primary, in view of the ability of carcinoids to form various polypeptide hormones (Milhaud *et al.,* 1974) (although not usually as much as was formed by Sweeney, McDonnell and O'Brien's tumour), and the finding of small amounts of amyloid in both our cases, Sweeney, McDonnell and O'Brien's case may be another carcinoid of the larynx forming an unusually large amount of polypeptide hormone and, secondarily to that, large amounts of amyloid."

—We disagree, we think.

The Flagpole Award

"The common practice of misdiagnosing deep vein thrombosis clinically should be abandoned."

—Agreed.

The Safe All Around Award

". . . unproductive diagnostic measures are unnecessary."

—Agreed.

The "It Ain't Over Til It's Over" Award (a tie)

"Very obviously, mouse connective tissue is not necessarily human connective tissue . . ."

—Very obviously.

and

"Shock never developed if the disease was not serious . . ."

—Seriously?

The Out in Left Field Award

"However, none of the subjects indicated any localized muscle pain or soreness of the delayed type at these times that they experienced later."

—We, however, wish to indicate diffuse pain and soreness of the immediate type brought about at this time by the statement above that we experienced earlier.

The Batty Title Award (four-way tie)

"Early Gastric Cancer in a United States Hospital"

—Presumably the hospital's chief complaint was pain in the middle of the corridor at the level of the ninth floor.

and

"Bacteremia in a Long-term Care Facility"

—Did the organisms enter through the front or back door?

and

"Stability of Prevalence"

—Your guess is as good as mine.

and

"Training Effect in Elderly Patients With Coronary Artery Disease on Beta Adrenergic Blocking Drugs"

—Are trained drugs more effective than untrained drugs?

The Long Fly to the Pitcher Award (a tie)

"The acquisition of new observations makes it appropriate for us to re-evaluate our existing knowledge base and to make such modifications as are necessary to form a reasonably coherent theoretical whole."

—In short, knowledge begets knowledge.

and

". . . she experienced a rapidly fatal outcome."

—In short, she died.

The Make-Up Game Award (a tie)

"The role of the congested prostate in infertilogenesis is presented."

—Neologically speaking, the author of that statement need not worry about infertility.

and

"The conclusions from the present work, drawn from systematic protocolized gathering of data . . ."

—Questionologically speaking, are protocolized data gathered through a protocoloscope?

The No Runs, No Hits, Two Errors Award

Until such a determination is made, physicians should inform their patients as to what the research to date do and do not show . . ."

—Well, what *do* it show?

The Switch Hitter Award

"The importance of classification is academic since none to date can handle all of the described anomalous possibilities."

—Anomalous possibilities are definitely harder to handle than possible anomalies.

Epilogue:

We draw two conclusions, one happy and one sad: The memory of Old Diz will be around for a long, long time. And so will dizzy medical writing.

* * *

Additional Readings

1. Quay E: Verbal hyperplasia: new thoughts on an old disease. JAMA 1965; 192(2):126–128.

Verbal hyperplasia is one of many disorders that result from an excess or deficiency of those enzymes needed for clear speech and writing. The most important enzymes are verbiase, which breaks S-bonds (syllable bonds) and C-bonds (clause bonds) and various transferases which attack dangling participles, excessive prepositions, and lyse the passive voice. Most of these diseases exist in a heterozygous and homozygous state.

2. Reece RL: Space-occupying gambits for medical writers. JAMA 1967; 200(1):162–164.

The author presents 10 techniques for turning clear writing into masterworks of ambiguity. In summary, "Say nothing well and don't stop saying it."

3. Yankelowitz BY: Making visual aids work for you. Br Med J 1980; 281(Dec 20–27):1718.

The author provides a number of suggestions on how to create effective graphs for scientific papers. For example, "In biology it is good to have at least three (preferably all) your data points not lying on the best fitting curve. This gives the reader the impression that you did not fudge the results or 'dry lab' the experiment altogether."

POETRY

Physicians like poetry. At least that's what my research shows. Although it is not well indexed, I found a considerable amount of poetry in columns, as white space filler, and in the correspondence section of many journals. Most physicians are not poets of course, and their technique is usually simple and straightforward. Such simplicity does not interfere with their message, however, particularly in the case of humorous poetry which makes up about 15–20% of the poems published in medical journals. As the following examples show, a poem is an ideal form for the expression of ones medical wit and humor.

'Twas the Night Before Match Day*

'Twas the night before Match Day, and all through the
   school
Not a student was certain, not even a fool,
Of the choices he'd put on his match list with care,
In hopes that St. Medicus soon would be there.

Significant other and I in my scrubs
Had just settled down for some starry-eyed love,
When suddenly I rose to the sound of the drone
Of the clamoring ring of my red telephone!

The call gave grave news from a bleary-eyed dean.
I begged him and wailed, "Sir, what do you mean?"
I *had* to have matched at least one or more!
After all, on my list were 104!!"

"There, there now," he soothed, in a tone
   professorial,
"We've a slot just for you out at Peau-Dunque
   Memorial!"
"Please, not *there*, sir" I cried, "where each bed has a
   saddle
And the interns get bruised starting IVs on cattle!"

"Well, we still have a flexible out in Corfu
That comes with a nice on-call room with a view. . . ."

"But *they're* much too cheap to buy beepers or
   phones—
To wake interns they tug on strings tied to their toes!"

"For ecology fans there's Mount Bogus," he said,
"Where to save paper and trees they keep charts in
   their heads. . . ."
"Not for me, sir," I wavered, "but thanks just the
   same—
After one night on call I'd forget my own name!"

"You're awfully picky when put to the test.
But there is something that must be confessed:
As dean of our jovial medical school,
The reason I called was to play April Fool!!

"The fact is: you matched at Mass General, I heard!
Good luck there, my boy, you will need it, you nerd!"
"Thanks a lot, sir," I said, "I am proud and relieved.
That's a jolly good joke to be so deceived. . . ."

"You're welcome, my boy. Now rest your swelled head.
For this year is the last you will see of your bed!"
And I heard him exclaim 'fore he hung up the phone:
"HAPPY CAREER TO ALL! AND REMEMBER YOUR
   LOAN!"

Kevin E. Vitting, M.D.

Keeping Informed†

One thing that is really not difficult, friends,
Is keeping abreast of new medical trends,
New treatments, new gadgets, new antibiotics,
New cures for the ailing, including neurotics.

And if you don't learn from attending a meeting
Or glancing at journals, though glances be fleeting.
Or talking with colleagues, you'll not be without it,
For surely your patient has read all about it.

Richard Armour, Ph.D.

Wise Guy*

Who knows each illness, knows each cure?
Who never doubts, is always sure?
Who gives advice to learned scholars
And shrugs aside their thanks and dollars?

Who is this learned fellow, friends?
Who is the chap who condescends
To chat with men like Mayo? Who?
It is the intern, young and new,

Who knows more than all other men.
He'll never know so much again.

Richard Armour, Ph.D.

To the Editor: I read Michael Crichton's article in the December 11, 1975, issue of the *Journal* regarding the quality of English usage. I took the article for what it was worth until I saw the taunting review of his article in this week's *Time* magazine. Since the criticism received such wide publicity (not that the *Journal* needs defense) I felt compelled to write this little verse:†

I've read *The Journal* for many years
Completely unaware
Of the dreadful English usage,
Nor did I really care.

But now that Michael Crichton
Has pointed out the flaws
As I peruse each article
I find I often pause.

And ask myself these questions:
Is this paper worth my while?
How can I rely upon
An author with poor style?

Is the message crystal clear,
Or is it obfuscated?

Is the man illiterate,
Or is he addle-pated?

How *did* such dismal copy
Pass editorial eyes,
Of Dr. Ingelfinger
And all those other guys?

To improve the *Journal* style
And make it more grammatical,
Perhaps the editorial staff
Should take a long sabbatical.

Of course I write this all in jest.
I'll make a safe prediction,
The Journal style will stay unchanged.
And Mike will stick to fiction.

Milton J. Chatton, M.D.
Department of Rehabilitation

San Jose, CA

Number 1 et al*

To the Editor: The commentary of Dr. G. M. Bernier et al (New Eng J Med 281:567, 1969) entitled "On the phenomenon of having the names of as many as eight authors appearing on a single paper" inspired this gentle rejoinder, humbly submitted.

It's 2 times 4
And 4 times 2
And what is more
Just who is who?

Assuming 1 is the driving force
And number 8 the chief, of course.

The who is 5,
What did he do
That makes him 5
Instead of 2?

Pity poor 7 and 6 and 3
Their place suggests obscurity.

In time's recall
Said paper shall
Be know to all
As such and such by 1 et al.

Donald T. Quick, M.D.
University of Florida
Gainesville, Fl   J. Hillis Miller Health Center

Multiple Authorship
On the *NEJM* COVER†

The outer front cover
May soon not provide
Enough space to list
All the authors inside.

Original articles
Should not as a rule,
Be authored by half
Of a medical school.

It is nice to give credit,
Where credit is due,
But on the front cover
Restrict it to two.

Milton J. Chatton, M.D.
San Jose, CA   Santa Clara Valley Medical Center

*Reprinted with permission from The New England Journal of Medicine, ©1969; 281(16):911.
†Reprinted with permission from The New England Journal of Medicine, ©1980; 302(25):1425.

Lyophallization*

Although it is not referenced, this poem was written in response to a letter by Dr. Melvin Hershkowitz, "Penile Frostbite, An Unforeseen Hazard of Jogging" (see p 106).—*H.B.*

There exists an MD who jogs
Wearing his everyday togs;
Without care or worry,
'Round the park does he scurry,
A full 30 minutes he logs.

All went well 'til December
(A night I'm sure he'll remember);
He challenged Jack Frost
And undoubtedly lost
As Frostie nipped the doc's member.

Now being a scholarly chap,
He profited from his mishap.
He penned a description
Of this new affliction,
Which had dropped right into his lap.

This syndrome's not rare, I would guess,
And more cases will soon come to
    press;
I'd say, then, in short,
That this first report
Shows the tip of the iceberg, no less.

Now, our jogger's immortalized,
And always will be recognized
By the medical clan,
As the very first man
Ever to be lyophallized.

Denver, CO

Michael Silverman, M.D.
University of Colorado
Medical Center

See No Evil†

A "double-blind" study has merits galore
(Especially one well controlled);
The critics and skeptics are satisfied more
When the story's objectively told.

All unconscious biases will be screened out
(I'm sure conscious ones don't exist).
It's clear there is no valid reason to doubt
The results of a randomized list.

So bear this in mind and you won't be deceived:
If data are worth the pursuing,
Those doctors can be without question believed
Who really don't know what they're doing.

Bronx, NY

Richard A. Rosen, M.D.
Albert Einstein College of Medicine

*Reprinted with permission from The New England Journal of Medicine, ©1977; 296(14):825.
†Reprinted with permission from The New England Journal of Medicine, ©1971; 285(17):975.

Help?*

When doctors doctor, and nurses nurse,
Most patients get better, though some get worse.
The system's not perfect, but one of the facts is
That no one is suing the nurse for malpractice:
She knows what her job is, and does it with grace,
While doctors make sure that she stays in her place.

Now nurses start doctoring: Junior Physicians?
Noctors? or Durses? Nurdocs? Nursicians?
What will their work be? And how shall we choose them?
How to be certain the public will use them?
And how to get doctors (traditional, staid)
To accept as their colleague this new Medi-Maid?

Problems aplenty, but what's even worse is:
If one of them's sued, they'll wish they were Nurses.

Michael M. Stewart, M.D.
Rockefeller Foundation

Bangkok, Thailand

A Pulmonologist's Valentine†

To the Editor: Last year my husband, a pulmonary fellow, sent me a valentine; he thought that the cardiac system was receiving far too much attention on that day. I thought that your readers would enjoy the valentine:

Roses are red
Violets are blue
Without your lungs
Your blood would be too.

David D. Ralph, M.D.
(Submitted by Susan Ott, M.D.,
Mrs. David Ralph)

Seattle, WA

*Reprinted with permission from The New England Journal of Medicine, ©1971; 285(24):1384.
†Reprinted with permission from The New England Journal of Medicine, ©1981; 304(12): 739.

During my research, I found that humorous poetry generally fell into two categories: either spontaneous reflections on medical topics or responses to previously published articles. The following poems show that the clever author can not only use verse to review a book, but also to review the reviewer!—*H.B.*

Introduction to Surgery*

An Introduction to Surgery. Edited by David H. Patey, M.S.(Lond.), F.R.C.S.(Eng.). (Pp. 228 + xi; illustrated. 17s. 6d.; student's edition 9s. 6d.) London: Lloyd-Luke (Medical Books) Ltd. 1958.

This useful little book is meant
For those on surgery intent,
To tell them what they ought to know
Before into the wards they go;
Within small compass, too, it packs
Much that the student often lacks,
And stresses well the "human touch"
Which to the patient means so much.
To every dresser then we say—
Read through this book without delay;
The hours in reading it you spend
Will pay a handsome dividend.

Zachary Cope, M.D.

Rhymed Review†

How pleasant to the eye and mind
A lucid book review to find,
So apt and pithy with its rhyme,
Saving a column's reading time.
Such verse appropriately used
Would Brighten those who have accused
The *B.M.J.* as dull and glum,
Too vague, prolix, and wearisome.
Then with your grace may we all hope
That others follow Zachary Cope.

Basingstoke   I. Atkin, M.D.

*Reprinted with permission from the British Medical Journal, ©1958; 2(Oct 18):958.
†Reprinted with permission from the British Medical Journal, ©1958; 2(Nov 1):1106.

Laments of a Clinical Clerk*

Dermatology
or
Give Me a Man Who Calls a Spade a Geotome

I wish the dermatologist
Were less a firm apologist
For all the terminology
That's used in dermatology.

Something you or I would deem a
Redness he calls *erythema;*
If it's blistered, raw and warm he
Has to call it *multiforme.*

Things to him are never simple;
Papule is his word for pimple
What's a *macule,* clearly stated?
Just a spot that's over-rated!

Over the skin that looks unwell
He chants Latin like a spell;
What he's labeled and obscured
Looks to *him* as good as cured.

Julia Bess Frank, M.D.

Laments of a Clinical Clerk—V†

Infectious Disease

Of all my consultants, most easy to please
Is the fellow who comes from infectious
   disease.
His wants are so simple! His needs are so few!
Just gather some sputum, blood cultures
   times two,
X-ray the patient from guggle to zatch,[1]
Examine the urine, both cath and clean catch;
It takes but a moment to do an L.P.,
Swab wound, throat and cervix, yank out the I.V.

When all of the data at last are collected,
The last culture plated, the last slide inspected,
The attending arrives to review and recap
(While intern and student enjoy a brief nap);
He broods with the air of a scribe with papyrus
And gives his opinion: "Most likely a virus.
Don't bother to fix it; can't treat it, can't cure it,
Though superinfection may later obscure it.
Should there be recurrence of fever or pain
Go back to square one and start over again!"

Julia Bess Frank, M.D.

[1] For the location of these anatomical landmarks, see James Thurber's
The Thirteen Clocks, New York, Simon and Schuster, 1950.

*Reprinted with permission from The New England Journal of
 Medicine, ©1977; 297(12):660.
†Reprinted with permission from The New England Journal of
 Medicine, ©1978; 298(18):1009.

Prostatic Resection,
Or Lines for My Urologist*

Now that, at last, I lie so meekly here
 My nether half benumbed, a prey to fear,
Good Doctor, I beseech you, have a care
 As you explore those tubes and ducts down there!
I hope that in your cystoscopic quest
 (As three diplomas on your wall attest)
With sponge, resectoscope, hawk-billed coudé
 You know just what you are about today!
Oh, do be careful as you probe and shove
 With catheter and sound and rectal glove,
While in my dank and murky depths you grope
 With tiny, incandescent telescope,
With practiced eye and craft superior
 To reconnoiter my interior.

I know you have, as yonder parchments state,
 The arcane skills that they certificate.
You dilate, snip, excise and cauterize;
 Such arts unfeignedly I eulogize
I do not doubt your virtuosity,
 But ponder, sir, what this can mean to me!
If you should falter—no offense!—I plead
 To what calamaties can all this lead?
What piercing pangs may we precipitate,
 What surging ecstasies abbreviate?
What dire impairments may your blade inflict,
 What cherished sins in future interdict?
As to the mark your nimble scalpel swoops,
 The word I do not wish to hear is "OOPS!"

Richard Bardolph
University of North Carolina
at Greensboro

Greensboro, NC

*Reprinted with permission from The New England Journal of
 Medicine, ©1980; 303(11):647.

The next two poems are medical takeoffs of the nonsense poem Jabberwocky, written by Lewis Carroll. The poem, which appears in his book *Through the Looking Glass,* is felt to be the most famous nonsense poem ever written. After Alice reads the poem she says, ". . . it seems to fill my head with ideas—only I don't know exactly what they are." Although one needs footnotes to understand all the words in Lewis Carroll's poem, Geniewacky and Gynawocky are a little easier to figure out.—*H.B.*

Geniewacky*

'Twas genic and the acrocents
Did twine and twist and gyrotate
To lub and lubber's recompense
A truly metaphasic plate.

Yes, seek them out, mosaics rare
And non disjunctions panoplied
But of the beast you must beware
Lest you be vittles for his greed.

A thunder through the spital thrums
With bowing nurds on either side
Behold the great Granteater comes
With multiforms upon his hide.

He comes with outstretched geltigrab
Antennae tuned to visiteams
Engorged by a research lab
Fulfulled of fluff and borrowed dreams.

Quick on him cast the potent drug
Oh, cleanish boy with eyes of green
His gulps now steam upon the rug
No man has such a colchicine.

'Twas genic and the acrocents
Did twine and twist and gyrotate
No trace of dollars or of cents
Did there remain to translocate.

Samuel P. Bessman, M.D.
University of Maryland Hospital
University of Maryland

Baltimore, MD

*Reprinted with permission from The New England Journal of Medicine, ©1968; 279(4):220.

Gynawocky*

From the 1943 University College Hospital, London

'Twas gynig and the slithy vulvs
Did grease and glather in the glare;
The midderstuds, like hungry wolves,
Waved dettol-fingers in the air.
One by one they came to grips
With problems of the Gynaequest;
Caressed the os with sensitips,
As from above they fundiprest.
The Gynaeprof, all fidgetas,
Could feel, he thought, a viscerop.
'Twas but a bulkypelvimass
Projecting 'bove the symphitop.
"Tell me, good Muth, your menstridates:
I fear you have a graviwomb.
You must come up to antenates
That we may test for albimune.
We'll closely watch your pressiblood,
And you will tell us, if you would,
Your foetipulse and fundiheight,
The times you uripass at night.
Your swellifeet, your mornipulse,
Are all of interest to me;
Though trivisympts to you they look,
Preclamptitoxisigns they be."
The months passed by and pendybell
Grew bigger every day.
No toxisympts, and all was well
Until the estiday.

From noctislumb a listiclerk
By telebell was woke:
"Arise, good sir, quick off the mark!
The membribags have broke."
All slumberfull he stumbled down
And flustertripped upon the stair;
He hurriscrubbed and caught the crown
In time to stop a peritear.
"Now rapipant," cried midderstud,
"An foetipush no more."
But with a mighty spurtiblood
A prematinf she bore.
"Now, fundigrip with all thy strength
Before the flacciwomb distend."
The umbicord increased in length—
Placenta came, and 'twas the end.
"Well now, my dear," said Gynaeprof,
"In case your womb descends
I'll fit you with a cervipop;
'Twill not defeat your ends."
"In three months time return to me."
In three months time she came.
"Now let me see what I can see;
Turn on your back again."
The Gynaeprof, all fidgetas,
Could feel, he thought, a viscerop.
'Twas but a bulky pelvimass
Projecting 'bove the symphitop. . . .

Anonymous

*Reprinted from JAMA, ©1948; 137(7):A38, with permission from the American Medical Association.

Methanosis*

To the Editor: Dr. W. C. Duane freely admits in the paper he co-authored with Dr. M. D. Leavitt, "Floating Stools—Flatus versus Fat" (N Engl J Med 286:973, 1972) that his consistently floating stools were fortuitously noted to be associated with "a CH_4 excretion rate of near record proportion." This forthright admission of a high methane rating from one of our professional colleagues inspired the following trio of limericks:

Our thanks to frank Doctor Duane
Who takes the time to explain
Just how he had noted
That his stools often floated
Before they were flushed down the drain.

He must have thought first, "Mama mia!
Do I suffer from steatorrhea?
But it cannot be that—

There is no trace of fat."
Which led to another idea.

Well aware of the gas he unloosed
The doctor quite shrewdly deduced,
(Almost clairvoyant)
His feces were buoyant
Because of the methane produced.

San Jose, CA   Milton J. Chatton, M.D.

A month before "Methanosis" was published, Joseph Teller offered his own poetic response to Dr. Duane's article.—*H.B.*

Floaters and Sinkers†

To the Editor: The recent article "Floating Stools—Flatus versus Fat." inspired me to embrace the Muse as follows:

While safe's the stool that comes a sinker,
The floater's apt to be a stinker.

So it's not fat but, rather, flatus
Imparts the elevated status.

Freehold, NJ   Joseph D. Teller

*Reprinted with permission from The New England Journal of Medicine, ©1972; 287(2):362.
†Reprinted with permission from The New England Journal of Medicine, ©1972; 287(1):52.

The Surgeon*

The public views his status regal,
In the profession he's "The Eagle."
With super-supple fingers slim
(Pus, blood, and guts don't bother him),
Up to his elbows, filled with glee,
With snick and slice sadistically,
Into a jar, up on a shelf
He puts a fragment of yourself.
For him no diagnostic doubt—
He'll operate, and so find out.

Edgar L. Dimmick, M.D.

Ode to Room 459†

They test your blood by pints and quarts
They fill you up with barium,
And watch your blushing innards flip
Like fish in an aquarium.

They puncture you like needlepoint
They steal your clothes and drag you
From whatsiscope and whosiscope
They pummel, thump and gag you.

For there's a test for every ill
To help the doctor cure it.
But few except the well and strong
Are able to endure it!

Gainesville, FL   Leonard Reaves III, M.D.

Hamlet's Soliloquy on Allergy‡

To sneeze, or not to sneeze; that is the question.
Whether it is nobler in the mind to suffer
The stings and lachrymation of outrageous hay fever
Or to take shots against a sea of troubles
And by much needling end them? To cry, to sneeze
No more, and by a sneeze to end
The headache and the thousand devilish symptoms
The flesh is heir to; 'tis a consummation devoutly to be
    wished
To cry, to sneeze,
To sneeze, perchance to stream; ay, there's the rub
For in that sneeze allergic when it comes what
    streams
May run from noses and from eyes
Must give us pause. There's the aftereffects
That make the antihistamines of so long action
For who would bear the pills and sprays all the time,

The skin tests wrong, the proud man whealy,
The pangs of needles shoved, the doc's delays,
The impotence of medication and the side effects
The patient suffers from the things he takes
When he himself might his own relief obtain
With a sterilized Luer? Who would patch tests bear
To itch and scratch under an unknown allergy
But that the dread of something worse to come,
That undiscovered remedy by whose boon
No victim's yet been cured, puzzles the will
And rather makes one bear the wheals one has
Than risk some others that he knows not of?
Thus allergy doth make cowards of us all
And thus the native tan of healthy hide
Is siklied o'er with pale lumps of "hives"
And proprietaries of great promise and advertisement
Their doses go awry and fail to get desired action.

Dunmore, PA   E. L. Dimmick, M.D.

*Reprinted from JAMA, ©1967; 199(6):A274, with permission from
the American Medical Association.
†Reprinted from JAMA, ©1963; 184(7):A242, with permission from
the American Medical Association.
‡Reprinted from Obstetrics & Gynecology, ©1962; 20(1):148, with
permission from the American College of Obstetricians &
Gynecologists.

The Formulary Song*

(To be sung to the tune of Gilbert and Sullivan's "I am the Very
Model of a Modern Major-General")

There's Aldomet and Atromid and Antivert and Atarax
And Dexamyl and Donnagel and Demerol and Dulcolax.
There's Tylenol and Tegretol and Riopan and Regitine
And Pertofrane and Pavabid and also Pyribenzamine.
Now if you're down there's Dexedrine and Benzedrine and Elavil,
And if you're up there's Librium and Valium and Vistaril.
There's Thorazine and Stelazine for calming schizophrenics with;
There's Seconal for sleeping and for mania there's Eskalith . . .
There's Benadryl and Gelusil and Placidyl and Peritrate
And Decadron and Parafon and Sinequan and Sorbitrate
And Miltown, Motrin, Medrol, Maalox, Myleran and Miradon
And Mycostatin, Micronor, Mandelamine and Mylicon.

There's Omnipen and Principen and Tegopen and Torecan
And Versapen and Betapen and Pyopen and Percodan.
There's Robitussin, Garamycin, also Butazolidin
And Furadantin, Coricidin, even Triaminicin.
There's Dimetane and Dimetapp and Dymelor and Dimacol
And Diuril and Dialose and Diamox and Disophrol.
There's Darvocet for headaches when you really want to stay at home,
But if the other end is sore, the one you need is Proctofoam . . .
I know you must be weary and this song is getting pretty grim
With all these pharmaceuticals from Actifed to Zyloprim.
But just imagine what would happen if I tried to fan the flames
By starting over once again and using all generic names!

Mark L. Cohen
Pennsylvania State University
College of Medicine
Milton S. Hershey Medical Center

Hershey, PA

*Reprinted with permission from The New England Journal of
Medicine, ©1977; 296(9):520.

Urinalysis*

Some bring their sample in a jar,
    Some bring it in a pot,
Some bring a sample hardly ample,
    While others bring a lot.

Some hide it in a paper bag,
    Some wrap it like a treasure,

Some, quite undaunted, proudly flaunt it
    As if it gives them pleasure.

Some cork it up so tightly that
    It's quite a job to spring it,
Some let it slosh, almost awash,
    And some forget to bring it.

Richard Armour, Ph.D.

The journal *Survey of Ophthalmology* began publishing a poetry column in 1983 called "Time Oph." Although most of the poems are geared toward ophthalmologists, the following one has broader appeal.—*H.B.*

Roundsmanship†

Envy has me in its grip—
I'm just no good at roundsmanship
I never enter in the fray
With brilliant quotes, ex temporé
Lest all those agile minds around me
Use their rebuttals to confound me.

Each week, somehow, it's still the same—
The pundits stand forth and declaim
They speak of obscure things like quarks
(One can almost hear quotation marks)
And each one notes, in his oration,
The year and place of publication.

Only seldom is it noted
That any author's been misquoted
And, apart from him who has misspoken,
The silence in the room's unbroken
Because the speaker is adepter
At specifying verse and chepter.

I'd love to quote, and as I please,
Beginning with Hippocrates,
Passages from any text

. . . What went before and what comes next . . .
And pick the minutest of particles
From long-forgotten, obscure articles.

If only I could have my druthers,
I'd scintillate before the others
I'd quote the literature verbatim
At rounds, they'd whisper: "How we hate him.
His absence would be quite idyllic
And we'd all seem less imbecilic."

But, in the grip of my aphasia,
I hurry back to my fantasia
And, as the scholars comments sear me
I look at all those seated near me
And even though I'm not clairvoyant,
I realize why they're not too buoyant.

Their interest is counterfeited,
Their eyes becoming heavy-lidded
Though their attendance is requested,
Most of them will leave well-rested.

Ben Milder, M.D.

A New Personality Type*

To publish in your learned journal
One doesn't need a truth eternal.
A recent issue[1-3] made us see
Your editors like poetry.

What kind of people, you might ask,
Would spend their time on such a task
Composing lines that barely rhyme?
My goodness what a waste of time!

This group of people must be rare,
Compulsive, but with time to spare.
We've discovered they must be
Personality type, non-A non-B!

David Baer, M.D.
Debra Judelson, M.D.
Stephen Mizroch, M.D.
San Francisco, CA
Kaiser Foundation Hospital

[1] Frank JB: Laments of a clinical clerk—V. N Engl J Med 298:1009, 1978
[2] Schnitzler ER: "Honeymoon cystitis." N Engl J Med 298:1035, 1978.
[3] Editors: *Journal* usage under attack. N Engl J Med 298:1038, 1978.

A Referenced Poem†
by Poets Three[1]

The journal we all hold prestigious.
Whose articles both long and terse
Sport lists of authors quite prodigious,
Now gives us multi-authored verse.
Did David Baer the poem compose,
Fair Judelson his inspiration,
While Mizroch (senior author) chose
To lend his name and approbation?
How antic seem the poets of old,
Given to wry and solitary feats.
How richer *Ode to Autumn*'s gold
If writ by Shelley, Hunt *and* Keats!
A referenced poem by poets three
Is surely the best of poetry.

Frederick L. Jones, Jr., M.D.
Danville, PA
Geisinger Medical Center

[1] Baer D, Judelson D, Mizroch S: A new personality type. N Engl J Med 299:558, 1978.

*Reprinted with permission from The New England Journal of Medicine, ©1978; 299(10):558.
†Reprinted with permission from The New England Journal of Medicine, ©1978; 299(24):1372.

Off to the Yearly Convention*

Oh, we're off to the medical meeting
Where there's never a problem with seating—
Except in the bar,
Where friends from afar
Are exchanging their annual greeting.

Since the IRS didn't complain
When we held our convention in Spain,
We'll talk antibiotic
In some place exotic
And not in Dubuque or Fort Wayne.

If the papers get to soporific
We'll steal off to watch the Pacific
And we'll toss down a few—

Tax-deductible too!—
In a toast to La Vie Scientific.

And what if we do run up bills
For dinners with all of the frills?
A fine bill-of-fare
Will help us prepare
To "improve our professional skills."

So we're off to the yearly convention,
Eager to turn our attention
To the holy alliance
of Pleasure and Science
And sundries we don't need to mention.

David Goldblatt, M.D.
University of Rochester
Rochester, NY

*Reprinted with permission from The New England Journal of Medicine, © 1974; 290(24):1385.

*   *   *

Additional Readings

1. Eyerer R: Clinico-pathological exercise. J Maine Med Assoc 1965; 56(12):279–281.

An otherwise serious clinico-pathological-case (CPC) of which 50% is written in rhyme.

The following four poems are all enjoyable, but longer than what I wanted to include in the book.

2. Bean WB: Omphalosophy: an inquiry into the inner (and outer) significance of the belly button. Arch Int Med 1974; 134(5):866–870.

3. Butterfield WC: Know any bawdy old medical limericks? Med Economics 1973; 50(Jan 8):166.

4. Green L: Requiem for the eponym. Skeletal Radiol 1989; 17(8):589–590.

5. Rankin HJ: Successful treatment of a compulsive limerick composer by behavioral methods. Behav Res Ther 1976; 14(2):167.

6. Armour, Richard: The Medical Muse.* New York, McGraw-Hill, 1963.

For those who would like a little more of Richard Armour, this book is a collection of poems published in *Postgraduate Medicine* from 1951 to 1963.

7. Cope, Zachary: The Diagnosis of the Acute Abdomen in Rhyme.* London, Lewis, 1962.

In this fascinating book, Dr. Cope addresses the diagnosis and treatment of the acute abdomen. Although the subject is serious, his style gives it a light touch and makes it a pleasure to read.

8. Farnum, Charles G: Medicine Could Be Verse.* New York, Exposition Press, 1949.

Dr. Farnum's poems are insightful, witty, and thoroughly enjoyable.

*These books are no longer in print but should be available through interlibrary loan.

CASE
REPORTS

Soon after they hit the wards, medical students become familiar with the language of the hospital, including that all-purpose medical label: "The Interesting Case." Patients who become Interesting Cases are the ones who remain undiagnosed, presented in an unusual manner, or developed an uncommon complication of their disease. Although they are frequently the subject of much discussion, in corridors and elevators, over lunch, etc., no one should strive to become an Interesting Case. Nevertheless, medicine being what it is, there is rarely a shortage of such patients in the hospital. And what should one do with an Interesting Case? (That is, besides trying to diagnose it.) Why, write it up of course!

Et Al and the Case Report*

THEODORE KAMHOLTZ, M.D.

The urge to contribute to medical literature is motivated by more than a desire to wear the professorial stole. It's as inexplicably compelling as the suicidal drive of lemmings to the sea. If the bug has really bitten you, you don't stop scribbling until, with parkinsonian hands, you caress your volume of Collected Writings.

But in order to collect your writings, you must have something to write about. And even the most gifted clinician can't discover penicillin *and* unearth a new disease *and* find the cure for coryza *and* perfect a new operation *and* so on—for article after article.

Old hand and neophyte alike must pad. Padding comes in all sizes and shapes. In medical literature, its most familiar shape—do you recognize it?—is the case report.

By definition, a case report is proof of the precept that anything can happen and eventually does. Coincidentally, it's apt to feature the first patient you meet in the hospital after the literary fever hits you.

Having selected your case—trichinosis, let's say, in a 24-year-old white male—you must next pick your co-authors. Note the plural. Of course, it is you (singular) who will write, type, and proofread the article. But for publication purposes, the chief of service, who has never seen the case, gets top billing in the by-line.

Next comes the attending physician, who made rounds once and almost saw the case. Then the associate, who *did* see the case and contributed several grunts.

Low man on the totem pole is, of course, you—properly thankful not to be included merely as "et al" (along with "ibid" and "anon," perhaps the largest authorship fraternity in the world).

Leading off the article is your introductory review of the literature. If you are saving yourself for a solo article later, you state that a search of the literature "of the past ten years has neglected trichinosis in 24-year-old white males, though incidence of the disease in such patients is not as uncommon as the meager attention it has received would lead one to believe."

Your chief, who has gone through the same initiation, may suggest that you sweeten this up a bit. If so, you extend yourself, thus: "A search of the literature of the past *twenty* years . . ."

The question of what references you've used is a touchy one. It is not quite cricket to lift someone else's bibliography intact. Besides, you don't know where *he* got it; and you certainly don't want to fall victim to the reader who insists upon checking all references and who may then write the editor to point out that an article you've cited (presumably on trichinosis) deals actually with impotence in bald-headed men. Although a nuisance, then, it's probably best to include only those references you've validated yourself.

You've reached the peak of successful writing when your bibliography is longer than your article. This gives your work an impressive mathematical flavor: "Trichinosis[17,23,4,97] has been said[81,56,27] on several occasions[5,32,74] to be a disease[108,69,13] characterized by fever,[77,10,15] pain[11,43,91] et cetera.[16,96,103,111]"

As for the case itself, you describe it in a series of rigid clichés, following a procedure not unlike filling out a life insurance form. For example: "This was the *n*th admission of an *x*-year-old *white male* who was admitted to the *Blank* Hospital complaining of *fever and migratory joint pains.*"

You go on in this vein until, in due course, "he was discharged on the *n*th day after admission, *completely relieved of his symptoms.*"

It is wise not to depart from this classic form, unless you want to wind up in the Reader's Digest and out of your local society.

It is likewise *de rigueur* to make the patient seem as controlled as a test tube in the laboratory. You say

*Reprinted with permission from Medical Economics, ©1952; 29(June):93–97. Copyright by Medical Economics Company, Inc., Oradell, NJ 07649.

nothing about your discovery, following a sugar tolerance test one day, that the patient had eaten breakfast beforehand. Nor do you mention the BMR that was done while the patient in the next bed delivered precipitously. Nor the sputum report that came back marked "No free acid."

In a report case, then, there are no Sunday visitors, no temperamental orderlies, no misplaced specimens, no recalcitrant patients. This requires a kind of vigorous selectivity; you must omit every detail that even smacks faintly of the human touch.

Your laboratory reports, on the other hand, must omit *nothing*. They must include every test that was performed, whether it had anything to do with the case or not. For one thing, you may as well get credit for your thoroughness. For another, someone is always ready to pounce on that lone missing test as the really important one. You're damned if you didn't perform an opsonic index; and you're damned if you did—but more faintly.

The muttered oaths directed your way from the laboratory itself are something else again. They're a tribulation to be borne during the clinical rather than the literary work-up of the case.

The next major division in the article comes under the heading of *Discussion.* Here you may—indeed, must—divulge your motive for writing the report. The medical profession does not appreciate the disease, you say. Doctors are not aware of its incidence, morbidity, mortality, curability, pathology, and so on. It has

therefore occurred to you that here is a fine illustrative case to enlighten all and sundry. So runs the *stated* motive. Quite coincidental is the fact that you're going to get your name into print.

Next comes your *Summary,* a matter of delicate balance and verbal cunning. If you tell too much, the reader's interest will pall. If you tell too little, he won't be enticed either. You must show the import of your case—but tantalizingly. If in doubt, have this part of the article edited by the Coming Attractions writer at your local theatre.

Finally—the title. If you're a junior assistant, you may appropriately head your report "Trichinosis in a 24-Year-Old-Male." If you're an assistant with some standing, you rate a more comprehensive title—say, "Fundoscopic Findings in Thirteen Consecutive Cases of Trichinosis."

The associate physician can take the liberty of writing about "The Psychodynamic Aspects of Trichinosis." The title of the attending's article is "Trichinosis: Its Cause and Cure." The chief of service simply asks, "Whither Trichinosis?"

Once your seniors have given the nod, the article should be mailed immediately to a medical journal. If postmarked later than midnight, it may fail to establish your priority. In fact, if you put it off for even as much as the wink of an eye, the same article may appear under a different title and a different authorship. This will not happen because of plagiarism but merely because genius these days is such a common thing.

Chicken Soup Rebound and Relapse of Pneumonia: Report of a Case*

NANCY L. CAROLINE, M.D.
HAROLD SCHWARTZ, M.D.

A case is reported in which a previously healthy individual, having received an inadequate course of chicken soup in treatment of mild pneumococcal pneumonia, experienced a severe relapse, refractory to all medical treatment and eventually requiring thoracotomy. The pharmacology of chicken soup is reviewed and the dangers of abrupt termination of therapy are stressed.

Chicken soup has long been recognized to possess unusual therapeutic potency against a wide variety of viral and bacterial agents. Indeed, as early as the twelfth century, the theologian, philosopher and physician, Moses Maimonides wrote, "Chicken soup . . . is recommended as an excellent food as well as medication."[1] Previous anecdotal reports regarding the therapeutic efficacy of this agent, however, have failed to provide details regarding the appropriate length of therapy. What follows is a case report in which abrupt withdrawal of chicken soup led to severe relapse of pneumonia.

Case Report

The patient is a 47-year-old male physician who had been in excellent health until 8 days prior to admission, when he experienced the sudden onset of rigors followed by fever to 105°F (40.5°C). He was seen by a physician at that time, when physical examination revealed a severely toxic man, unable to raise his head from the bed. Pertinent physical findings were limited to the chest, where rales were heard over the right middle lobe. Chicken soup was immediately begun in doses of 500 ml po q 4 hours. Defervescence occurred in 36 hours and a chest x-ray film taken 5 days prior to admission was entirely normal. Because he felt symptomatically improved, the patient declined further chicken soup after this time. He continued to feel well and remained afebrile until the night prior to admission, when he developed right upper quadrant pain, nausea and vomiting while on a visit to Vermont. His vomiting persisted through the night, and the following morning he boarded a plane for Cleveland.

En route, he became severely dyspneic, and by the time he deplaned in Cleveland, he was cyanotic and in severe respiratory distress.

He was brought immediately to the hospital where physical examination revealed an acutely ill man, febrile to 104°F (40.0°C), breathing shallowly 60 times per minute, with a pulse of 140. Physical findings were again chiefly limited to the chest, where bilateral pleural friction rubs, bibasilar rales and egophony over the right middle lobe were heard. Chest x-ray examination showed consolidation of the right middle lobe, infiltrates at both bases and a questionable right pleural effusion. White cell count was 7700 without a shift to the left. Electrolytes were within normal limits. Arterial blood gases on 6 liters/min of nasal oxygen were pH = 7.51, P_{CO_2} = 20 torr and P_{O_2} = 50 torr. Gram stain of the sputum showed swarming diplococci, and multiple cultures of sputum and blood subsequently grew out type 4 Pneumococcus.

Chicken soup being unavailable, the patient was started on one million units q 6 hours of intravenous penicillin. Failure to respond led to increases of the dose up to 30 million units daily. Nonetheless, the patient remained febrile and his chest x-ray film showed progressive effusion and infiltration. On the twelfth hospital day he was taken to the operating room for a right thoracotomy. He thereafter made an uneventful recovery, maintained on 30 million units of penicillin daily during his postoperative course, and was discharged on the 25th hospital day.

Discussion

The therapeutic efficacy of chicken soup was first discovered several thousand years ago when an epidemic

*Reprinted with permission from Chest, ©1975; 67(2):215–216.

highly fatal to young Egyptian males seemed not to affect an ethnic minority residing in the same area. Contemporary epidemiologic inquiry revealed that the diet of the group not afflicted by the epidemic contained large amounts of a preparation made by boiling chicken with various vegetables and herbs. It is notable in this regard that the dietary injunctions given to Moses on Mount Sinai, while restricting consumption of no less than 19 types of fowl, exempted chicken from prohibition.[2] Some scholars[3] believe that the recipe for chicken soup[4] was transmitted to Moses on the same occasion, but was relegated to the oral tradition when the Scriptures were canonized. Chicken soup was widely used in Europe for many centuries, but disappeared from commercial production after the Inquisition. It remained as a popular therapy among certain Eastern European groups, however, and was introduced into the United States in the early part of this century. While chicken soup is now widely employed against a variety of organic and functional disorders, its manufacture remains largely in the hands of private individuals, and standardization has proved nearly impossible.

Preliminary investigation into the pharmacology of chicken soup (Bohbymycetin[R]) has shown that it is readily absorbed after oral administration, achieving peak serum levels in two hours and persisting in detectable levels for up to 24 hours. Parenteral administration is not recommended. The metabolic fate of the agent is not well understood, although varying proportions are excreted by the kidneys, and dosage should be appropriately adjusted in patients with renal failure. Chicken soup is distributed widely throughout body tissues and breakdown products having antimicrobial efficacy cross the blood-brain barrier. Untoward side effects are minimal, consisting primarily of mild euphoria which rapidly remits on discontinuation of the agent.

While chicken soup has been employed for thousands of years in the treatment of viral and bacterial illnesses, there have been no systematic investigations into the optimal course of therapy. The present case illustrates a possible hazard of abrupt chicken soup withdrawal: a previously healthy man, having received what proved to be an inadequate course of chicken soup for clinical signs of pneumonia, experienced a virulent relapse into severe bacterial pneumonia. It was not possible in this case to determine whether the relapse was caused by resistant organisms, as chicken soup was unavailable at the time treatment had to be restarted, and a synthetic product of lesser potency was used instead. Further study is needed to determine the most efficacious regimen for chicken soup. Pending such investigation, it would probably be more prudent to give a ten day course at full dosage, with gradual tapering thereafter and immediate resumption of therapy at the first sign of relapse.

References

1. Rosner F: Studies in Judaica: The Medical Aphorisms of Moses Maimonides. New York, Yeshiva University Press, 1971. Treatise 20, aphorism 67.

2. Leviticus 11:13–19.

3. Caroline Mrs Z (my mother). Personal communication.

4. Bellin MG: Jewish Cookbook. New York, Garden City Books, 1958, pp 19–20 (recipe).

The Chicken Soup Controversy*

The following letters were written in response to the article by Drs. Caroline and Schwartz. Although the four best are reprinted here, eight were originally published in the journal. Interestingly, the editor of *Chest* stated that an even greater number of letters were submitted though not published. Is there anyone who still doubts the therapeutic efficacy of this wonder drug?—*H.B.*

To The Editor:

The report of Caroline and Schwartz (*Chest* 67:215–216, 1975) is timely and alarming, for it suggests that chicken soup-resistant pneumococci may be emerging in nonhospitalized populations and that this time-honored therapeutic modality may have to be abandoned in favor of less relishable treatments. However, the authors failed to obtain *in vitro* sensitivities of the organism against chicken soup, so the presence of chicken soup-resistant pneumococci and/or the question of emerging resistance remains unanswered.

Spurred by the report by Caroline and Schwartz, our laboratories tested 100 recently isolated strains of pneumococci against chicken soup[1] serially diluted in brain-heart infusion broth (BHI). The minimal inhibitory dilution (MID) was defined as that dilution of chicken soup which visibly inhibited growth after incubation for 24 hours at 37°C. Using inocula from a 1 ㏒dilution of an overnight broth culture, 99 percent of the strains were observed to be inhibited at a dilution ≤ 1:64 (well within the range of levels achievable in the serum). However, one isolate was not inhibited at this dilution or, for that matter, even by undiluted chicken soup. Further examination of this putatively chicken soup-resistant Pneumococcus revealed it to contain a plasmid (labeled CS) which coded for chicken soup resistance. Not surprisingly, this CS plasmid was found to be linked directly to a plasmid coding for resistance to tea leaves (*Camellia sinensis*) and one coding for resistance to whole-wheat bread mold (*Penicillium chrysogenum?*). Regrettably, though, this multiresistant plasmid, CSTLBM, was spontaneously lost at such a high frequency that we could not preserve it for confirmatory studies; however, we urge others working in this field to maintain a constant vigil for the emergence of such chicken soup-resistant strains.

R. J. Duma, M.D.; S. M. Markowitz, M.D.;
and M. A. Tipple, M.D.
Division of Infectious Diseases
Medical College of Virginia
Virginia Commonwealth University, Richmond, VA

Reference

1. Bellin MG: Jewish Cookbook. New York, Garden City Books, 1958, pp 19–20.

To the Editor:

As a longtime chicken-souper, I appreciated reading the article entitled "Chicken Soup Rebound and Relapse of Pneumonia: Report of a Case" (*Chest* 67:215–216, 1975).

Us chicken-soupers have long been aware of the therapeutic efficacy of chicken soup. Our data, however, have consistently been ignored by the bulk of organized medical opinion whose practitioners, as you know, are predominately affluent steak eaters.

We would like to undertake a research program to bring chicken soup into its rightful place in medical therapy. Adjunctive to this study might be the investigation of how the use of happy or unhappy chickens affects the beneficial efforts of chicken soup. In this respect, we have communicated with a contact in the chicken industry, in the hopes that he might want to finance this study with a lifelong supply of chicken legs for the researcher. Unfortunately, research within our contact's company devoted to improving the breed precludes their participation in our program. We hope that improvement of the breed includes attitudinal programs designed to produce *happy* chickens. With

---

*Reprinted with permission from Chest, ©1975; 68(4):604–606.

the evidence presently available concerning the results of talking to flowers and plants, it is certainly reasonable to expect some degree of extra therapeutic effect from chicken soup derived from happy chickens. We must expect that even chicken brain will respond better than a weed! In any event, if chickens and plants ever take over the world, isn't it good sense to build some advance good will for ourselves?

On behalf of the Chicken Soup Institute, we thank *Chest* for its interest in chicken soup and humanity.

Ralph Packman
Chicken Soup Institute, Philadelphia

To the Editor:

I read with interest the article, "Chicken Soup Rebound and Relapse of Pneumonia: Report of a Case" (*Chest* 67:215–216, 1975).

You might be interested to know that we have successfully treated male impotence with another chicken-derived compound, sodium cytarabine hexamethyl-acetyl lututria tetra-zolamine.

This compound, when applied in ointment form to the penis, not only cures impotence but also increases libido and prevents premature ejaculation. In respect to the latter, preliminary studies indicate that its effects are *dose* related inasmuch as intercourse continues for five minutes when 5 percent ointment is applied, 15 minutes when 15 percent ointment is applied, and so forth. We had hoped that it might also cure Peyronie's disease, but thus far our results have been disappointing.

We have received a grant in the sum of $650,000 from the National Scientific Foundation to carry out a prospective, randomized, controlled double-blind study. Unfortunately, we are unable to obtain a suitable number of subjects inasmuch as each volunteer refuses to participate unless we assure him that he will be a subject rather than a control.

Laurence F. Greene, M.D., Ph.D.
Anson L. Clark Professor of Urology
Mayo Medical School
Rochester, Minn

To the Editor:

I have read the interesting report of Caroline and Schwartz (*Chest* 67:215–216, 1975) on the adverse reaction to abrupt withdrawal of chicken soup in the therapy of pneumonia. While the data presented are convincing, several additional points should be made, and it need not be emphasized that we at the Mount Sinai Hospital have had extensive experience in this form of therapy.

1. Are there any data on the bioavailability of the product used? I assume, perhaps presumptuously, that Caroline produced and administered the drug to Schwartz. The question must be posed: does a girl from Presbyterian Hospital really know the laboratory methods well enough, Mrs. Z. Caroline (reference 3) notwithstanding? We have treated many patients with short-term (one to three day), parenteral, pyrogen-free chicken soup (see the following) without recrudescent disease ever being noted.

2. Was the product used in the monomeric or polymeric form? We have observed that, in the absence of mixed soup greens (Bronx Terminal Market, stall 47, Bronx, NY), only polymeric drug is produced in the fermenter vat. This tends to coalesce into oil-like droplets on the surface of the medium, and there is a tendency for some manufacturers to skim off this deposit and discard it. This, in fact, removes the major biologically active fraction from the drug.

3. Because of the growing awareness of the efficacy of chicken soup, the lack of R-factor mediated resistance, and the broad spectrum of activity, we have been faced with a severe shortage of purified drug. As indicated in the paper by Caroline and Schwartz, this is apparently a national (perhaps international) problem. We have, therefore, developed an affinity chromatography method for recovery of chicken soup from the urine. This is based on the selective adsorption of chicken soup to unleavened bread in the form of finely pulverized microspherules (Sephardex) catalytically activated with beaten eggs. The active drug may be eluted with a sodium chloride gradient using large macrocrystalline salt.

We hope this information will prove of value so that properly controlled clinical trials can be initiated.

Gerald T. Keusch, M.D.
Associate Professor of Medicine
Mount Sinai School of Medicine
of the City University of New York

Almost everyone in medicine knows the name of William Osler. What many people do not know, however, is that Osler's reputation is not limited to his role as physician, author, and medical educator. Throughout his long career, he was also admired for his sense of humor. Osler often expressed his less serious side with the help of an alter ego, the fictitious Army surgeon Egerton Yorrick Davis. The following letter is a perfect example of Osler's wit. According to Lawrence Altaffer (see Additional Readings), Osler sent the letter to Theophilus Parvin, a fellow editor at *Medical News* who had previously written an editorial on vaginismus in the journal. Osler disagreed with using editorial space for such an obscure topic and fabricated the case as a way of satirizing the condition. Osler did not intend for the letter to be published, but Parvin misinterpreted his hoax as a true case report.—*H.B.*

Vaginismus*

Through the courtesy of the Editor of *The Canada Medical and Surgical Journal,* we are in receipt of the following note:

Dear Sir: The reading of an admirably written and instructive editorial in the Philadelphia *Medical News* for 24th November, on forms of vaginismus, has reminded me of a case in point which bears out, in an extraordinary way, the statements therein contained. When in practice at Pentonville, Eng., I was sent for, about 11 P.M. by a gentleman whom, on my arriving at his house, I found in a state of great perturbation, and the story he told me was briefly as follows:

At bedtime, when going to the back kitchen to see if the house was shut up, a noise in the coachman's room attracted his attention, and, going in, he discovered to his horror that the man was in bed with one of the maids. She screamed, he struggled, and they rolled out of bed together and made frantic efforts to get apart, but without success. He was a big, burly man, over six feet, and she was a small woman, weighing not more than ninety pounds. She was moaning and screaming, and seemed in great agony, so that, after several fruitless attempts to get them apart, he sent for me. When I arrived I found the man standing up and supporting the woman in his arms, and it was quite evident that his penis was tightly locked in her vagina,

and any attempt to dislodge it was accompanied by much pain on the part of both. It was, indeed, a case "De cohesione in coitu." I applied water, and then ice, but ineffectually, and at last sent for chloroform, a few whiffs of which sent the woman to sleep, relaxed the spasm, and relieved the captive penis, which was swollen, livid, and in a state of semi-erection, which did not go down for several hours, and for days the organ was extremely sore. The woman recovered rapidly, and seemed none the worse.

I am sorry that I did not examine if the sphincter ani was contracted, but I did not think of it. In this case there must have been also spasm of the muscle at the orifice, as well as higher up, for the penis seemed nipped low down, and this contraction, I think, kept the blood retained and the organ erect. As an instance of Jago's "beast with two backs," the picture was perfect. I have often wondered how it was, considering with what agility the man can, under certain circumstances, jump up, that Phineas, the son of Eleazar, was able to thrust his javelin through the man and the Midianitish woman (*vide* Exodus); but the occurrence of such cases as the above may offer a possible explanation.

Yours truly,

Egerton Y. Davis,
Ex. U.S. Army

Caughnawaga, Quebec, 4th December, 1884

*Reprinted from Medical News, 1884; 45:673.

Prolonged Haemorrhage Following Nail Clipping*

J. L. Burton, B.Sc., M.D.

The popularity of the annual report of the various medical defence societies testifies to the fact that *schadenfreude*[†] is one of the more pleasurable emotions experienced by doctors. This regrettable fact prompts me to report the case of a two-year-old male who almost died from blood loss after a simple surgical procedure (nail-clipping) carried out by a surgeon with inadequate knowledge of a common anatomical variant.

Case-Report

The patient was a two-year-old male green budgerigar,[‡] employed as an entertainer at a local primary school. He was the result of a normal mating between only slightly related parents, he hatched normally, and his developmental milestones, such as the ability to ring a little bell by nodding his head and stand on one leg while shelling a peanut, had been normal. He presented at the insistence of the surgeon's child's schoolteacher, who needed to find a home for him during Easter vacation. The patient had no symptoms at the time, but the surgeon's wife noticed that he had a tendency to fall off his perch because his claws were too long. Further testing revealed that he dropped his peanuts too. After due consideration of alternative therapeutic possibilities (eg, thicker perch, walnuts instead of peanuts) it was decided that claw-clipping would be the safest and quickest palliative procedure. It was felt that this operation was within the competence of the average dermatologist, and the author (who is a *very* average dermatologist) duly carried out this procedure with scissors without an anaesthetic (other than a gin and tonic) at 9 PM the same evening. It has to be noted with regret that a consent form was not signed, the procedure was not fully explained to the patient, and the surgeon had never previously seen this operation performed on a budgerigar, though he had previously done a pretty good job on the school rabbit's claw, apart from lacerations of the forearm (the surgeon's forearm, not the rabbit's). Mitigating circumstances include the fact that the first assistant for the operation (the surgeon's wife) was a consultant pathologist who is not at all afraid of blood and has had considerable experience in clipping the toenails of squirmy little two-year-olds.

The immediate postoperative recovery was uneventful. The tachycardia of both surgeon and patient quickly settled, ruffled feathers were preened, and both settled comfortably on their respective perches. About 15 minutes later small beads of blood were observed at the end of each of the budgerigar's claws, and a small red stain was seen in the sawdust beneath the perch. The usual nursing observations were immediately instituted, but some difficulty was experienced because neither of the medical attendants knew how to feel a budgerigar's pulse. The carotid was not readily palpable, and attempts to locate other pulses were abandoned when the patient viciously pecked a small piece of flesh from the surgeon's finger. Palpation of the heart by the simple expedient of picking the patient up revealed that the rate was too fast to count, and it was felt that this manoeuvre, if repeated, was likely to excite the patient unduly and thus increase the blood loss. In retrospect a knowledge of the pulse rate would not have helped, since the preoperative rate was not recorded and neither of the medical attendants knew the normal pulse rate for a budgerigar.

The pallor proved equally difficult to assess. Grey beaks and green feathers are a notoriously unreliable guide to the haematocrit, and neither the conjunctiva nor the tongue were readily accessible without the risk of another painful nip.

The bleeding could scarcely be described as torrential, but the blood that slowly oozed from the tips of the claws did not clot, and the dark stain on the sawdust steadily increased in size. The blood volume of a budgerigar is not large, and most of it seemed to be slowly accumulating as a sticky dark-red pool on the floor of the cage. By 11 PM the patient's condition was causing considerable concern, since he seemed to be weakening and his head was repeatedly drooping. Whether this was due to blood loss or whether it was simply past his bedtime was not clear. At this stage cauterisation was considered, but where there are capillaries there may be nerve endings, and the surgeon did not wish to add a charge of cruelty to that of negligence. Various other

---

*Reprinted with permission from the Lancet, ©1983; 2(Dec 24–31):1484–1485.

[†] Enjoyment obtained from other's troubles.

[‡] A small Australian parrot.

possibilities were discussed, such as bone-wax as used by neurosurgeons and autotransfusion as used by desperate obstetricians, but eventually it was decided that the most satisfactory solution would be to get up early the next morning before the children awoke, and if the patient had dropped off his perch during the night, a near-identical budgerigar would be purchased and surreptitiously substituted. Experienced surgeons usually sleep soundly while patients struggle through their first postoperative night, but in this case the patient slept well, while the surgeon and his first assistant both spent a restless night, taking it in turns to tiptoe downstairs at regular intervals to check the progress of the tell-tale stain in the sawdust.

Fortunately by 6 AM the patient was considered to be out of danger, and he had completely recovered by breakfast-time, although the surgeon's fingertip continued to be painful for some days. At the end of the school vacation the budgerigar returned to full-time employment, and the teacher was so pleased with his shortened claws that the surgeon was invited to operate on the other four budgerigars. The offer was declined for ethical reasons.

Discussion

The human nail-plate is avascular, and haemorrhage does not normally follow nail-clipping, even when performed by fumble-fingered dermatologists. Budgerigars are different. They have a pink centre to each claw which represents the corium, equivalent to the human nail-bed. The corium is rich in blood vessels, and since birds have a longer clotting-time than mammals, careless clipping can kill. The corium is also rich in nerves, so that enthusiastic chiropody resembles an ancient Chinese torture. The claw should be clipped about 2 mm distal to the pink corium, but this can be difficult to see if the nails are pigmented. Most veterinary surgeons at some time or another have over-pruned the nails of various animals, including birds and tortoises. Few birds bleed to death, but the shock of handling can cause them to die from heart failure.

Dermatologists, unlike surgeons, receive very little formal instruction in common anatomical variants, which can so easily precipitate a surgical disaster. Most surgeons, as a result of their prolonged training, would probably realise that budgerigar claw-clipping requires special skills, which they may not possess. This case illustrates the danger of allowing a non-specialist to operate on a case that was clearly beyond his competence. It also confirms that technical incompetence does not prevent the building-up of a large private practice, providing the cage-side manner is good.

I thank Mr A. I. Wright, BVSc, MRCVS, for technical advice after the event.

The Hazards
of Daily Living

Anyone who reads *The New England Journal of Medicine* is aware of certain "Letters to the Editor" that turn up occasionally in the journal's correspondence section. These letters are different from what usually appears in the journal and range in topic from unexpected complications of outdoor activities to humorous commentaries on previously unreported ailments. Although *The New England Journal of Medicine* is well known for publishing these unusual letters, they appear in other journals as well. In fact, as noted in E. R. Plunkett's book, *Folk Name & Trade Diseases* (see Additional Readings), physicians have been publishing this type of clinical material for well over a hundred years. What all of these letters have in common is a catchy title and a description of an unusual and sometimes strangely entertaining malady of daily living. Although the authors frequently end their communication with a sentence or two that is humorous, the letters themselves are usually serious. The ones that follow were written with a light touch throughout.—*H.B.*

Penile Frostbite,
an Unforeseen Hazard
of Jogging*

To the Editor: A 53-year-old circumcised physician, nonsmoker, light drinker (one highball before dinner), 1.78 meters tall, weighing 70 kg, with no illnesses, performing strenuous physical exercise for many years, began a customary 30-minute jog in a local park at 7 p.m. on December 3, 1976. He wore flare-bottom double-knit polyester trousers, Dacron-cotton boxer-style undershorts, a cotton T-shirt and cotton dress shirt, a light-wool sweater, an outer nylon shell jacket over the sweater, gloves, and low-cut Pro Ked sneakers. The nylon shell jacket extended slightly below the belt line.

Local radio weather reports gave the outside air temperature as –8°C, with a severe wind-chill factor.

From 7:00 to 7:25 p.m. the jog was routine. At 7:25 p.m. the jogger noted an unpleasant painful burning sensation at the penile tip. From 7:25 to 7:30 p.m. this discomfort became more intense, the pain increasing with each stride as the exercise neared its end. At 7:30 p.m. the jog ended, and the patient returned home.

Physical examination at 7:40 p.m. in his apartment at comfortable room temperature revealed early frostbite of the penis. The glans was frigid, red, tender upon manipulation and anesthetic to light touch. Immediate therapy was begun. The polyester double-knit trousers and the Dacron-cotton undershorts were removed. In a straddled standing position, the patient created a cradle for rapid re-warming by covering the penile tip with one cupped palm. Response was rapid and complete. Symptoms subsided 15 minutes after onset of treatment, and physical findings returned to normal.

Side effects: at 7:50 p.m. the patient's wife returned from a local shopping trip and observed him during the treatment procedure. She saw him standing, legs apart, in the bedroom, nude below the waist, holding the tip of his penis in his right hand, turning the pages of the *New England Journal of Medicine* with his left. Spouse's observation of therapy produced rapid onset of numerous, varied and severe side effects (personal communication).

*Reprinted with permission from The New England Journal of Medicine, ©1977; 296(3):179.

Pathogenesis of the syndrome was assessed as tissue response to high air velocity at –8°C, penetrating the interstices of polyester double-knit trouser fabric and continuing through anterior opening of Dacron-cotton undershorts, impacting upon receptor site of target organ to produce the changes described.

The patient continues to jog, wearing the athletic supporter and old tight cotton warm-up pants used in college cross-country races in 1939. No recurrences are expected.

Jersey City, NJ

Melvin Hershkowitz, M.D.
Medical Center

Although he didn't know it at the time, Dr. Hershkowitz's letter would inspire someone to write a poem about his unfortunate incident (see p.82)—*H.B.*

Martini Toothpick Warning*

To the Editor: We are writing to call attention to a new and potentially serious hazard associated with the hasty ingestion of martinis (or indeed Gibsons, as in the present case). One of us was partaking of a Gibson (gin, ice, essence of vermouth, and several cocktail onions speared on a flat wooden toothpick). As the beverage and onions were quickly consumed, the toothpick floated from the glass into the oral cavity and lodged, uncomfortably, in the posterior pharynx. An attempt to dislodge it by regurgitation resulted in transferring it up into the posterior nares, pointed end first. A trip to the emergency room brought the first author of this letter into contact with the second. Actually, this meeting occurred one hour later, after several encounters with other hospital personnel, who took the history by asking such questions as: "You have a toothpick caught where?" "Are you the man with a toothpick up his nose?" "This couldn't happen—why didn't the olive stop it?" Fortunately, the adroit second author was able to extract the offending obstruction deftly with an alligator forceps. The first author was sent home with the suggestion that he have a drink, sans toothpick. We caution imbibers to consider this potential danger at the end of a difficult day.

Daniel Malamud, Ph.D.
University of Pennsylvania
Mary Harland Murphy, M.D.
Philadelphia, PA   Lankenau Hospital

*Reprinted with permission from The New England Journal of Medicine, ©1986; 315(16):1031–1032.

Telephone Transmission of Hepatitis B?*

To the Editor: Saturating medical literature in recent years has been speculation about a remarkable variety of theoretical transmission mechanisms for the hepatitis B virus. Interestingly enough, investigators have incriminated infusion, illicit injection, inapparent inoculation, ingestion, intercourse, intimacy, insects and, ironically, icteric illness from eye instillation[1] of the infectious ichor. A recent report[2] has gone so far as to imply that even nuns, although not habit-ually important in disease dissemination, may have a greater propensity to serologic evidence of hepatitis B infection than prostitutes from the same urban area. One hardly knows where to call for help. In the light of the growing complexity of the problem, we report still another potential mode of hepatitis B acquisition—telephone transmission.

In the process of a telephone survey of transfusion recipients of a possibly contaminated commercial blood product,[3] one of us (D.B.N.), after multiple telephone calls during a single day, noted the gradual onset of lethargy, malaise, headache, otalgia, low-back pain, gluteal rash, profound anorexia, and a gnawing sensation in the upper abdomen. Interestingly enough, there was no diminished taste for cigarettes or coffee. In an attempt to relieve these distressing symptoms, the interviewer medicated himself with a sizable quantity of ethanol. This therapeutic modality temporarily ameliorated the symptoms. By the next morning, however, new symptoms had appeared—dry mouth, nausea, and a slight darkening of the urine. A transaminase in serum drawn at that time was slightly elevated. Although it was suggested that a hepatitis B antigen determination be done, the subject refused on the basis of possible medicolegal implications.[4]

Because of the nature of the telephone contacts, we have reason to believe that this case may represent the first report of telephone transmission of hepatitis B. The unusually short incubation period seen in this case may reflect the speed of sound, with the virus somehow traveling synergistically within this framework.

Although some may question the obviously theoretical nature of our conclusions, further observations in other members of the investigatory team have led to additional case-finding and possible epidemic proportions of similar illness. Unfortunately, we have as yet been unable to obtain a single blood specimen for antigen determination.

A Bell-shaped curve of the epidemic has confirmed our hypothesis, and all reputable investigators have been tapped for further ideas. We would willingly discuss our data by telephone with any interested antigen-negative person.

Phoenix, AR

Atlanta, GA

Charles P. Pattison, M.D.
Center for Disease Control
David B. Nelson, M.D.
Calvin A. Klein, M.D.
Center for Disease Control

1. Kew MC: Possible transmission of serum (Australia-antigen-positive) hepatitis via the conjunctiva. Infect Immun 7:823–824, 1973.

2. Adam E. Hollinger FB, Melnick JL, et al: Type B hepatitis antigen and antibody among prostitutes and nuns: a study of possible venereal transmission. J Infect Dis 129:317–321, 1974.

3. Center for Disease Control. Viral Hepatitis B Associated with Transfusion of Plasma Protein Fraction—Indiana, Morbidity and Mortality Weekly Report Vol 23, No 11. Atlanta, Georgia, The Center, March 16, 1974, pp 98–99.

4. Chalmers TC, Alter HJ: Management of the asymptomatic carrier of the hepatitis-associated (Australia) antigen. N Engl J Med 285:613–617, 1971.

*Reprinted with permission from the New England Journal of Medicine, ©1975; 292(1):50.

Dog-Walker's Elbow*

To the Editor: I have had a recent malady that I believe would interest readers of the *Journal.* This summer and fall, I had a rather stubborn lateral epicondylitis of my left elbow, and in turn a medial epicondylitis of my right elbow. A rare game of tennis played right-handed (although perhaps not too handily) did not seem likely to be the cause, nor did leaf raking (too early for this) or wood chopping (my son had attended to the wood pile).

Ah! Then it came to me! My black Labrador, Hogan, had a cumulative GPA of about 1.1 in obedience school. Since I had undergone extensive neck surgery in the spring, we increased considerably the amount of time that we walk together. Hogan's residual training causes him to walk on my left side, but he tugs constantly to sniff most bushes, poles, trash containers, fireplugs, and dogs both male and female. Cats and squirrels in particular increase his catecholamine release and thus the traction on my arms.

I usually hold his leash in my left hand with my forearm pronated and the arm extended about 150 degrees. When my left arm became sore, I shifted the leash to my right hand. My right arm was supinated and was again held at about 150 degrees of extension. Needless to say, there was almost constant tension on one or both extremities, with occasional vigorous contractions and involuntary extensions. Multiple microtrauma—the sort of injury responsible for chondromalacia, shin splints, stress fractures, tendinitis, and, yes, tennis elbow—seemed to be the likely cause. To paraphrase Pogo, "We found the enemy, Hogan, and it was us."

Several solutions suggested themselves: stop walking the dog—an option unacceptable to both of us; recycle Hogan through obedience school—perhaps not a bad idea, but he objected; or get a longer leash and assume a "get tough" attitude on my part through firmer commands. This is what we have done, and now my wife walks with us and handles his lead—let him pull *her* epicondyles a bit. Hogan is happy, my arms are better, and all three of us enjoy being out together.

We call the condition "Hogan's elbow," but let us not add another eponym to the medical literature. Dog-walker's elbow, I expect, would be more widely acceptable.

Philadelphia, PA

William M. Mebane, III, M.D.
Chestnut Hill Hospital

*Reprinted with permission from The New England Journal of Medicine, ©1981; 304(10):613–614.

Poster Presenter's Thumb*

To the Editor: Presentations at national meetings can bring prestige and peril. The hazards of slide presentations include recalcitrant audiovisual equipment and obnoxious skeptics. Anxiety attacks and wounded egos are common. Physical injury is rare. Poster presentations decrease some psychological and technical risks but pose a unique hazard.

A 38-year-old right-handed man used 80 Push Pins (Douglas Stewart Co., Madison, Wis.) to mount his scientific presentation on a standard, unreceptive, 1.2-by-2.4-m poster board. On completion of the task, the patient noted painful erythema on the volar aspect of his left thumb. In 15 minutes, a 6-by-7-mm blister appeared; it ruptured during the subsequent dismantling of the poster. The patient recalled similar trauma associated with his use of standard thumb tacks at previous meetings. A poll of other poster presenters revealed numerous similar unpublished cases. Prolific patients had multiple recurrences.

Considering the widespread use of poster sessions, thousands of similar cases must occur annually. Organizations that invite such sessions should provide user-friendly boards to reduce the incidence of "poster presenter's thumb."

Laurel C. Preheim, M.D.
Creighton University
School of Medicine

Omaha, NE

*Reprinted with permission from The New England Journal of Medicine, ©1986; 314(23):1518.

Syndrome-Reader's Scowl*

To the Editor: Recently, I found a colleague of mine in a dark mood that I mistook for ordinary depression. Upon consultation with a specialist I was horrified to learn that he suffered from syndrome-reader's scowl.

"Note the pained curl of the brow, the wandering, fearful eyes, the cowering posture," said the specialist.

"C'mon, Brandon," I said to my friend. "You just need to have a little fun. How about some exercise?"

"Not on your life," shouted Brandon. "I might get tennis elbow, runner's knee, or frisbee finger."

I had never known Brandon to refuse exercise. "Let's catch a movie, then," I offered.

"No, no, no! Haven't you heard of popcorn-eater's grimace?"

"Intense, repetitive movements of the tongue and facial muscles in response to a morsel of popcorn lodged near the tonsils," explained the specialist. "Some victims have been known to insert a finger into the posterior pharynx and induce a gag reflex."

"Sounds beastly," I said. Brandon was agitated and weeping. "Forget the movie," I said, trying to calm him. "We'll go to the opera instead."

"Never! If I enjoy it I'll get applauder's palms."

"Painful, erythematous swelling of the hands in response to a bravura performance," said the specialist.

Brandon limped away complaining loudly that his orthotics needed adjustment.

"Your friend is very ill indeed," said the specialist, shaking his head.

"Is there nothing that will help him? What about psychotherapy?"

"He'll never submit to psychotherapy if he's heard about shrink-seer's sputter. It's an uncontrollable compulsion to speak openly about one's feelings."

The specialist was correct. We never heard from Brandon again. There were rumors that he had fled to the Bowery, where he has allowed a bad case of tipper's elbow to progress to doorway-sleeper's hip.

As for me, I sit before the pile of unopened journals on my desk, tapping my fingers, fearful of the next revelation. Finally, I can bear the pain no longer. I return to the specialist. He looks at my hands.

"Procrastinator's fingertips," he says sternly. "Be very careful."

David Bateman, M.D.
Harlem Hospital Center

*Reprinted with permission from The New England Journal of Medicine, ©1981; 305(26):1595.

Additional Readings

1. Doering EJ, Fitts CT, et al: Alligator bite. JAMA 1971; 218(2):255–256.

A case report about a farmer who got free of an alligator bite by "beating it about the head with the family bible." The case prompted a field trip and bacteriologic study in which those with lesser academic rank had to capture and hold open the mouths of the alligators while the senior members obtained the cultures.

2. Greengold MC: Letter from Copenhagen. JAMA 1968; 204(1):155–156.

The author presents three case reports that show what might happen if fictional characters ever ended up in medical hands instead of literate ones. The unfortunate "patients" are: The Princess and the Pea, The Ugly Duckling, and The Emperor's New Clothes.

3. Moskow, Shirley B: Hunan Hand & Other Ailments (Letters to the New England Journal of Medicine). Boston, Little Brown and Company, 1987.

This collection brings together 20 years of letters published in the journal. The letters range from silly to serious, but together provide an interesting commentary on a way of looking at health that is unique to our profession.

4. Pedoe EJ, Lightman S: Hazards of paternity: an unreported syndrome. Lancet 1981; 2(Dec 19–26):1427.

The authors describe the "Sucker-daddy Syndrome" which occurs when enthusiastic fathers attach suction toys to their foreheads. The resulting lesions progress from petechiae to purpura and are not amenable to treatment. Prevention can be achieved by using a pin to airvent the toy or, alternatively, the parent's forehead.

5. Plunkett ER: Folk Name & Trade Diseases. Stamford, Barrett Book Company, 1978.

From "Bowler's Thumb" to "Hula Hoop Syndrome" to nearly 1500 other ailments, this book is a dictionary of conditions that have afflicted people for well over a century. Each entry is accompanied by a brief description and its original citation. Although this is not a book on medical humor, it does make for interesting reading.

6. Simkin PA: Simian stance: a sign of spinal stenosis. Lancet 1982; 2(Sept 18):652–653.

A serious article that provides a light touch: a black bar is drawn across the eyes of an illustration (a chimpanzee) to conceal its identity.

The following references provide some additional examples of the type of reports presented in the "Hazards" section of this chapter.

7. Dembert ML: Sick Santa syndrome. JAMA 1986; 256(23):3216–3217.

8. Kamins ML: Proofreader's prostatitis. N Engl J Med 1969; 280(20):1130.

9. Pinals RS: Genu amoris. Arthritis Rheum 1976; 19(3):637–638.

10. Regalbuto G, Hamada P: Pseudo-enuresis recumbens. N Engl J Med 1982; 306(10):615–616.

11. Shear NH: Snoring and calf pain. N Engl J Med 1987; 317(13):840.

12. Spitzer DE: Horseradish horrors: sushi syncope. JAMA 1988; 259(2):218–219.

The following articles provide additional insight into William Osler's sense of humor.

13. Altaffer LF: Penis captivus and the mischievous Sir William Osler. South Med J 1983; 76(5):637–641.

14. Bean WB: William Osler: The Egerton Yorrick Davis alias. In McGovern JP, Burns CR (eds): Humanism in Medicine. Springfield IL, Charles C Thomas, 1970, pp 49–59.

15. Blumer G: The jocular side of Osler. Arch Intern Med 1949; 84(1):34–39.

16. Cullen TS: The gay of heart. Arch Int Med 1949; 84(1):41–45.

17. Nation EF: Osler's alter ego. Dis Chest 1969; 56(6):531–537.

MEDICAL RESEARCH

Considering the amount of research that gets published every year, I did not find that much humor written on the subject. Perhaps that's because researchers are too busy writing grants to find the time to be funny. Or because no one can guarantee that a parody will get funded, and guffaws and chuckles will not feed the mice. Then again, some might argue that a lot of research is amusing anyway, especially if you read it a decade or more after it is published. One example of this type of humor can be found in an article that was published in 1879 by Dr. Allen W. Hagenback: "Masturbation as a Cause of Instanity" (J Nerv Mental Dis 1879; 6:603–612). In the conclusion to this interesting treatise, Dr. Hagenback makes a number of final remarks, the most illuminating of which is:

> That in a small percentage of masturbators, certain physical findings are present due to the vice which may prove valuable in confirming the diagnosis.

Is it possible that this is the origin of the Hairy Palm Theory? The articles that follow make some interesting claims of their own. I wonder how they'll hold up over time?

"Cephalomalacia Obfuscate," A Fourth Generation Cephalosporin*

BRUCE K. RUBIN, BSC, MENG, M.D.

A new fourth generation cephalosporin, cephalomalacia obfuscate, has been synthesized. Limited testing has shown this new class of antibiotic to have substantially greater bacteriopathic properties than the third generation antibiotics. The role that these properties may play in host defense is discussed.

Introduction

Since the early 1960's the cephalosporins have enjoyed great clinical success as a family of antibiotics. Laboratory manipulations have produced successive generations of this antibiotic, each more powerful than its predecessor (Fig. 1). The synthesis and testing of what we believe to be of a fourth generation of cephalosporins are reported here. We have named this antibiotic "cephalomalacia obfuscate" and hope to market it under the trade name Killacillin.

Synthesis

One of the newer third generation cephalosporins, "cephalohaematoma," was obtained from the manufacturer (Ersatz Pharmaceuticals) and a side chain was added as an offshoot to the method described by Stalin.[1] This side chain is known to both traumatize and immobilize many bacteria *in vitro*.

A phagocytic moiety was then added (Fig. 2) to produce a new class of antibiotics: the fourth generation cephalosporin.

Methods and Results

Bacteria exhibit avoidance activity in the presence of adversive stimuli. This activity has been quantified crudely in the past using the Kirby-Bauer method[2] where noxious agents in the form of antibiotic discs are placed into a colony of microorganisms, encouraging them to move away. A major difficulty with this method is that it does not measure the rate at which the bacteria migrate, but only the total distance travelled.

CEPHALOSPORIN PEDIGREE

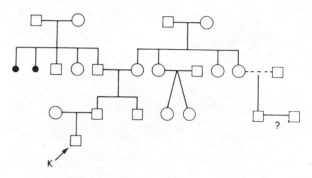

Figure 1. Cephalosporin pedigree. "Cephalomalacia" is marked with the arrow.

Many researchers believe that this technique better reflects the stamina of the specific microorganism (B. K. Rubin, personal communication). To overcome this problem we implanted microphones into the cell walls of a fixed number of bacteria in a colony using standard microsurgical technique. When these microphones were connected to highly sensitive acoustically shielded recording and amplifying devices, we found that the rate of migration correlated well with the amplitude of the sound produced which, to our ears, sounded not unlike millions of tiny screams.

By this methodology we were able to obtain pain tolerance curves for several of the more pathogenic bacteria (B. K. Rubin, unpublished data).

A double blind experiment was then undertaken (Fig. 3) using alternate challenge with either "cephalomalacia" or one of the highly touted third generation

*Reprinted from the Pediatric Infectious Disease Journal, ©1983; 2(6):424–425, with permission from William & Wilkins, Baltimore.

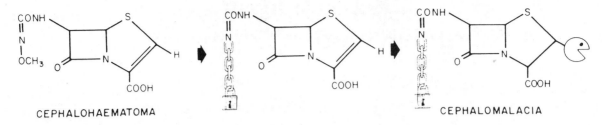

CEPHALOHAEMATOMA

CEPHALOMALACIA

Figure 2.   Synthesis of "cephalomalacia obfuscate." Funding seems to be the rate limiting step.

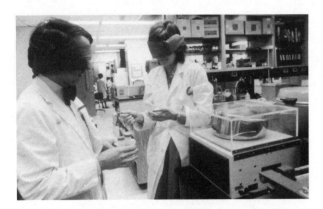

Figure 3.   Behavioral bacteriology laboratory during double blind research into pain thresholds. Dr. Ford-Jones (R) is attempting to "pin the tail" on Dr. Biggar.

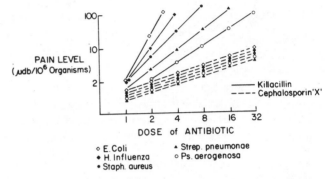

Figure 4.   Bacteriopathic properties of the third and fourth generation of cephalosporin. Antibiotic dose was increased to the limit of the organisms pain tolerance.

cephalosporins (identified as cephalosporin "X"). The results as shown in Figure 4 show clearly that "cephalomalacia" produces more bacterial pain per unit dose in those organisms tested.

Discussion

Behavioral bacteriology is the name given to the science born of the marriage between microbiology and psychology. This field is rapidly changing our concepts of the unicellular organism. We present here both a new antibiotic and an appropriate laboratory tool for measuring an important facet of microbial socialization. This method has been used to test a new class of drug, the bacteriopathic antibiotic.

There are many factors that influence host defense. One of the most important and perhaps most overlooked is the psychologic state of the host or "will to live." Unexpected recovery from terrible disease has often been attributed to a patient's tenacious fight for life. It would be beneficial for many patients to know

not only that the medicine being taken is killing an infecting microorganism but also that it is making those organisms suffer. We anticipate that this sense of revenge could be valuable to the overall healing process. In this regard we feel that "cephalomalacia," the first of the bacteriopathic cephalosporins, represents a significant advance in antimicrobial therapy.

Acknowledgments

Thanks to Drs. E. L. Ford-Jones and D. Biggar of the Division of Infectious Diseases, The Hospital for Sick Children, Toronto, for performing double blind experimentation. Thanks also to Drs. A. S. Rebuck and K. Chapman of the Respiratory Division, Toronto Western Hospital, for guidance.

References

1. Stalin J: The annexation of Eastern Europe. In World War II, 1945.
2. Bauer AW, Kirby WMM, Sherris JD, et al: Antibiotic susceptibility testing by a standardized single disc method. Am J Clin Pathol 45:493–496, 1966.

Retraction on
Cephalomalacia Obfuscate*

To the Editors:

Readers of PEDIATRIC INFECTIOUS DISEASE have been writing requesting the raw data on which my article was based. When we went to review these data we found that my research fellow, whose name was regrettably left off the preliminary publication because of an editorial oversight, had in fact "dry labbed" the entire experiment and pocketed most of the funds. The bottles of what we thought were Killacillin were in fact merely outdated tetracycline which was to be discarded. Needless to say we are all embarrassed over this incident and the research fellow has resigned his position to take a job with the government. I must therefore retract much of the data presented in the article but I am pleased to announce at this time that we are doing some exciting research into outdated tetracycline.

Regretfully our methodologist and symptomatologist both resigned their positions because of this incident, so in the future we will be forced to report on methods and symptoms rather than methodologies and symptomatologies.

Bruce K. Rubin, M.D., F.R.C.P.(C)
Queen's University
Department of Paediatrics

Kingston, Ontario, Canada

*Reprinted from the Pediatric Infectious Disease Journal, ©1984; 3(3):283, with permission from Williams & Wilkins, Baltimore.

The Teething Virus*

HOWARD J. BENNETT, M.D.
D. SPENCER BRUDNO, M.D.

A prospective study was carried out on 500 teething infants which demonstrated that a new infectious agent, the human teething virus, is responsible for the febrile response that accompanies the eruption of deciduous teeth. Speculations are made concerning whether or not primary care physicians will began prescribing amoxicillin instead of Jack Daniel's to treat teething infants and their parents.

Introduction

Teething has been the subject of intense interest in the medical and nonmedical community for centuries.[1] Controversy has resulted not only over the signs and symptoms associated with teething but also over the tooth fairy's impact on the family.[2,3] But perhaps the greatest controversy of all is whether or not teething causes fever. Unfortunately all of the research in this area suffers from serious methodologic flaws. McCartney et al.[4] reported that teething was responsible for fever in 20% of infants with temperatures $\geq 40\,°C$. That study was carried out in an emergency room setting, however, and therefore is not applicable to all infants. In addition, the authors failed to quantitate the amount of drooling that residents had to contend with and whether or not this interfered with optimal observation of the patient. More recently, Shorts[5] examined 240 teething patients in a suburban practice and concluded that teething does not cause fever. His population included school-aged children as well as infants, however, and it is well known that older children will feign illness in order to get stickers and other rewards from the doctor's office.[6]

Early in 1982 one of us was doing histopathology research on the brain cells of hairless mice that had been subjected to 36 hours "on-call." Inadvertently a sample of saliva from a teething infant (via a soggy bagel) was put under the electron microscope. To our amazement this accident uncovered a new viral particle (HJ Bennett, unpublished revelation). This discovery led to the diversion of all previously acquired grant funds into the search for the mythical teething virus. In this report we present the results of a prospective study of teething infants and young children undertaken during the Washington, DC teething outbreak of 1983 and 1984. We report our findings, which prove conclusively that the human teething virus (HT virus) is the hitherto elusive agent responsible for the fevers associated with teething.

Patients and Methods

The study included 500 infants who were followed prospectively from birth through 2½ years of age. The patients were selected from consecutive term births at our medical center. Primiparous women were interviewed by one of the authors sometime during the third trimester—usually on the way to the delivery room. The mothers-to-be were asked two questions regarding possible entry into the study: (1) If you have a baby, would you like to participate in a study of teething in infants? (2) Do you believe in Santa Claus? A positive response to either question made the infant eligible for the study.

A total of 506 mother/infant pairs were initially included in the study. The patients were matched for socioeconomic status, educational background and whether or not both parents watched "Dallas" on Friday nights. Two infants with natal teeth were subsequently excluded, though it is worth noting that in both cases the mother experienced a "warm uterine feeling" 2 weeks prior to delivery. An additional four babies dropped out of the study for unknown reasons. Their mothers reluctantly withdrew from the project as well.

*Reprinted from the Pediatric Infectious Disease Journal, ©1986; 5(4):399–401, with permission from Williams & Wilkins, Inc., Baltimore.

Mothers were instructed to bring their baby to the clinic at the first sign of teething. During this visit vital signs were taken and the infant was examined for physical evidence of teething using the method described by Leech.[7] Briefly, this technique involves having the infant breastfeed for 5 minutes in the office. If the mother's cry exceeds 90 dB, the baby is teething. The threshold is adjusted to 120 dB in nonnursing mothers. Infants were seen regularly during the teething period, and parents kept a diary of relevant symptoms.

Saliva was obtained on the fourth and sixth teething days by adsorption onto teething rings impregnated with human embryonic lung and human embryonic kidney. The specimens were processed using a revolutionary technique that is currently under investigation by a rival laboratory and therefore is not available for publication. Additional saliva was obtained from the subjects' mothers and in between episodes of teething such that each patient served as his or her own control. Serum specimens were not obtained due to parental squeamishness. All subjects and specimens were handled in a triple blind fashion: patients did not know why they were in the study, technicians did not know what was being studied and the authors didn't care but hoped to get published anyway.

Results

Basic research. The HT virus is a uniquely shaped viral particle with a diameter of 140 nm. The envelope surrounds a helical nucleocapsid that is covered with spherical studs (Fig. 1). Though superficially resembling a slice of white bread, the HT virus is actually the

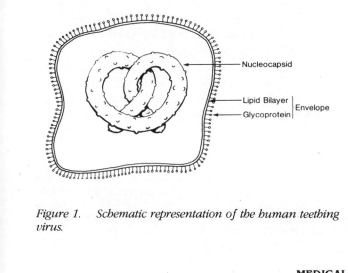

Figure 1.   Schematic representation of the human teething virus.

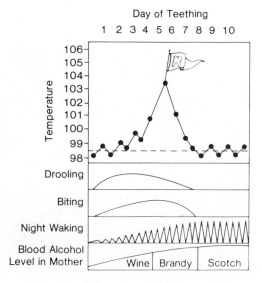

Figure 2.   Schematic diagram illustrating the clinical sequence of teething.

first recognized member of a new family of RNA viruses to be named the masticoviridae. Details of the virus' life-style and reproductive habits will be the subject of another report.[8]

Clinical research. The 500 patients in our study experienced repeated bouts of teething during the first 2½ years of life. Teeth erupted at a rate of approximately 10 per year, which provided us with 5000 tooth-years of data. Eighty-four percent of patients became febrile during the teething process. The clinical course of these patients is shown in Figure 2. All patients recovered uneventfully from this developmental nuisance. Unfortunately, however, at least 15 divorces could be directly attributed to "irreconcilable differences" on how to manage a teething baby at three o'clock in the morning.

The HT virus was isolated by electron microscopy from well over 99% of febrile teething patients (Table 1). In fact there was only one febrile infant in whom the HT virus was not isolated, and the technician who handled that specimen admitted to misplacing the patient's teething ring and secretly testing his own saliva (J Cama, personal confession). The HT virus was not isolated from any of the nonfebrile teething patients, though it was seen in two samples taken from the mothers' group. In both cases, however, the mothers admitted to kissing their febrile babies just prior to submitting their own specimens for study.

Figure 3. The modern treatment of teething: an ice and alcohol bath.

Table 1. Isolation of the human teething virus by electron microscopy in control and teething patients.

Group	No. of Samples Tested	No. Positive for HT Virus	% Positive for HT Virus
Mothers	500	2	< 1
Nonteething infants	1000	0	0
Nonfebrile teething infants	800	0	0
Febrile teething Infants	4200	4199	>99[a]

[a] P < 0.000001 by Toddler's t test and the Fisher-Price test.

Discussion

Infants acquire their primary teeth by 30 months of age. Teething occurs off and on for 24 of these months—mostly on, according to parents. We have shown that 84% of infants develop fever when teething and that it is the HT virus which causes this fever. There appears to be little doubt, therefore, that parents have been right all along. Fortunately, however, teething phobia can now be approached intelligently instead of with the irrational treatments of the past (Fig. 3).

A few questions still remain, however, concerning the pathogenesis of the HT virus. We believe that primary infections with the virus occur early in life in the majority of children. These infections are probably subclinical most of the time but undoubtedly are also responsible for many of the "idiopathic" conditions of infancy, colic and difficult temperament, to name a few. Once the primary infection subsides, the virus becomes dormant within the alveolar ridge. Then, at future points in time, the aggressive movements of erupting teeth disturb the sleeping virus who retaliates by producing local and systemic effects. The pattern of transmission is not horizontal, as one might expect, but gravitational, this of course owing to the aerodynamics of drooling babies.

As a result of this study, we have revised the anticipatory guidance given at 6 months of age. Parents are encouraged to check for teething at the first sign of fever and to quickly begin their prophylactic Valium[R] if the baby's Leech test is positive. Finally we recommend that practitioners approach their 2 a.m. calls as a time to educate parents about the positive aspects of teething.[9] This advice will minimize the hoarding of left-over amoxicillin until such time as a vaccine is developed to rid mankind of this pesky little virus.

Acknowledgments

This work was supported completely by a grant from the makers of Orajel[R] and Goldstein's Bagel Shop. Special thanks to Judith Ratner, M.D., who somehow found the time to review our manuscript in between pelvic examinations in her adolescent clinic.

References

1. Radbill SX: Teething as a medical problem: Changing viewpoints through the centuries. Clin Pediatr 4:556–559, 1965.

2. Skinner BF: The tooth ransom: Are today's children holding out for too much money? J Pediatr Bribery 86:314–316, 1980.

3. Westheimer R: Is 50¢ a tooth enough to get children to sleep in their own beds at night? J Parental Celibacy 69:123–128.

4. McCartney PL, Flintstone F, Rubble B, et al: Do teething infants need a CBC and blood culture? J Dubious Invest 59:463–468, 1977.

5. Shorts RH: Teething and fever: Another myth debunked. PMD Bull 21:459–463, 1982.

6. Munchausen BV: Factitious teething as a means to visit the pediatrician. Acta Idiotica Scand 70:212–213, 1978.

7. Leech LA: The clinical application of breastfeeding reflexes: "Let-down" means the milk is in, "Let Go!" means the teeth are coming. The Breast 36:24–34, 1982.

8. Bennett HJ, Brudno DS: The masticoviruses: Have we bitten off more than we can chew? Popular Virol, in press, 1986.

9. Weissman MI: Tootharche, menarche, and anarchy: Three developmental milestones of childhood and adolescence. Curr Prob Nightcall 12:1–7, 1983.

Single-Blind/Double-Blind Radiographic Analysis: New Viewing Techniques*

MICHAEL H. REID, M.D.
ARTHUR B. DUBLIN, M.D.

In 1982 Oestreich[1] described the cupped hand method for excluding extraneous light when viewing radiographs. Several advantages were ascribed to this simple procedure. We report two variations: 50% and 100% light exclusion.

To test the utility of these variations, we applied them to 1,000 outpatient skull films randomly selected from the discard film bin of a large university teaching hospital. These films were then viewed by two techniques on a standard radiographic viewbox independently by two radiologists as illustrated in figure 1. The results were then tabulated and compared against the original interpretation in the hospital record by a third radiologist who elected to remain anonymous. The hospital record could not be found in 55 instances.

Of the 1,000 films, 182 were normal, 58 were possibly normal, 91 were possibly abnormal, 389 were suggestive of being possibly abnormal, 82 were equivocally suggestive of pathognomonic abnormality, and 78 were uninterpretable. Of the 922 interpretable films, 318 were considered technically acceptable and should not have been discarded.

Student's t-test and Wilcoxin's paired-difference test were applied to the data. Not unexpectedly technique B (single blind) had a 50% sensitivity, while technique A (double blind) had no false positives (100% specificity).

Interpretive errors in the radiographic analysis of poor quality skull radiographs have always been a problem, and our data confirm this. While there have been many recommendations to improve viewing conditions for the radiologist, we believe our techniques are unique.

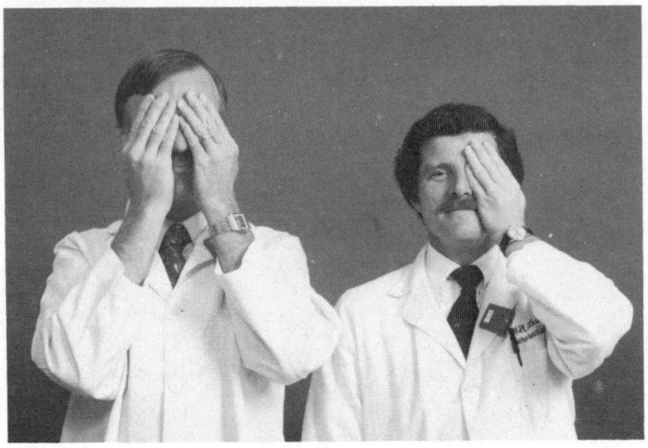

Figure 1.   Anonymous radiologists demonstrating technique A (left) *and technique B* (right).

The contribution of technique A is the low false-positive rate (also low false-negative rate). The radiologist using technique A also complained less of eye fatigue and excessive glare. The principal disadvantage of technique A is that comparison with previous films is difficult.

We conclude that technique A (double blind) is superior when a negative interpretation is desired. Another method, technique C (no blind, not shown), has been investigated thoroughly on acceptable films but not on discarded films. Such a study, compared with techniques A and B is in progress and will be the subject of a future report.

References

1. Oestreich AE. Use of the cupped hand for improved viewing of radiographs. Radiology 1982; 143:563.

*Reprinted from the American Journal of Roentgenology, ©1983; 140(4):825, with permission from Williams & Wilkins, Inc., Baltimore.

For the last ten years, the *British Medical Journal* has published a special issue each December that features, in addition to some serious articles, a number of lighter medical pieces. You can easily spot this issue because it sports an artistic cover instead of the journal's traditional blue and black. Although a lot of the material is regional, some of it does travel well. Three of the articles in the book (including the next one) and a number of "Additional Readings" were originally published in the *BMJ*'s Christmas issue. For those who do not get the journal, it may be worth a trip to your local medical library when the holiday season rolls around. Actually, considering the time it takes to cross the Atlantic, you might want to wait until late January—*H.B.*

Biology, Blind Men, and Elephants*

BERRIL YUSHOMERSKI YANKELOWITZ, M.D.

Newton watched an apple fall and discovered the Law of Gravity (*A*). Biologists would attack such a problem more scientifically. A typical scientific approach would be as follows.

Introduction

Apples would seem to appear to fall to the ground.[1-50, 52,54,57] This suggests the possibility that there is some property of apples which might result in this phenomenon. It is well known that apples falling from a height have apparent changes in tissue turgor pressure.[51,55,56-80] This might well reflect changes in intracellular water and electrolyte losses. It, therefore, appeared reasonable to determine the relationship between the apple's fall, its tissue turgor pressure, and the intracellular electrolyte content.

Materials, Methods, and Results

A total of 500 apples were randomly selected from an orchard in the State of Washington with another 500 from Wisconsin as controls. The apples were stratified by colour, number of seeds, worm content, and baseline tissue turgor pressure and intracellular electrolytes measured by methods we have previously described.[53, 81-200] Each apple was numbered and randomly placed in brown bags (obtained through the courtesy of Cheatem Markets). The bags were then dropped from 1, 10, 20, and 100 feet (respectively 30, 300, 600, and 3000 cm) by an investigator who did not know their contents. Post-drop tissue turgor pressure and electrolyte concentrations were then remeasured by another method we have previously described.[53,201-430]

Results were analysed by the χ^2, Student's test, Wilcoxon, covariant analysis, and multiple linear regression techniques with appropriate strata. There was a highly significant difference in the worm content of red apples as opposed to green ones ($P < 0.05$). Furthermore, green apples with more than 10 worms and less than five seeds showed a much greater decrease in post-fall tissue turgor if they were from Wisconsin than if they were from Washington State ($P < 0.00001$). By analysis of covariance and multiple linear regression, there was an almost linear relationship between height of drop and decrease in tissue turgor pressure (figure). When corrected for crush artifact, no differences could be observed for pre- and post-drop intracellular electrolyte concentrations. All apples that were dropped, fell. Consequently we could not determine whether the change in turgor pressure was statistically associated with falling. Nevertheless, the inadequate number of drops may have led to a substantial type two error; in a more extensive trial, it is expected that a sufficient number of apples would rise to actually determine this effect.

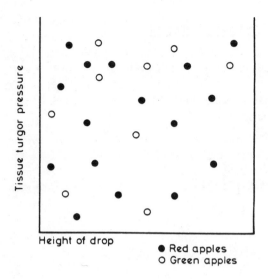

Height of drop

● Red apples
○ Green apples

Tissue turgor pressure (vertical axis label)

Comment

We plan to repeat the study with a larger number of apples and also measure apple shelf life before and after dropping them. Of course, there will be much criticism of our methodology—"the investigator failed to stratify by the type of apple—for example, Golden Delicious vs Beverly Hill vs Pippin, Roman." "The apples should have been allowed to drop from trees." "In our study[1-20] we found a significant correlation with temperature and season of the year—the current investigation cannot be interpreted without such data."

But once the criticism dies down, there will be a flurry of activity, investigators repeating the study with pears, prunes, pumpkins, and watermelons to show the generality of the results. The original investigators will spend six months a year on speaking tours in both the scientific and lay communities. Grant money will flow in vast rivers from both public sources and private charitable foundations. A Nobel prize should be forthcoming. In his dotage, the author should be interviewed for his political and social opinions to which he was more than entitled by virtue of his previous achievement.

Statistics is not truth. Statistical science exists only because we don't know what questions to ask of nature or because we haven't devised appropriate ways of testing our hypotheses.

But, while it is quite true that this type of science doesn't provide any satisfying answers, it does produce all that marvellous data that we all like so much. Also, it puts bread on the table of the researcher. So, with that, I must return to my laboratory to predict elephants by examining their tails (*B*).

A Newton, Sir Isaac, personal communication.
B Aesop, personal communication.

How to Live with Statistics*

(Without Having to Marry Them)
RICHARD P. PERKINS, M.D.

In the ever more complex world of medical research and data analysis, it becomes necessary, no matter the reluctance to do so or the asthenia of spirit or capacity, for the reader to have a working familiarity with the nature of modern statistical tests. Armed with this insight, he or she can, without fail, ascertain any bias of the author or, in other cases, of the reviewer's statistical consultant. The following is in the nature of a user's manual of modern methods. Caveat Emptor.

The Simpler Tests

The Chi-Line Test

This analytic tool, previously called the Chi-Square Test before going straight, is a method by which simple associations can be given credibility by surrounding them with many similar comparisons, thus requiring the data to organize themselves into linear arrangements for continuity and recognition. Thus associated, they can be more easily attached firmly to the observer's bias for easier presentation. Because any two points can determine a line, this is a convenient way to establish convincing correlations between any datum point and any other. The acceptability is improved by linking items at great distances from one another which, through the intercession of crowding, all but eliminates the escape of one point from another during random association (ie, by limiting the degrees of freedom to unity). Conversely, because any line, if long enough, can be made to find two points, random and otherwise meaningless associations can be made to assume any significance desired, frequently by chance alone, with this test.

The Student's Tea Test

This simplified version of Grogan's Multiple Punctiliation Analysis requires at least three students and a small amount of illegal substance rolled into a convenient form for gradual consumption of the vapors released when burned. If while smoking the "tea," the results become progressively more salutary, the test is validated by the simultaneously executed affidavit of the participants (if notarized).

The Fisher's Exacta Test

In this time-honored method, all possible associations are listed singly on slips of paper and cast into a large bin. The required number of critical associations is then determined and one volunteer (ideally one without any connection with the research in any other capacity than perhaps to dispose regularly of discarded data) is selected to plunge his or her hand into the collected mass and retrieve blindly three slips of paper on three occasions. These data items are thereby proved, by random and unbiased selection, to be correlated significantly.

The More Complex Tests

Logistic Digression

This technique has been in use for many years under various other names, depending upon the strategy employed. The fundamental method requires the selling of one's point by a series of distracting maneuvers presented in the guise of ancillary information, tension-relieving anecdotes, or extensive exposition of data already declared irrelevant (but possibly of interest in some other context). If done skillfully, the listener will be lulled into a deep delta state in which all conclusions seem plausible; alternatively, he will completely confuse which data were to be preserved as pertinent and which were to be discarded.

If the discussion is regularly punctuated with a succession of cleverly chosen and optimally unobtrusive tangents, the technique is called Multiple Digression

*Reprinted from Obstetrics & Gynecology, ©1988; 72(3):422–424; with permission from the American College of Obstetricians & Gynecologists.

Analysis. This method has been used by many, often serendipitously, while presenting largely unprepared material.

A more sophisticated approach, requiring some preconception, involves the careful alignment of non-pertinent material in a seemingly logical sequence eventually leading back to the main topic. This device called Circular Digression Analysis, avoids the dreaded complication experienced by its primary proponents in their earlier days—the progressive and unrelenting distancing from the main concept, to such a degree that the principal thematic material can never be rediscovered. This statistical debacle, known as Linear Digression, essentially guarantees that its innocent victim will never again publish anything.

A secondary benefit of tests in this category is the ability to determine the statistical validity of a "digression line" drawn among a large number of data points on an X-Y axis. It is here that the test truly demonstrates its ascendancy, for any analytic technique that can display the relevance of the inclination of a flagpole in a blizzard as reflecting the force and direction of the wind is of singular utility in modern scientific inquiry. This is also referred to as the bias of bias.

The Stepwise Indiscriminate Analysis

This technique is all but self-explanatory. Data are arranged in any convenient order, and the presenter then forges through them, discarding any items that appear to unsettle his prejudices or threaten the credibility of his argument. The remaining items, therefore, are seemingly far more illustrious, much as blowing out the other fellow's candle that yours might shine the brighter, a well-recognized maneuver in dimly lighted circles.

Power Analysis

No article on understanding statistics would be complete without an explanation of power analysis, that champion of the rueful objector who, finding his own life's work in stark conflict with presented and irrefutable data, cries "Foul!" and declares that there are too few subjects in another's report to constitute a satisfactory data base. He usually goes on to point out that his own population of 17 individuals, being made up of some of the best people in his community, is much stronger and more powerful than the 3216 indigent subjects reported from the research hospital in another state. He backs up this contention by showing that, after combining his data with those of the author, his conclusions remain unaltered, proving beyond question the strength of his results. Alternatively, he can show that if his population were increased by a factor of 200, the new distribution would unequivocally engulf that of the current study.

Such is the power of Power. It proves the truth of the adage seen on the wall in the fireworks factory: "It is far better sometimes to curse the darkness than to light the wrong candle."

Trendy Tests

Finally, a potpourri of the latest tests, the so-called staying power of which is yet to be shown.

Waldemar's Three-Tailed Test for Non-Parametric Variables takes data bearing no relationship to one another and finds common ground. For example, using this test, it is possible to compare apples and oranges or, for that matter, an entire fruit salad for, say, the predispositions of its various ingredients to contribute meaningfully to the maintenance of bowel regularity. It was by this innovative approach that the fallacy of the previously held concept that "an apple a day keeps the doctor away" was proved; in consumers over the age of 50, it clearly requires 2.7 apples to assure this result in statistically significant frequency.

The newer concept of Relative Risk (RR) deserves mention. It shows readily that, faced with the circumstance of a head-on collision between a 150-lb jogger running at 10 mph and a 12,000-lb tractor trailer traveling at 70 mph, the RR to the jogger is infinitely greater than to the truck. However, the test fails miserably in attempting to predict the RR to the jogger from a repeat encounter (RR2), therefore being of no use in equations involving second-order kinesiology. This regrettable shortcoming has limited the popularity of this test among other modern methods.

Last, a word about Confidence Limits. More and more, we are seeing reports in which these are displayed, and their meanings and functions touted as most informative and relevant. This is a healthy trend, and we applaud it. The wider the limits of confidence, the better, we say, and good news to all. Keep up the good work.

Dedication

This review is dedicated to the author's teacher, confidant, consultant, and fishing buddy, Samuel J. Null, PhD, discoverer and elucidator of the Null Hypothesis, upon which all subsequent work has been based and without which none of the foregoing would have been possible.

X-Ray Gogs:

Preliminary Evaluation of a "New" Imaging Modality*

DAVID K. EDWARDS, III, M.D.

"X-Ray Gogs," which apparently reveal internal anatomy without radiation, ultrasound, or magnetic fields, were compared with conventional imaging modalities in evaluating a variety of pediatric conditions. Conventional techniques were preferable in terms of diagnostic accuracy and image quality, and are thus recommended in most settings. Because of low cost and lack of ionizing radiation, "X-Ray Gogs" are recommended in cases where radiography is not indicated, or where the results of radiographic study will not influence patient management, or where the diagnosis has already been established by other means.

X-RAY GOGS. You saw these advertised in comic books as a child. And you wanted them with all your heart. And your parents objected. And you yielded. And since then life has not been very happy for you, has it? We offer a second chance to buy, own and operate the famous X-ray glasses. According to the package, it is: the "scientific marvel of the century." Not sold to communist countries on the restricted list that also prohibits sales of Cray Supercomputers. $1.25 each.

Quoted with permission from *Catalog #5*[1]

In this age of rapid advances in imaging techniques, it was mildly surprising to read the above advertisement and to realize that X-Ray Gogs (XRG), which have been available to the lay public for many years, have evidently not been examined in medical context.[2] Because of parental skepticism and parsimony, the author never owned XRG, and indeed life was not riotously happy thereafter. However, a childhood friend with less frugal parents recalls that XRG permitted visualization of not only digital bones but also the lead in a wooden pencil (Bobby "Bubba" Young, personal communication).

The intent of this preliminary study was to compare XRG with conventional imaging modalities in a variety of clinical pediatric settings.

Materials and Methods

The XRG as received from the vendor (Archie McPhee & Co., Seattle, WA) consisted of plastic frames with cardboard inserts containing 5-mm openings in which a red, translucent, striated material acted as a lens (Fig. 1). The striated material proved to be part of a red feather.[3] To permit a correct interpupillary distance and to compensate for myopia, I removed the cardboard inserts and affixed them to prescription spectacles (Fig. 2).

A miscellaneous variety of pediatric sonographic ($n = 30$) and radiographic ($n = 97$) examinations (list available on persuasive request) were performed with simultaneous or near-simultaneous XRG observation. The bright light required by the XRG studies was intermittently turned on and off during fluoroscopic procedures.

The Human Subjects Committee responded to routine petition in an uncouth, jocular manner that was interpreted as approval. Because of the benign nature of XRG studies, informed consent was considered implicit. Pediatric patients (age, 1 day to 10 years) were employed both because of the author's area of specialization and because adults, encountered in hallways, responded adversely to the examiner's appearance (Fig. 2), whereas children seemed intrigued, and infants oblivious. The passive voice was used wherever possible in this report.

The obviously harmless character of XRG allowed bypassing tedious laboratory investigation involving rodents and other vermin. Following the model of the similarly seminal early communications of Wilhelm

*Reprinted from the American Journal of Roentgenology, ©1988; 150(4):731–734; with permission from Williams & Wilkins, Baltimore.

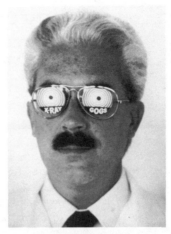

Figure 1.   Obverse of X-Ray Gogs and package label, photographed on corduroy (5.5 ridges/cm). Reverse of package label (not shown) contains instructions and faintly distasteful insinuations about seeing through clothing.

Figure 2.   X-Ray Gogs modified for use with prescription lenses.

Roentgen,[4] this study was not cluttered with annoying gibberish about line-pairs, ROC curves, sensitivity/specificity, and similar incomprehensibilities.

Results

Preliminary Evaluations

When used as instructed (i.e., viewing structures against a strong light), the XRG displayed the soft tissues of the fingers in a pleasing pink, with darker central regions that were surely either bones or something else (Fig. 3). Similarly, a wooden pencil thus viewed revealed pink edges and a dark central line that suggested the pencil's graphite core. The potential, hinted by the manufacturer, of seeing through clothing was explored with selected female staff members to the point of eyestrain, without success. Continual wearing of the XRG offered the advantage that the eyes remained dark-adapted; however, it was difficult to find one's way about the department in what seemed a dense red fog, hounded by the jeers of one's colleagues.

Comparative Study

The results comparing XRG and conventional studies are presented in Table 1. Conventional studies were notably superior in furnishing the correct diagnosis. The XRG studies provided the correct diagnosis only in those instances when the conventional study also revealed no abnormality. An important reason for this disparity appeared to be image quality, which was invariably inferior with XRG. Indeed, on no occasions were axial skeletal structures, soft tissue–gas interfaces,

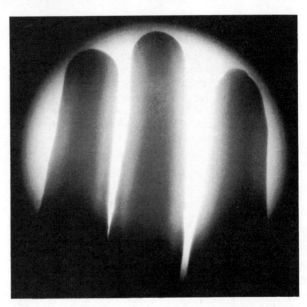

Figure 3.   Three of the author's fingers viewed through X-Ray Gogs.

or administered contrast materials discernible with XRG; all that was seen was a pink, patient-shaped blur.

On the other hand, XRG was superior in terms of ease of examination (one had only to look at the patient with a bright light in the background), cost (negligible), and radiation dose (nil). With these advantages in mind, the cases were reviewed retrospectively to define the actual benefit afforded the patient by the imaging study; 13 cases (10%) were found in which the benefit of the XRG study was at least the same as that of the conventional study. These were cases in which at least one of the following pertained: (1) the

Table 1.   *Comparison of X-Ray Gogs and Conventional Radiographic Techniques (127 Examinations)*

	Correct Diagnosis[a]	The preferred study in terms of:			
		Image Quality	Ease of Examination	Cost of Examination	Radiation Dose[b]
Conventional techniques	112 (88%)	127	0	0	0
X-Ray Gogs	60[c] (47%)	0	127	127	97
Significance of difference	$p \ll$ tiny[d]	$p <$ SC[e]	$p <$ SC	$p <$ SC	$p <$ SC

[a]Pathological, surgical, or clinical confirmation.

[b]30 sonograms not included.

[c]Where the correct diagnosis was "no abnormality seen," or thereabouts.

[d]Conventional techniques were correct and X-Ray Gogs wrong in 61 cases, while X-Ray Gogs were correct and conventional techniques wrong in 9 cases.

[e]SC = smoking computer: the clone, using the sign test and attempting to compute the infinitestimal "p" values of chi-square in the megaton (100+) range, began to smoke: heavily, indoors, and in defiance of local ordinance and several clearly visible signs.

radiographic study was not indicated; (2) no change in patient management would occur whatever the results of the radiographic study; or (3) the diagnosis was already firmly established by other means. Examples of such cases follow.

Exemplary Case Reports

Case 1.—A 4-year-old girl presented to the Emergency Room with a hurt finger. The intern, swamped with patients, injudiciously ordered radiographs before examining the child. The finger proved to have been hurt by a bee sting.

X-Ray Gog Examination: Soft tissue swelling dorsal to distal phalanx. No bony injury seen.

Radiographic Examination: Ditto.

Comment: No imaging examination was indicated.

Case 2.—A 3-year-old boy was evaluated for unexplained fever. Examination revealed otitis media, purulent nasal discharge, and tenderness over the left maxilla. The discharge was sent for culture, and the patient was begun on antibiotics and decongestants. As the child was leaving the clinic, a Waters view of the paranasal sinuses was requested and obtained.

X-Ray Gog Examination: No abnormality seen.

Radiographic Examination: Radiopacity of the left maxillary antrum.

Comment: The XRG diagnosis was clearly wrong. However, the clinicians proposed to treat the child the same whatever the radiographic study showed. The film added nothing except a nebulous entity called "baseline."

Case 3.—A 1-month-old boy presented with projectile vomiting. Examination revealed mild dehydration,

peristaltic waves across the upper abdomen, and a palpable mass ("olive") in the right abdomen. Sonography demonstrated a lengthened pyloris with a wall thickness of 5.5 mm; pyloric stenosis was diagnosed. However, an upper gastrointestinal series (UGI) was demanded and, after unseemly shouting and flexings of ego on the part of the clinicians and radiologists, grudgingly performed.

X-Ray Gog Examination: Barium sulfate suspension, administered by bottle and nipple, was not seen to flow freely through a normal esophagus. The filled stomach was not observed in several projections. Pyloric lengthening and marked narrowing ("string sign") were not noted. Distal to the narrowing, a normal duodenal sweep and ligament of Trietz were not appreciated. Hypertrophic pyloric stenosis was not diagnosed.

Fluoroscopic Examination: Ditto, deleting the word "not."

Comment: The diagnosis of pyloric stenosis was established prior to further study, if not clinically then certainly by sonography. The unnecessary UGI cost $203 and inflicted an active marrow radiation dose of perhaps 0.1 rad (0.001 Gy).

Discussion

Red goggles, long a radiologic mainstay until the development of image intensifiers, are now useless save possibly for staring at the superficial veins of breasts;[5] indeed, if tinted goggles are to be worn, they probably should be yellow, to enhance depth perception.[6] Breasts were not visualized in the current study (although not for want of trying), and any potential advantage of XRG in maintaining dark-adaptation was vastly outweighed by several painful collisions with both fixed and animate objects.

The imaging ability of XRG, when judged by the limited, picayune standards of diagnostic accuracy and image quality, is admittedly abysmal. Nonetheless, this study suggests a definite role for XRG in the diagnostic imager's armamentarium. The modality is invaluable in the following common settings: (1) where radiography is not indicated but someone badly wants it anyhow; (2) where the results of radiographic study will not influence patient management; and (3) where the diagnosis has already been established by other means (i.e., "The more times you run over a dead cat, the flatter it gets."[7]).

It is recommended that every radiologist purchase XRG and modify them to his or her ocular needs. Then, when one of these settings is encountered, the radiologist should vigorously recommend to the clinician an XRG examination in lieu of whatever conventional radiation-laden and/or costly study is requested. This recommendation may be enhanced by slowly and portentiously donning the XRG, gazing solemnly about, and finally stumbling off in the general direction of the patient. Then, having performed the XRG examination, only one diagnosis need be pronounced: *"No abnormality seen."* The advantages to the radiologist, and especially to the patient, are obvious. However, further investigation supported by substantial and tax-exempt grants is needed (and isn't it always?).

Acknowledgments

Gratitude is expressed to the unknown founder(s) of April Fool's Day; to the *AJR* editorial staff for helping commemorate it;* and to Carol A. Edwards and Marcia L. Earnshaw for their photographic assistance.

References

1. Anonymous. Catalog #5. Archie McPhee & Company, Box 30852, Seattle, WA 98103, 1987:20.

2. In other words, if X-Ray Gogs *were* previously tested, the report is buried somewhere beyond reach of the author's bibliographic search service and (one hopes) beyond reach of the reader's memory as well.

3. Yes, a feather. I know little of matters avian, but my parents did provide a childhood toy microscope, and I do know feathers. X-Ray Gog barbicels and hamuli were clearly discernible at 30X.

4. See any comprehensive medical history text. Direct citation of Dr. Roentgen might imply that I read German, or have read translations, which I don't and haven't. Give me a break.

5. Dunn FH. Red goggles and the mammographic physical examination. Radiology 1970; 95:618.

6. Kinney JA, Luria SM, Schlichting CL, Neri DF. The perception of depth contours with yellow goggles. Perception 1983; 12:363–366.

7. Schreiber MH. Wilson's law of diminishing returns. AJR 1982; 138:786–788.

---

*Since 1983, *AJR* has published a humorous article in all but two of its April issues.—*H.B.*

Additional Readings

1. Foraker AG: The temptation of Dr. Faust. Perspect Biol Med 1970; 14(spring):473–476.

Dr. Faust loses his funding from two institutions that had accepted his grants for years: The Geltmore Foundation and The National Omphalological Institute. While he is frantically preparing a new application, he is visited by that well known subspecialist from below.

2. Fraser AG, Rees A, et al: The haggis tolerance test in Scots and Sassenachs. Br Med J 1988; 297(Dec 24–31):1632–1634.

This study examined the lipemic effect of haggis, the national dish of Scotland, on two groups of subjects. Haggis is made from lamb's heart and lung, pig's liver, beef perinephric fat and oatmeal that are seasoned and boiled in a sheep's stomach. Although one probably needs to be British to actually eat haggis, the article itself is quite palatable. To quote the authors, "This study was ill conceived and badly designed, but brilliantly executed."

3. Greenberg DS: Grant Swinger's innovations. N Engl J Med 1977; 297(8):459–460.

A dialogue with Grant Swinger, the Director of the Center for the Absorption of Federal Funds. He suggests two innovations that would improve the climate for scientific research: (1) The Fund for Dubious Projects (2) The Journal of Rejected Manuscripts.

4. Greenstein JS: Studies on a new, peerless contraceptive agent: a preliminary report. Can Med Assoc J 1965; 93(Dec 25):1351–1355.

A new contraceptive is inadvertently discovered while the author is working to control the odor problem in his animal research lab. The agent is 100% effective and, except for increasing the libido, is totally free of side effects.

5. Iverson OH: Volvolon: a recently discovered peptide hormone from the pineal body. Can Med Assoc J 1982; 126(Apr 1):787–790.

A new hormone is discovered that regulates body movements during sleep (Lat. volvo: I roll). A number of isomers exist which explains why people turn in both directions at night. The effect of volvolon stops after death, which puts to rest the old belief that the actions of young people make their fathers turn in their graves.

6. Onestone AP: Further studies on the antirhabdomyelic effect of iso-2-pallallic acid. Obstet Gynecol 1956; 7(3):361–362.

This article satirizes some of the complexities of scientific research, including the propensity for different researchers to refute each other's work.

7. Umpierre SA, Hill JA, et al: Effect of coke on sperm motility. N Engl J Med 1985; 313(21):1351.

The authors compared the spermacidal effects of four different types of Coca-Cola. Diet Coke was best, but in comparing New to Classic Coke, the authors found that Classic Coke "is it."

8. Warburton FE: The lab coat as a status symbol. Science 1960; 131(3404):895.

In this amusing editorial, the author provides some insight into the evolution of the scientist's lab coat: "When work is unavoidable, he will be found in his shirt sleeves, in a coarse brown smock, or in plastic. His lab coat, clean, pressed, possibly even starched, hangs safely behind the door, to be worn only when he is lecturing or greeting official visitors."

SURGEONS & OTHER SPECIALISTS

Of the 11 articles in this chapter, more than half were written by or about surgeons. Whether this implies that surgeons are more revered than other specialists or less, I'm not sure. In any event, the chapter does offer a revealing look at the consulting process and some of the specialties. The reason each organ system is not fully represented is that a lot of humor never makes it out of the cath lab. It's clear from the following excerpt, however, that no one in medicine gets off scot-free.

> "Humor is quite common when house officers refer to specific rotations and hospitals to which they are assigned . . . No specialty is spared. Radiology becomes radioholiday, while nuclear medicine is known as unclear medicine. Gastroenterology is referred to as scoping for dollars and anesthesiology is known as doping for dollars. Urology probably has the most nicknames, such as stream-team and whiz-kids, to name a few. Orthopedic surgeons have to be strong as an ox and only twice as smart, and think that the sole function of the heart is to pump antibiotics to the bones."
>
> From "Humor and the Physician" by Fred D. Cushner, M.D. and Richard J. Friedman, M.D. (see Appendix).

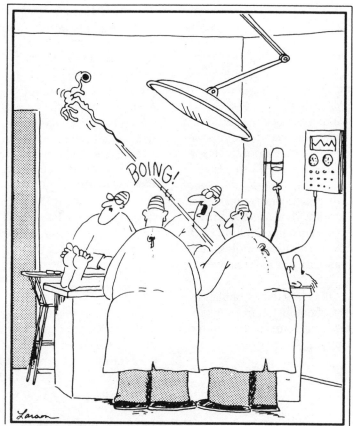

"Whoa! Watch where that thing lands — we'll probably need it."

Communicating with Surgeons, Once You Learn the Language, Is Possible Most of the Time*

PATTY SWENSON, R.N.

An area close to my heart (and quite possibly my ulcer) is "Communicating in the OR." The reason there are difficulties in this area can be directly traced to the fact that most OR nurses sign on with only their mother tongue as a means of communication. Although the job descriptions never mention it, fluency

*Reprinted with permission from AORN Journal, 1984; 40(5):784–785, Copyright ©AORN Inc., 10170 East Mississippi Ave., Denver Co. 80231. Edited from the original.

in "Surgeon Speak" and its several dialects—one for each surgeon—is easily the key to on-the-job success or failure.

For example, the manufacturer's catalog will refer to a certain instrument as a Mayo clamp, but only a fool will ever expect to hear it called by that name. Instead surgeons will ask for heavy curves, curved sixes, fat Kellys, and in moments of intense concentration, "that one over there." Kitners, kuntners, peanuts, and occasionally, cherries, all refer to the same blunt dissector. Schnitz, snits, and tonsils are the same stroke to different folk.

One surgeon will call an instrument by many pet names, depending upon how it will be used. Alone it's a right angle; feed a piece of suture into its little beak and you have a tie on a mixter. The list is endless, and I will bet there are some regional variations that would bring tears to my eyes.

But conversation in the OR is less than stimulating, despite the occasional burst of confusion from instrument names. Most of the exchanges are hardly enough to keep the mind alive. I quote:

"Give me a tie."
"What kind?"
"Any kind."
"Here's 3-0 silk."
"Terrific!"
"You're welcome."
"I didn't ask for a rope. I asked for a tie."
"You have it."
"Then what is THIS?"
"Three-0 silk."
"Man oh man. This sure doesn't FEEL like 3-0."
"What DOES it feel like?"
"It feels like 2-0."
"Trust me."
"I TRUST you. But next time I want thin 3-0."
"Ooookay."

Surgeon Signal

Next we have "Surgeon Signal." This is a series of hand signals substituted for the spoken word, used to request objects with perfectly good given names. They are used instead because: (a) the surgeon in question doesn't know the real name, (b) is saving his voice for bigger and better things, (c) assumes the scrub nurse is deaf, or (d) all of the above.

Among the more common signals are

• the forefinger and middle finger moving up and down against each other in a scissors-like fashion meaning, "I wish to cut."

• the thumb and forefinger meeting one another in a rapid pinching motion usually indicating the desire for a pickup or is a sure sign of burnout.

• the hand formed into a semi-fist, whipped rapidly in a partially clockwise direction, quaintly requesting a needle and thread on a needle holder. Now really, wouldn't the simple use of the word suture be a lot less wearing on everyone?

One of my favorite surgeons has a habit of simply holding out his hand, as if to make a left-hand turn, giving you the option of placing in it whatever you think will strike his fancy.

Surgeon Snag

To me, the average surgeon's concept of time is the eighth wonder of the world and something for which there is no rational explanation. "Surgeon time" is not necessarily "clock time" as I know it. There is no established rule for converting one to the other, but a safe guideline is if your surgeon says, "This will only take 45 minutes," DOUBLE it! In many cases—and these you quickly become familiar with or go mad—TRIPLING it is a more realistic approach to estimating when the room will be available for someone else. No matter what *they* say, *you* know better. And *they* know *you* know. And *you* know *they* know *you* know. Which is 75% of the reason for the half-crazed expressions worn by surgery supervisors during working hours and why they are so often observed babbling pathetically to no one in particular.

The remaining 25% of the cause contributing to the downfall of even the brightest and best OR supervisor is directly traceable to the "Supply and Demand Equation." This boils down to something like, "The number of supplies and instruments a surgeon says he will need is inversely proportionate to the amount he will ultimately require." This law is most effective after 3 pm and on weekends.

All in all, after years of research, observation, and personal experience, I can safely say that communicating with surgeons, once you learn the language and establish a few ground rules, is possible most of the time.

Come Back Dr. Curmudgeon*

KENNETH R. MORGAN, M.D.

The old-time practitioner was a fiery autocrat compared to today's colorless counterpart, says this Connecticut OBG man. If the trend towards docility continues, these ghastly scenes may occur.

In the days between World Wars I and II, no surgeon worth his salt ever left an operating room unless the scrub nurse was in tears, the anesthetist cowering in a corner, and the assistants nursing their bruised knuckles in ashen dismay. When he stomped down the corridor, glowering left and right, the orderlies ran for cover, and the medical students took to the hills like frightened deer. It's a pity this splendid prima donna has disappeared from our midst.

An occasional pallid imitation still wields his knife in the amphitheatre, but the spirit has seeped out of him. He knows in his heart that the scrub nurse will tolerate his ferocity only so long as it amuses her; that the intern, if he is lucky enough to have one, will break scrub and find more congenial company unless the old bomber remembers to be polite; and that the anesthetist will treat him with lordly disdain at the first sign of pique.

I won't be at all surprised if a few years hence the typical operating room scene will be played out something like this:

SURGEON: Suture!

SCRUB NURSE: Say please.

SURGEON: Suture, *please!*

SCRUB NURSE: Once more. And no sarcasm this time.

SURGEON: Please?

SCRUB NURSE: That's better. *(She forks it over.)*

SURGEON *(to assistant):* Would you mind sponging the wound so I can see?

ASSISTANT *(bursting into tears):* I can't stand it! Orders, orders, all day long! Never a kind word!

SURGEON: There, there. After the operation we'll have a little chat about a raise in salary, and I'll try to be a little more understanding in the future.

ASSISTANT: All right—as long as you promise.

SURGEON *(to anesthetist):* The patient seems to be getting a little light. Muscles are kind of rigid.

ANESTHETIST: It's not necessary to reflect on my ability. You'll notice that I refrain from criticizing *you.*

SURGEON: No criticism intended. I simply meant that because of my own ineptitude I need more muscle relaxation for exposure than most surgeons do.

ANESTHETIST: In that case I accept your apology.

SURGEON *(concluding operation and beaming at everybody):* Thank you, thank you, one and all! You've been most tolerant this morning. . . .

In the old days, the atmosphere was as tense outside the operating room as in. For example, what floor nurse would have dared remain seated when old Tyrannosaurus rex stormed into the ward trailed by his house staff? At the first sound of approaching thunder she tossed her copy of Elinor Glyn into the wastebasket and leaped to attention, reciting a catechism of temperature readings, pulse fluctuations, and bowel movements as if entranced.

Nowadays, the doctor making rounds goes through a sort of ritual courtship of the head nurse before extracting the requisite information. It won't be long before you can expect the nurses' station to be the setting for this short drama:

DOCTOR: I hate to disturb you, Miss Imperious, but how is Mrs. Brown doing?

NURSE *(busy manipulating six ball-point pens of different colors to make an artistic time sheet showing who will be on night duty next week):* I wish I could tell you, Doctor, but as you well know—or should— Miss Globetrotter is in charge of all patient information. Get clearance from her, and I'll tell you. You'll find her in the south building.

*Reprinted with permission from Medical Economics, ©1962; 39(Jul 16):188–200, Medical Economics Company, Inc., Oradell, N.J. 07649.

DOCTOR: Thank you ever so much. Before I look for her, perhaps I ought to glance at the chart—if I may?

NURSE: The chart will be back from Miss Granite shortly. She's using it in a student nurses' class. Perhaps you'd care to sit and wait.

DOCTOR: Why, that's very nice of you, Miss Imperious. You don't find that kind of hospitality everywhere in this hospital! . . .

When it came to getting along with patients, the curmudgeon was in absolute command. Perhaps you've heard the story about the postpartum patient who called the senior obstetrician to state indignantly that she'd just removed a sponge from her vagina. Did he apologize for his carelessness? Did he say the intern must have done it? No, sir!

"Damn it!" he shouted into the phone. "You mean you took it *out?*" He left her so filled with remorse and self-recrimination that, instead of suing him, she castigated all her previous accoucheurs for not having stuffed her with sponges.

What doctor today would show the same blithe unconcern about offending a patient? Compared to the formidable old party of yesterday, we're pathetic weaklings. I can imagine this scene being played at the consulting room desk of the future:

PATIENT (barging in, unannounced): Sit down, Doctor. Dr. Zircon in Springfield suggested that when I moved to Bridgeport I should shop around for an obstetrician.

OBSTETRICIAN: How nice! I see you have a stenographer's pad with you, and I imagine you want to ask a few questions. But before we begin, let me give you this booklet. It tells all about me—my early childhood, my struggling years in—

PATIENT: No, no, Doctor. My questions go deeper. I already know your medical background, basic experience, percentage of deliveries missed, and so forth. We *all* read Medical Consumer Reports.

OBSTETRICIAN: Yes, well, the reason Medical Consumer Reports gave me only an "Acceptable" rating last year was—

PATIENT: No need to apologize. I'm aware it was because the magazines in your waiting room were weeks old. Tell me, now: What do you think about when you deliver a baby at 4 o'clock in the morning?

OBSTETRICIAN: Often I think about George Muldoon, who sat next to me in high school and flunked out his second year, and who now makes $200,000 a year as a plumbing contractor.

PATIENT (writing furiously): I see. And how about your thoughts when you first hold in your hands the precious fruit of a mother's womb?

OBSTETRICIAN: Hold what?

PATIENT: The baby, the baby!

OBSTETRICIAN: Oh! Well—I think that if I can just get the episiotomy sewn up without sticking a vein, then maybe I can go home and get two hours' sleep before office hours.

PATIENT (sneeringly): Two hours' *sleep!* Doctor, you should be in some other line of work.

OBSTETRICIAN: Funny you should suggest that too. George Muldoon told me the same thing just the other day. . . .

But perhaps I'm being over-pessimistic. After a steady movement toward total docility, the medical pendulum could, I suppose, swing back again. For all I know, my colleagues have already started to lead the profession back toward wholesome curmudgeonism. Consider the following three conversations. Would you give Dr. A's responses or Dr. B's?

PATIENT (at 3 A.M.): I just thought I'd call and let you know I'm feeling much better, because I didn't want you to worry.

DR. A: You shouldn't have bothered. I like to worry.

DR. B: That's fine, but just to make sure you're O.K. I'll give my answering service instructions to call you every hour on the hour for the next five nights.

FLOOR NURSE (at 9 A.M.): How did *I* know I wasn't supposed to wake the patient to give her the Seconal?

DR. A: That's perfectly all right. I should have been more explicit.

DR. B: And how did I know the hospital hired an imbecile?

OFFICE NURSE (at 3 P.M.): I'm sorry. I forgot you had a plane to catch, or I wouldn't have squeezed in these five extra patients.

DR. A: That's O.K. Just cancel my trip.

DR. B: Well, you just go out there and tell those five patients that you failed your course in calendar-reading.

Are you a Dr. A or a Dr. B? If you're a Dr. B, you're a curmudgeon, and there's hope for the rest of us.

Consultmanship:

How to Stay One-up on Colleagues*

ANTHONY SHAW, M.D.

The art of consulting involves, of course, a good deal of medical one-upmanship. Such feats as feeling a spleen that's eluded all previous palpators or hearing a diastolic murmur that has previously gone undetected will score points for almost any consultant.

My first experience with the heady joys of consultmanship came when, as a senior surgical resident, I put on the consultant's hat. Often I'd be summoned by quaking medical residents to face down hemorrhage or to grapple with pus. Writing in a bold, steady hand, I'd speedily summarize a problem that had baffled another service for weeks, dismiss all the diagnostic possibilities studding the chart, and offer the correct diagnosis. Then in a spirit of noblesse oblige, I'd invite one and all to troop up to the O.R. and witness the cure. Now it's been some years since I was a surgical resident, and it may not have been exactly like that, but that's the way I prefer to remember it.

From my initial night emergency consultation, though, I emerged not one-up, but definitely one-down. It started with an urgent call from the psychiatric wing of my medical center. The psychiatry resident, a young woman, had a patient—also a young woman—who'd suddenly started to hemorrhage from somewhere down below. She wanted a surgeon to come over and check it out. Not wanting to steal a case from GYN (especially at 4 A.M.), I asked which orifice the blood appeared to be coming from. There was a pause, during which I heard some whispering at the other end.

"She doesn't know," answered the psychiatrist.

"I see," said I. "Would you have a look and call me back?"

Her shock and dismay came through loud and clear: "Do you mean you want me to examine her perineum?"

"Well, yes," I said, falling back on my best 4 A.M. weapon, sarcasm. "I believe that even psychiatrists can tell which is which."

"Doctor," she said (you're in trouble when another doctor calls you Doctor), "I *never* examine my patients. It would ruin our rapport!"

I've told this story to a number of psychiatrists, and the first one has yet to laugh, which certainly must be an indication of something or other.

The techniques of consultmanship vary from specialty to specialty, but within each field of practice, certain consistencies may be recognized. Take the matter of consultation notes. The ophthalmologists' are comprehensible only to other ophthalmologists, being in code. Orthopedists' notes are brief. Typically, they say: "Chart read and patient seen. Will return after reviewing X-rays." Since the X-rays usually can't be located, this may be all there is to the note. One pediatrician got back at the orthopods. When he was called to see a young orthopedic patient with bilateral facial swelling, his entire succinct note read, "Mumps."

Neurologists' notes are paragons of organization, covering at least three sheets and ending with an offer to return and reevaluate the patient—if any change in condition should be observed. I don't think I've ever read a neurologist's note all the way through because I've always had to see another patient or have lunch or something. Nonetheless, as The New York Times ads say, "You don't have to read it all, but it's nice to know it's all there."

In many consultants' notes, various diagnoses are suggested not in order to establish them but to rule them out. Following a consultant's description of the physical findings of a patient howling with abdominal pain, one may read:

"Impression:

*Reprinted with permission from Medical Economics, ©1970; 47(Aug 31):162–168, Medical Economics Company, Inc., Oradell, N.J. 07649.

"1. Rule out peptic ulcer.
"2. Rule out acute pancreatitis.
"3. Rule out appendicitis.
"4. Rule out PID.
"5. Rule out twisted fallopian tube.
"6. Rule out splenic infarction."

"Rule out appendicitis" is a favorite pediatric note for a youngster with abdominal pain, McBurney's point tenderness, fever, vomiting, and elevated white blood cell count. I think this notation reduces the burden of guilt the pediatrician may feel when his little patient is carted off to be cut up by wicked surgeons. After all, he didn't say it *was* appendicitis, so he can't be blamed for what happens in that tiled chamber of horrors upstairs.

Every woman seen in the emergency room with abdominal pain and a little fever has pelvic inflammatory disease until the attending OBG man on call makes his appearance to rule it out. "Put her up in stirrups, and I'll be right over," comes the advance telephone warning. Most seasoned OBG's tend to affect a tremendously effective air of utter boredom that lends great authority to their consultive notes. Somehow they seem to be able to tell over the phone that young women awaiting them in the emergency room have pristine pelvic organs. While this clairvoyance rarely relieves them of the obligation to make the trip to the E.R., it does enable them to rouse themselves at 3 A.M., amble over, in and out of the E.R., write "No GYN pathology" on the chart, and return home to slide back in the sack, having scarcely disturbed a good night's sleep.

Internists strain to outdo the neurologists in producing truly comprehensive consultative notes—a talent they acquired while surgeons were practicing square knots on bed posts. I remember one budding internist back in residency who would see a patient, and for two days no one could approach him nor would he discuss the case.

At the end of this time, an exquisitely typed "case report" would appear on the patient's chart. It not only would include the findings along with a diagnosis but also would provide a full review of the literature and bibliography on all diseases in any way related to the patient's. Sometimes his note would appear too late to help the patient, but it would be very useful in the subsequent CPC. That man is now solidly esconced on Park Avenue where he's able, in a busy week, to see five patients in consultation. His opinions are generally considered the last 10,000 words.

Surgeons on the other hand rarely write elaborate notes. As a matter of fact, surgeons are often much too busy to write notes at all. When the typical surgeon appears on the medical floor at 8 or 9 P.M. after his day in the O.R., he has in tow his resident or intern, whichever has a pen and legible handwriting. "Looks like perforated ulcer"—or hemorrhoids, or femoral thrombosis, or whatever—he barks. "Get him typed and cross-matched and we'll take him up!" After making sure the house officer is getting it straight on the chart, he rushes off to the coffee shop.

Occasionally a consultant feels that, while he doesn't know what a patient has, he could handle it better if the patient were in one of the consultant's own beds. Thus, a medical consultant's note may read in toto: "A fascinating case of vitiligo, nausea, and amnesia. I will be happy to accept this patient on my service." Surgical consultants are prone to a similar type of brevity: "Patient has gallstones. Will accept for transfer."

Sometimes the above formalities are dispensed with altogether. In that event, the consultant may substitute what I've heard some surgeons call "active" consultation—others call it case-stealing—for the more common "passive" kind. For example, a plastic surgeon I know of was once asked to evaluate a lump on the wrist of a medical patient. The next day, while making rounds, the primary physician noted a dressing on his patient's wrist and a sling on his arm. The complete "consultation" note on the chart included operative findings and a pathology report. One-up!

Fellowshipmanship

A Concise Manual on How to Be a Specialist Without Studying*

IAN ROSE, M.B., B.S.

Long before Stephen Potter† described in print the principles of lifemanship, their application to certain branches of medicine was well known. Also before that time the College for Fellowshipmen was founded. The following short treatise constitutes the basic text for students of the College. The value of the principles to be described speaks for itself and cannot be enhanced by a lengthy introduction.

The Approach to General Practitioners

It is as well at the outset to decide to choose the image one intends to present to general practitioners. There are a considerable variety, but they all have the same basic intention of putting the G.P. at a psychological disadvantage. The father figure, the older brother image, the absent-minded professor type, and the hearty captain of the football team role are among the most popular personality types. Most Fellowshipmen (specialists) are accomplished in at least one of these personalities. We recommend, however, that three or preferably four should be studied and available for instant use by any of our graduates.

In this way it is generally possible during the first few moments of meeting a general practitioner to adopt the role that will most effectively sap his personal confidence.

Whatever role is assumed, the following rules must always apply:

1. The Fellowshipman must always appear to be fond of the general practitioner, in the same way as a good citizen is fond of his dog, or the Mountie of his horse.

2. The Fellowshipman must never openly disagree with the general practitioner on matters pertaining to medicine because there are far more effective ways of demonstrating his error and because the general practitioner is sometimes right. (This last eventuality, of course, must never be admitted openly to the general practitioner.)

Mannerization I

Some nondescript and totally meaningless mannerism should be carefully developed, such as a tut-tutting noise made with the tongue against the teeth, a significant but ambiguous raising of the eyebrows, or a rubbing of the side of the nose with the right forefinger. Such mannerisms are invaluable in circumstances where a categorical "yes" or "no" might lead one to commit oneself to a definite opinion which, as will be seen later under "General Rules," should never be expressed by the Fellowshipman. [Note: This is, of course, the alternative to the negative opinion, which can be quite effective, or the double negative opinion, which in the right circumstances may be classed as one of the master strokes.]

It is generally wise to ask the general practitioner to outline the history before going to the patient, so that he has to recount it from memory without the use of his notes.

If the history is presented in a sketchy manner the Fellowshipman should pursue it to great lengths, asking as many questions as possible, particularly emphasizing the sketchiness of the past and family histories that he has been given. On going to the bedside, the Fellowshipman should sit down and take the history in detail again from the patient.

If, on the other hand, the history is presented efficiently and clearly, the Fellowshipman should yawn, shift from foot to foot, examine his nails and make it clear that he feels it all to be a waste of time. A number

*Reprinted with permission from the Canadian Medical Association Journal, ©1962; 87(Dec 8):1232–1235. Edited from the original.
†Potter, S: Lifemanship, Holt, Rinehart and Winston, Inc., New York 1951.

of history-devitalizing questions can be used to interrupt and break up the flow of the general practitioner's presentation. For example, during the description of the first examination of the patient by the general practitioner, the Fellowshipman should suddenly take an interest and say: "Just a minute. Was there a gag reflex present at that time?" or "I suppose the father wasn't a glass blower, was he?" or "Is the patient red-green colour blind?"

The Presentation of the Diagnosis

This is the crucial point of the consultation. Even if the consultation has been requested by the general practitioner for the purposes of advice regarding treatment, or in order to make a good impression on the family of the patient, this is the pivot of the Fellowshipman's activity. His whole approach should rise to a crescendo, the peak of which is the pronouncement of the diagnosis, and all that may follow should be diminuendo in an atmosphere of glory and adulation.

By the time the diagnosis is to be presented, the general practitioner must be in a state of complete subjugation and intimidation. Any audience that may be present will by this time be regarding the general practitioner as either a doctor who never did know much about medicine or one who has forgotten what he did know.

Bamboozlization

The opening gambit in presenting the diagnosis is of extreme importance. It should be calculated to intrigue and mystify. It can be of two kinds, which will be described under the separate headings of A and B:

A. The Fellowshipman, having completed his history and physical examination and any remarks that he wishes to make regarding these, leans back, lights a cigarette or cigar, or takes a pinch of snuff, or whatever may be his particular penchant, and then says: "Well, it isn't a Weir-Westergrand-Jones syndrome."

Any other names may be used to designate this non-existent syndrome, and any questioning regarding it may be passed off as of no significance, since the

Fellowshipman has just said that this is not the diagnosis in any case.

B. The second diagnostic opening is a gambit which is best described by quoting from some of the creations of Kingley-Spillsbury-Gunderson, author of our privately circulated pamphlet entitled "The Raw General Practitioner and How to Cook It." It was he in fact who dubbed this gambit with the name by which it will ever be known, that of "Obviousmisting." Having completed all his preliminaries, he would begin by uttering some such remark as: "It is of course essential to note that this patient has normal vision." Alternatively, "It is not without significance that the liver is not enlarged."

This gives the general practitioner something very puzzling to consider during the rest of the discussion.

Circumstances will dictate the final method of presenting the ultimate diagnosis. There are a number of rules to be considered, of which the most important is that under no circumstances should a positive diagnosis be given, however obvious it may be. In fact, the more obvious it is the more it should be obscured. Thus, it is not permissible in the case of a patient who has consolidation of his right lower lobe, a fever of 104°F., and pneumococci in his sputum, to make the diagnosis of lobar pneumonia.

In such a case, the double negative diagnosis may be used to some effect. Thus: "It is impossible to say that this patient does not have pneumonia."

There are many variations of the double negative and these should be committed to memory. A most common method is to select a special investigation that has not been performed (it is quite immaterial how irrelevant such an investigation might be), then turn to the general practitioner and ask him for the results of this procedure as though it were quite inevitable that he should already have performed it. On being informed that it has not been done, the Fellowshipman then suggests that it should be ordered immediately, with the implication that if this had been done previously there would have been no need to disturb the Fellowshipman from his Thursday afternoon golf.

Sometimes, a wily old general practitioner, and some specialists—in particular those who may have picked up a little Fellowshipmanship along the way*—

*The Fellowshipman need never be concerned that he will be opposed in consultation by another Fellowshipman. It will be seen under "General Rules" that a Fellowshipman never asks for a consultation.

will have ordered all possible investigations that could be performed. This presents a relatively difficult situation, and the best way of dealing with it is to suggest boldly that one of the examinations previously performed be repeated, with the assurance to all concerned that this will solve the diagnostic problem.

Standard Counters

A. Any reference to a specific report in the literature may be countered by inquiring who wrote it and, on being told, saying: "Well!"—followed by a hollow laugh.

If, in spite of this, the matter is still pursued, the general practitioner should be asked if he ever met Svenglehoffer (or Brown, or whoever wrote the article). This effectively stops the flow of argument, and the whole subject can be closed by saying: "If you ever had . . ."

B. On being pressed for an opinion as to the desirability of surgery, the Fellowshipman should shrug his shoulders and say: "Surgery! The final refuge of the therapeutically destitute physician!"

Stethoscope Symbolism

The stethoscope is the most important property (to use the terminology of the theatre) of the Fellowshipman. His personality should blend in with his stethoscope and his stethoscope with his personality. His attitude towards it and his manipulation of it must be carefully studied and made perfect by constant usage. These will vary in relation to his particular specialty. The following is a quick guide to the stethoscope. (A detailed analysis of the whole problem may be found in our booklet entitled "The Use and Abuse of the Stethoscope." Graduates and advanced students wishing to study this subject further are referred to the paper by Schmidt-Gobel-Schmidt published in 1948 and entitled "Fetishism and the Specialist.")

1. The *Fellowshipman cardiologist* should wear his stethoscope ostentatiously and use it reverently. He should have the latest model and see that it is polished and cleaned daily. We recommend that his stethoscope stand out and dominate his whole personality. The more modern models incorporating automatic transmission make excellent conversation pieces. At the same time we do not advise the use of gilt or jewels, as this may be regarded as vulgar by some.*

2. The *Fellowshipman chest physician* should carry an old battered stethoscope. It is quite a good idea if his stethoscope is patched in several places with contrasting coloured adhesive tape. He must learn to use it in an offhand way, giving the suggestion that the process of auscultation is just a formality.

Gordon Tingley-Martin, a Fellowshipman graduate of 1947 and author of that admirable article entitled "Breath Sounds to be Heard in Unusual X-ray Appearances", was a master of stethoscopic manipulation. He would fumblingly insinuate the ear pieces into his ears backwards and, while placing the bell idly on the patient's chest, murmur: "These things really belong in a museum."

It is probably wise for other Fellowshipmen practising specialists, such as gastroenterologists, dermatologists, syphilologists, etc., not to carry a stethoscope. If a general practitioner demonstrating a case wields a menacing stethoscope, it is safe for the Fellowshipman to adopt the attitude of Gordon Tingley-Martin and generally deprecate any conclusions drawn from auscultation by references to the variability of auditory interpretation and pitch capacity.

If, on the other hand, the general practitioner does not appear to have a stethoscope, the Fellowshipman should ask to borrow one from him, and when this is not available it can be made subtly clear that the Fellowshipman always expects the general practitioner to provide a stethoscope for this very important phase of the examination.

Fellowshipman Neurologists

The only other property that requires mention for the Fellowshipman is the patellar hammer for the Fellowshipman neurologist. This must be made even more a part of his personality than the stethoscope for the cardiologist and chest physician. While individual taste should have some play, we recommend that the following broad rules be followed. If the Fellowshipman is a large, heavy-set individual, he should purchase a very small steel patellar hammer which he manipulates

---

*It is to be noted that the cardiologist is the only Fellowshipman that need be able to hear through the stethoscope.

in an idle way most of the time, occasionally, during conversation, throwing it up and catching it or picking his teeth with the pointed end. If on the other hand the Fellowshipman is a diminutive individual, he should then purchase the large wooden-handled type of hammer which he should carry in the pocket of his white coat at all times, with the handle protruding laterally, catching on things and people as he passes.

We have been asked on occasion what advice we have in this regard to the Fellowshipman neurologist of medium size. After many years of experience we strongly urge that all Fellowshipman neurologists of medium size change their specialty.

Fellowshipmanship and the Specialist

It is essential to know, before meeting the specialist, his age and where he trained; and any papers he may have published should be studied. The names of one or two senior men of his medical school should be committed to memory.

The opening gambit in these instances is most important. Even if it is not possible to intimidate the specialist in this early stage, it is quite essential to place him in an inferior light to any others present. Any one of the following may be used:

Fellowshipman: What medical school did you go to?

Specialist: Upperwoldingham and Ham . . .

Fellowshipman: Well, then, you must have known Stinky Carpenter! (Carpenter was the Professor of Medicine at the time the Specialist was a medical student.)

Another useful opening is: "I think I read a paper you wrote in such and such a journal a few months ago." The specialist will then eagerly supply the title at which the Fellowshipman looks a trifle embarrassed and immediately suggests they get on with the business at hand.

Mannerization II

A negative mannerism should also be cultivated. This is an essentially personal movement which each will have to work out in his own way. As an example we may cite that developed by Garth Pindermoss,* one of our honoured graduates and author of the book "Fellowshipmanship and the Smith-Petersen Pin, or A Primer for Fellowshipman Orthopedicians."

*This mannerism is sometimes referred to as the Eltsihw Complex.

A warning should be issued that the student should not attempt anything as elaborate as Pindermoss' negativeannerism for some time, as this type of complexity, while being highly effective, is beyond the reach of most students for many years. However, Pindermoss would entice a fellow specialist into describing a recent operation he had performed. At a crucial point he would ask an apparently simple question, such as: "Did you undersew the superior inverted flap?" Whether the specialist says he did or did not, Pindermoss would then respond with the full negativeannerism. This, when analyzed, consists of a half closing of the eyes, a partial frown, a slight shaking of the head which leaves it turned half way to the right shoulder, and the sound produced by drawing the breath sharply through pursed lips (this sound is produced by inspiration through the lips in the position of whistling). This whole movement was beautifully executed by Pindermoss and could generally be guaranteed to have a paralyzing effect on the other specialist. During the subsequent course of the description of the operation, it was never necessary for Pindermoss to re-execute the entire maneuver, but at any time he could engender a similar emotional catastrophe in his opponent by making use of any one of the separate parts, such as half closing the eyes, shaking the head or sounding the eltsihw.

If the argument is progressing to the Fellowshipman's disadvantage, a number of moves are available. For example, the Fellowshipman first lulls the specialist into a sense of false security by seeming to be persuaded. This creates a favourable impression of impartiality and scientific open-mindedness. Then the following maneuver is executed:

Fellowshipman: "Very interesting. A new approach! It totally invalidates the fundamental work of Rosengrats and Gildenstern." (Other names may be substituted.)

Specialist: "How do you mean?"

Fellowshipman: "Well, it's obvious isn't it." (Pause.) "You don't mean to tell me that you are putting forward this theory without comparing it to their work?"

At this point it is very simple to show that the specialist has never given adequate thought to his thesis. The faith of the audience in the specialist is completely shaken, not only in relation to the present argument but in relation to his general standard of reasoning.

Roles of the Fellowshipman Surgeon

Surgeon Fellowshipmen, like any others, must present specific personalities. However, unlike other specialists, the popularity of surgical types varies with professional demand from year to year and, one might almost say, from season to season. It therefore presents considerable difficulty to recommend specific roles for our Fellowshipmen surgeons in a manual of this kind which is subject to revision only about once in five years. Since the inception of this institute, we have recommended many different roles to our surgical graduates. Amongst the most outstanding of these have been the small, imperial bearded surgeon with a trace of a foreign accent; the gangling, mustached, tweedy English surgeon-farmer type; and the highly successful stockbroker-diplomat-plastic surgeon character of 1948.

However, in this day and age we feel that it is becoming necessary to leave the Fellowshipman surgeon wishing to keep abreast of changing fashions to his own chameleon-like devices. Our biannual bulletin will in the future include notes and bar graphs showing the current trends in surgical personalities. But we intend here to delineate two primary surgical personalities that have stood the test of time:

Type I is the *hearty life-of-the-party* type who practises by the seat of his pants. He must never be tired and always be ready for 18 holes of golf at the end of the day's work—a beer and whisky drinker from way back. He has large unkempt hands and his hobbies involve the use of the chainsaw.

It is the view of two members of our advisory board that this type of surgeon is becoming rather *vieux jeu* and is no longer suitable for the larger centres. This is not the opinion of the entire board, but we feel it necessary to quote it in order to retain impartiality.

It is the unanimous opinion of the board that Type II is altogether the coming thing and we unanimously recommend it as a life study.

Fellowshipman Surgeon—Type II

Type II is *the pale, highly strung, introspective, bookworm type.* He must look decidedly ill. People are sorry for him. It is clear that he stands erect for operations only as a result of his will power and dedication to surgery. He never speaks but to quote the results from some German paper that has not been translated into English and that is usually unpublished.

His hands are delicate and he cherishes them. There is always a vague suspicion that they are insured for several hundred thousand dollars.

He is temperamental and loses his temper easily in a tired sort of way. He does not crush people with words but makes them feel guilty for having troubled him in his manifestly weakened state.

Finally, the Surgeon Fellowshipman must remember that he is the prima donna of the profession and give free reign to his emotions at all times. All urges and impulses should be irresistible. However, while the occasional scream may be regarded as effective, on the whole tears are to be avoided.

General Rules

1. Never commit a diagnosis.
2. The most recent work is always unpublished.
3. The most recent published work is always in German.
4. General practitioners are never right but may on occasion not be wrong.
5. All specialists (other than the Fellowshipman) are always wrong.
6. The most important symptom is one not related to the patient's present illness.
7. The most important sign is the one no one else has found.
8. No general practitioner is ever permitted to hear an early diastolic murmur.

Why Surgeons
Are Real Swingers*

E. F. DIAMOND, M.D.

Who among us has beheld one of his surgical brethren striding down the hospital corridor in his nonconductive shoes, his mask dangling at his throat, his green scrub suit draped and drawstringed, and hasn't said to himself, "There, but for the grace of God, goes God."

This imposing man has made the transition from barber/surgeon to bronze idol, from bloodletter to bankroller. He conquers without stooping. A stroke of his scalpel, and he wins admiration and gratitude far beyond that ever given some medical wretch for his decades of service to a family. On what meat doth this great paragon feed that even we who know better feel inclined to offer obeisance?

In these days of declining professional prestige, perhaps we nonsurgeons should stop worshipping from afar and instead examine him more closely and attempt to discover his methods. Maybe we could all learn to emulate him.

What are the ingredients of the surgeon's magic? Shielding my eyes, I see two main ones:

1. A sense of style.   Look around the doctors' lounge. There's the pediatrician with his galoshes and his hockey cap. On his last house call he was mistaken for the egg man. He's a young man, but his posture is bent forward from the effects of countless kicks in the groin from small boys. He sits in the corner with a vacant stare and a blanched complexion, terrified by the prospect of this afternoon's office hours.

The obstetrician shuffles aimlessly by. He's not yet been home to shave. His suit is rumpled by half a night's rest in the top bunk of the OB waiting room. His conversation is aimless and somewhat irrelevant. His only real animation comes when he asks, "How far apart are the pains?" Last year, when told that his house was on fire, he woozily inquired, "How far apart are the flames?"

Now comes the internist, stepping carefully. He never goes anywhere without his bag. Not a little bag, mind you, but a satchel with even a tuning fork and a direct-writing ECG machine inside. He's afraid that he'll miss something. When on emergency-room call, he makes everyone fill out the Cornell Medical Index, even those with 2-cm. lacerations. He wears sensible policeman's shoes, a belt with his suspenders, and he keeps asking us why we don't use our staff dues to invest in a computer.

Suddenly, the room is electric with the presence of the surgeon. He's careful to give a stroke or a pat to everyone with Class C surgical privileges who might have a ripe case of cholelithiasis in the house. He wears aviator sunglasses and Gucci loafers. (I once knew a neurosurgeon who wore a cape.) He recently traded in his Cadillac for a Ferrari that he parks grandly in front of the emergency entrance. "Keep an eye on it, Eddie!" he cries out to the lot attendant whose hernia he's promised to fix. He brings his own scrub nurse, a nearly mute Miss Clairol goddess so starched and efficient that she makes the home team of nurses feel like cretins. She helps Mr. Wonderful doff his mink-lined trench coat to reveal a resplendent fuchsia plaid sports coat. With a small smile for a not-too-funny remark by the internist, he moves on, waving his cigarette holder like Merlin's wand. What a performance, what *style.*

2. A grasp of dramatic values.   Much of what he does follows faithfully the cinematic or literary concept of what he should be. When he meets with a family while the patient is in the recovery room, he's careful to preserve the sense of high drama. With splendid humility in the face of overwhelming obstacles he intones: "I think we're going to be able to lick this thing," making a gastric resection sound like Custer's

*Reprinted with permission from Medical Economics, ©1977; 54 (Jan 10):200–207, Medical Economics Company, Inc., Oradell, N.J. 07649.

last stand. A relative leaps forward to grasp his hand gratefully, drawing a slight disapproving frown from His Eminence. She quickly withdraws, sensing that her impulsive gesture might have injured the delicate knuckles of those hands—those hands that can do so much.

Switch now to the fathers' room on the maternity floor. The obstetrician has just completed a midforceps delivery roughly equivalent to drawing a camel through the eye of a needle. "You didn't hurt his head, did you, Doctor?" queries the father. Reassured by an exhausted mumble, the father expands with pride and tries to buck up the perspiring midwife with a long story about a cousin whose wife was delivered by a policeman in a taxi.

Outside the nursery, the pediatrician informs the parents that finally the lungs have indeed expanded. "They really are tough little things, aren't they?" observes the father, while the mother adds such searching inquiries as "When will you fill out my baby book?" Grandma opines disapprovingly from the background that too much fuss has been made over something that she could have cured with "chamomile tea and lemon to cut the catarrh."

What sort of person is drawn to a surgical career? I asked one of our local psychiatrists about this. He said that the only rule is that there is no rule. He assured me that each case has to be individualized. He asked that no general conclusion be drawn from his personal observation. Finally, after running out of qualifications, he prepared the following list of prospective surgical candidates:

Rich students trying to maintain status. You can be a society surgeon, but who ever heard of a society pathologist?

Former all-Americans unable to adjust to empty grandstands.

Men who borrowed money from syndicate loan sharks while in training. At 10 per cent interest per month, you have to hit it big but fast.

Husbands of movie starlets. (It wouldn't be good for a rising young actress to be seen at a cocktail party with a proctologist. It wouldn't sound right in the gossip columns.)

Pool hustlers, safecrackers, finger painters, and other dexterous types.

This list shows from what a formidable pool of talent surgeons are drawn. After having considered the various high cards that the surgeon holds, I've decided that he can't be finessed. I think I'll go back, take a surgical residency, and become a swinger myself.

Fourth and Gall*

LEO A. GORDON, M.D., F.A.C.S.

"Good afternoon ladies and gentlemen and welcome to today's Southwestern conference matchup. We've got a dandy for you here. Dr. Floyd McKittrick, whom we've seen so many times before, will be going up against Lou Ronson—a big strapping hulk-of-a-guy with chronic biliary tract disease. We know you're gonna like this one. And doing the play-by-play is my good friend and colleague of so many American Surgical League broadcasts, the ol' Texan himself—Coach Dave Baker—David!"

"Good Morning Keith! And good morning everyone. It's a nippy November morning here in Houston. The room is in perfect condition and the participants are ready. You know, we've seen so many great match-ups on this very field. I believe you and I covered a GI bleeder here many years ago. McKittrick was just a student then, probably all wide-eyed watching the big boys. Now here he is himself—the main event. He is halfway through his eighth season in the American Surgical League. Most observers feel that he's just hitting his professional stride. He's got great hands and he's rugged. His greatest strength, though, is his innovative offense. He's not rigid, he adapts. That's been the key to his success in the league."

"Dave, how about this fellow Ronson?"

"Keith, Lou Ronson is a 52-year-old cost analyzer for an aeronautical research company. He has a long history of right upper-quadrant pain with two ER visits in the last month. Ultrasound shows stones in a contracted gallbladder with no other abnormalities. It's the general consensus of all players involved that cholecystectomy is indicated. He's a big man, 6 feet 2 inches, 195 pounds, and in good shape. He's eager and he's ready."

"How about the field conditions which you mentioned at the top of the broadcast?"

"The field is perfect, Keith. The lights are new. The table has recently been serviced. The floor is a bit slick, but otherwise playable. The suction is in peak condition. Temperature in the high sixties. Perfect biliary weather!"

"Thank you David. We'll be back with the starting line-ups after this commercial message."

Cut to commercial: Promo for "Greatest Surgical Legends" Special.
"Hello again, folks. The ol' Texan Davey Baker will go over the lineups. David!"

"Thank you, my friend! Floyd McKittrick will be working with his long-time first assistant, Dr. Calvin Duffey. They've been working together for years, although they are often viewed as unlikely teammates."

"How so?"

"Well, Keith, as you know, McKittrick is one of these Southwestern boys—good natured, low key, but not afraid to innovate in tight situations. Duffey is a product of that disciplined Northeast conference—very conservative on offense and unusually rigid on defense. Yet, when these two are on—when they really have it going—there is no finer duo in the league."

"How about anesthesia today?"

"Anesthesia controversy has dogged this conference for years. McKittrick has chosen his own for today's match. He's gone over his game plan repeatedly with the special teams and feels that they're ready."

"Thank you Dave. The patient is being induced. The prep is underway. The nursing staff is ready. We'll be back with the skin incision after these messages."

Cut to commercial: Promo for Network Investigative Report on "Medicine and Cognition—Fact and Fancy."
"Hello again everybody. Davey Baker and Keith Mattson bringing you a barnburner here from the rugged Southwestern Conference of the American Surgical League. McKittrick and company are going up against a tough rock-em sock-em bag of stones and we're going to stick with it all the way. Davey!"

"Here we go, ol' buddy. He's starting with a right subcostal."

"Yes. He's done this routinely for years. No reason to change with his record."

*Reprinted with permission from Surgical Rounds, ©1985; 8(11): 80–87.

"Pesky bleeder at the midline."

"Nicely handled with the cautery."

"Okay, he's in. The abdomen is open."

"Now watch McKittrick on routine exploration. Cool, methodical, updating the team at every move."

"Great, no abnormalities on routine exam."

"Remember the unexpected pancreatic head mass last season?"

"Yes indeedy. The boys in programming really caught heat from our viewers when they elected to pull away from the broadcast after the cholangiogram."

"Here we go. He's begun dissection at the porta."

"Let's watch Duffey. He's short, but what strong hands! He can hold that position for a long t . . ."

"Fumbl-l-l-l-l-l-le!"

"The duodenum has slipped up and covered the field. Hold on a moment. Who recovered? It's Duffey. Somehow he replaced his hand on the duodenum. He definitely has possession. The porta is visible again."

"Okay folks. McKittrick has identified the cystic duct. He's looking for the artery. Hold on to your tickets. Wait a minute. Yes, I thought so. Bleeding during cystic duct dissection. This could result in a delay-of-case call."

"Watch Duffey with the suction, Keith. Very few players use it so well. Gentle, not abrasive. There's the vessel. He's quick clipping. Here it is on the replay. Vessel, bleeding freely. Duffey comes down, slight curving motion, he's around it, gently, firmly, clipped . . . stopped. What a player!"

"McKittrick has the cystic artery now. He'll doubly clip it, but not divide it, as is his usual move. He'll go up top."

"If our overhead camera can get a view of the fundus, we'll see him dissect out the gallbladder from the liver bed. But before that, a word from our sponsors."

Cut to commercial: Promo "The Halsted Chronicles."

"Welcome back folks. While we were away, McKittrick began his posterior dissection. What do you think Dave?"

"He's beginning to. . . . Wait a minute Norma Jean! Lookee here!"

"He's passing! Not like him at all to do this at this time in the case. He definitely passed. The nurse is nodding in agreement—it's complete!"

"That was no lollipop pass either, buddy."

"No sireee. That was a straight-down-the-middle-head-on-thank-you-Suzie-meet-me-in-the-lounge-don't-take-no-for-an-answer pass."

"What's his passing percentage?"

"Last season, as the graphic on our screen shows, McKittrick was 48 of 63 from the field for a passing percentage of .762. Not bad for a 41-year-old who's a bit overweight and who has been accused of wearing a rug!"

"Be kind Keith. Don't forget the long bomb he threw earlier this season. New nurse . . . early in the case . . . he passes from way down town. . . . bingo . . . complete!"

"He's made his peritoneal incision. It's as thick as cow hide, buddy. Here he goes. Hold on . . . he's in the liver bed!"

"Not unusual in a match like this. Let's watch him work. Staying on the gallbladder as best he can. He's really in and out of it."

"Very dense inflammation."

"Yes, and you know how the men in the striped shirts can interpret that."

"Oh-oh! There's a lap on the play!"

"Watch McKittrick's face. He knows he must continue without arguing the call at this time. There he goes. The gallbladder is almost free. The vessel he clipped earlier is definitely the cystic artery."

"He's dividing it."

"What was the call?"

"Unnecessary roughness."

"Let's replay that on the monitor. There's the fundus. He dips behind. Well, the inflammation really obscured our angle. Let's just say it was close. Unnecessary roughness is subject to a lot of interpretation. This certainly wasn't the most obvious case."

"McKittrick kept his cool. He's fourth and gall. What do you think he'll call now?"

"No question in my mind."

"Cholangiogram?"

"Cholangiogram."

"Definitely. Cystic duct cholangiogram. The graphic shows McKittrick's record from last season. Thirty cholangiograms out of 39 cases for a cholangiogram rate of .769. Not bad."

"How about the positives?"

"Ten true positives last season."

"A great record."

"Here we go. Now watch Duffey duck out. He ducked out early, seeking the protection of the x-ray barrier. He's shown us just about his only fault as an assistant—leaving the field before the play is finished. That cost him last week."

"Okay. The gram is underway. No. He's hesitating. Oh-oh baby! Another flag."

"No question Keith—delay of case. No x-ray tech."

"Oh, that hurts."

"Here he is. The contrast is in . . . It's good!"

"Let's cut to the films for our viewers. There is the cystic duct entry. There's the distal duct with good emptying. There is the proximal duct. There's the right hepatic. There's . . . oh-oh-oh-oh Mama!"

"What?"

"Big stone in the left hepatic duct!"

"Great. We'll get a chance to see McKittrick shift from a one-one offense to a one-two with resident or nurse during the bile duct exploration."

"A real treat for our viewers—a common bile duct exploration. You're in for a thrill. We'll be back after these messages."

Cut to commercial: Promo for "Catgut Capers."

"Watch this folks, and watch it well. McKittrick routinely performs a Kocher during bile duct exploration."

"He Kochers as well as anyone in the league."

"There he goes. He'll get that distal duct and pancreatic head up lickety-split."

"Watch Duffey."

"Oh Sally-Jean! Duffey is out of bounds. He's over by the cava! O.K., he's recovering nicely."

"You think they'll call it."

"It's close. They'll let it go."

"McKittrick is opening the duct. He'll be using a biliary Fogarty. Here he goes. It's up. It's long enough. It's straight enough. Here it comes. It's GOOD! He's got the stone."

"How about a completion gram, Keith?"

"Floyd McKittrick is a wiley ol' fox of a player. He knows the value of a disciplined completion gram both for filling defects and, equally as important, for precise tube placement."

"O.K. Folks. In case you just joined us, we had a lulu of a hepatic stone extraction. Here's the replay of the stone extraction and completion gram. How about it Davey?"

"Here's the tape Keith. The catheter is up. It looked to me as if it veered to the right initially, but not so. Stone is out. The gram is perfect. Great placement and no other defects."

"Thank you Davey. We're back live. Oh-oh-oh Nellie! Just hold on. The field is really unsteady. McKittrick feared this in a pregame interview."

"It's the anesthesia problem again, Keith. Another flag. He's getting a ten-minute major misconduct for improper abdominal relaxation. This could definitely shift the momentum."

"O-o-o-o he's hot! McKittrick is arguing. Very unusual for him to do this. He prides himself on good communication with the entire team. He's settled down now. The field is stable."

"He's using a round Silastic drain Keith. Any comments?"

"Well, Davey. What can you say about a league that's spent the last 50 years arguing about a piece of rubber?"

"Right you are buddy. He'll use it and use it well."

"Ronson is drained. Let's watch the closure. Oh-oh. Wait a minute. McKittrick is stopping. He's motioning for the room to quiet down. Crowd noise can be a problem late in the match. He's still motioning. There he goes. His assistant can rely on audibles now. Here's the closure. Remember last season when several players were deemed ineligible because of closure problems?"

"I surely do. The famous 'cheap bite' controversy in the Midwest Conference really cut into the credibility of a lot of the players."

"Can't fault McKittrick here—monofilament, running, locking, two layer. Skin clips. Great match."

"He's done. He's leaving the table quietly. Quite a change from last season."

"Yes. The ACS rule against postmatch celebrations within three feet of the playing field has really stopped a lot of the hoopla."

"Remember that anterior resection in the Big Eight we covered two years ago? Who was it, Slauson?"

"That's right. Big Daddy Slauson—had the lesion licked and lost it all on a high-five that contaminated his left glove. What a mistake!"

"This has been a great match. Before we break, let's update our viewers on other action around the league today. Interesting development in the Southeast conference where Don Randall had to forfeit the first two cases of the season on an ineligibility rule. His hospital's review committee called back two cases because of lack of proper credentials."

"A tough call for Randall, but I got to hand it to the league commissioner."

"Drama, controversy, success, failure, we've got it all in the American Surgical League broadcasts. Stay tuned, folks, we'll be back with our postgame interviews and wrap-up after these messages."

Cut to commercial: Promo for the American Surgical League Playoffs.

"Welcome back, folks. We've been covering a real shoot-em-up for you here today. Things have gone well. We have Ahmal Ossard in the recovery area who'll be doing the postmatch interviews for us. Ahmal? Ahmal can you hear us?"

"Keith?"

"Ahmal?"

"Keith?"

"We seem to be having some tech . . ."

"Keith. I'm here in recovery with Lou Ronson who appears to be doing very well after the match. Vital signs are great, good respiratory effort. Clear bile in the bile bag. Lou, how do you feel?"

"Ahmal. I'm . . I . . . Where . . . The nurse. . . ."

"Well, Keith, Lou is a bit excited about the match. Perhaps we should come back to him."

"O.K., buddy. Maybe you could get over for a locker-room interview with McKittrick."

Cut to locker room.

"Floyd, you had problems early in the case. The bleeding around the porta, the poor relaxation, the unexpected hepatic duct stone. You came through. Things went well and the patient is fine. How do you feel?"

"Ahmal, it was tough. I had a great team in there today. We all worked together to get the job done and emerge with a win."

"Your assistant, Cal Duffey. What can you say about him."

"Cal was great. He protected me when he had to. He knew where I was during the entire match. His coverage was excellent, particularly last weekend. His retraction was superb during the exploration of the duct."

"We have that on tape. Watch the monitor. Here he is positioning the duct."

"Yes. He had just the right amount of tension. Real steady. The fumble during the duodenal retraction had me concerned, but after Cal recovered, I knew we would be all right. You know, Ahmal, everyone maligns the assistants, but they are key. Everyone in the league knows they can take a poor player and make him respectable, and take a mediocre player and make him a star."

"How about anesthesia?"

"We've had our problems with anesthesia all season. We shifted the line-up, brought up some rookies early in the year and I know we've been suspect. Dr. Stanton came through today."

"What about the delay-of-case call during the cholangiogram?"

"Look, I know the refs have a tough job. I thought it was unnecessary at that time. It's a judgment call. The x-ray tech was at lunch. You know how those things can happen."

"You looked real down after the unnecessary roughness call during the gall-bladder dissection."

"The patient had a lot of inflammation posteriorly. The gallbladder was partially intrahepatic. The line judge called it, I'm sure, because of the bleeding. You and the viewers realize that after years of inflammation, that plane can be hard to find and bleeding can result. I thought it was overcalling it, myself, particularly at the 150 cc line."

"What now Floyd? Where does Floyd McKittrick go now?"

"Ahmal, we did a great case today. I'll be stopping by recovery to review the orders and talk to Lou Ronson. Then I'll review everything with the family. After that, I'll go to the office to line up the rest of the schedule."

"We look forward to covering your cases in the future."

"Thanks, Ahmal. Can I say one thing?"

"Sure."

"Hi Mom!"

"Back to you Keith and Dave."

"Okay, friends—there you have it. A beautiful cholecystectomy with bile duct exploration and extraction of a left hepatic duct stone. A beautiful match with an early good result. Thanks for being with us. Please remember next week we'll be covering a big pancreatic tail lesion in the tough Western Conference. This is Keith Mattson and the ol' Texan, Davey Baker, saying good-bye for now."

The Abdominal Snowmen*

Anthony Shaw, M.D.

If public relations men had had their way, the first appendectomy would have been a different story.

Unfortunately for them, the citizens of the last century were denied the magnificent press coverage now given to surgical breakthroughs. One hundred years ago, surgeons gained recognition slowly—through the grueling process of publishing articles about their work in scientific journals and presenting the results of their work at medical meetings. If they were lucky, their colleagues eventually recognized their achievements. For example, it took more than a century of contributions by many physicians, often working independently of one another in different countries, before appendicitis was acknowledged as a cause of abdominal distress. One of these physicians was Rudolph Krönlein of Zurich, Switzerland.

How different it would have been for Krönlein (and the rest of us) if modern communications had existed 100 years ago:

April 7, 1886—Radio Bulletin—

We interrupt this program to bring you a special report. CBS-Geneva has just learned that Switzerland's first human appendectomy is being performed at this moment in a Zurich hospital. Authorities at the hospital refuse to divulge the name of the patient, but the surgeon is said to be Dr. Rudolf Krönlein, head of the hospital's new division of abdominal surgery.

April 8, 1886—Zurich Straatszeitung (Reuters)—

At 3:42 P.M. Swiss time, the first human appendectomy in Switzerland was performed at Zurich's Allgemeinische Krankenhaus by Dr. Rudolf Krönlein and a team of six specialists. All that is known so far is that the patient is a 17-year-old female who is presently under the care of a special team of 23 nurses in the hospital's intensive care unit. In an effort to avoid accusations of publicity-seeking, Dr. Krönlein and his associates will not speak to reporters until tomorrow, when a ward in the Krankenhaus will be converted to a pressroom and Dr. Krönlein will hold a nationwide TV conference.

April 9, 1886—Zurich Zentralblatt (UPI)— Appendix Woman Passes Gas.

In the first release since yesterday's surgical breakthrough, spokesmen for Dr. Rudolf Krönlein have announced that Irmagaard Gluck, the 17-year-old woman who underwent Switzerland's first appendectomy, has, in scientific terms, broken wind. According to famed American surgeon Dr. Mondrian Kantor, this is a necessary first step in her recovery. Dr. Kantor, who has performed many appendectomies on dogs and rabbits, has been trying to find a suitable patient for the first American appendectomy. In a confidential report to UPI, Dr. Kantor predicted that in the future many appendectomies will be performed.

April 10, 1886—WCBS-TV (By Telstar)

MC: Welcome to "Face the World." Our guest today was, until two days ago, an obscure doctor known only to his medical colleagues. Today, he is an international celebrity. Ladies and gentlemen, it gives me great pleasure to introduce the Swiss surgeon Rudy Krönlein. Dr. Krönlein, how do you feel?

*Reprinted with permission from MD, ©1986; 30(12):112–117.

K: Humble and proud, of course.

MC: Dr. Krönlein, can you now detail for us the events that led to this medical breakthrough?

K: I think there are many surgeons in the world today who are capable of removing the appendix from a living human being. The world is ready for this operation, and medical progress demands that it be done. We have done many appendix operations on mountain goats here in Switzerland, and when Ms. Gluck came into our laboratory—sorry, I meant hospital—we had our team ready to go.

MC: What was the most thrilling part of it all for you?

K: Toward the end—when I found myself looking into the right lower quadrant of a living human being and saw the big space where the appendix had been.

MC: Have you shown Ms. Gluck her appendix?

K: Of course. Her comments will be published in her autobiography, which she has sold to an American publisher for an undisclosed sum.

MC: Dr. Krönlein, you have been accused of doing this operation as a publicity stunt in order to get your grant renewed. Is it possible that Ms. Gluck did not need to have her appendix removed?

K: Why, my dear boy, our pathologists will tell you that I got it out just in time.

MC: Our reporter at the intensive care unit says that Ms. Gluck has peritonitis and pneumonia, has become jaundiced, and is hemorrhaging.

K: These are things that can happen to any patient and have nothing to do with the success of the appendectomy.

MC: Are you planning to perform any other appendectomies?

K: I have six patients awaiting the operation at the Krankenhaus right now, and, as soon as I finish my world tour, I plan to perform it on them.

May 14, 1886—Zurich Zentralblatt (AP)—Commission Formed.

In the wake of proliferating appendectomies during the past month, a distinguished commission of army officers, clergymen, and lawyers has been appointed to study the deep moral and ethical issues raised by the operation. Expected to testify are Dr. Mondrian Kantor, who only this morning performed an appendectomy on a newborn anencephalic; Dr. Hector Gomez of Venezuela, who favors partial appendectomy; and Sir Osler Worthington, who feels that since the appendix is the seat of the soul it should not be tampered with under any circumstances.

QUAC: A Modest Proposal for Optimal Use of CT Scanning Equipment*

MICHAEL H. REID, M.D.
ARTHUR B. DUBLIN, M.D.

Many articles have addressed the issue of cost containment in medical care, and the high cost of computed tomography (CT) has been used to illustrate this problem.[1-3] The impact of diagnostic-related groups (DRGs), preferred-provider organizations (PPOs), cost-conscious hospital administrations, and increased governmental controls is certain to affect the practice of radiology.[4] We describe a new technique that will enable increased diagnostic examination output in the face of limited resources and funds.

Current estimates suggest 1500–2000 body CT examinations per CT scanner per year as an appropriate patient load, but it is likely that budget limitations and the rising costs of CT facilities will necessitate heavier use. However, it is unlikely that CT efficiency can be increased with current operating techniques. We propose multiple simultaneous patient examinations—quantity uniaxial compositomography (QUAC)—as an alternative.

Technique

Figure 1A illustrates this new multiformat examination technique with four children in prone, supine, and right and left lateral decubitus positions symmetrically placed about the central CT axis. Occasionally, five children and rarely, only three might be accommodated. Figure 1B illustrates two adult patients and figure 1C, the resulting image. Using the format shown in figure 1B, 4000 examinations per year could be performed with a single scanner. In a children's hospital with smaller patients, this figure would be 6000–8000 or even higher. For neuroradiologic studies, the number of examinations possible with the QUAC technique rises precipitously, particularly in practices restricted to patients with small heads.

Manufacturers should be encouraged to develop CT scanners with large padded apertures with low-friction Teflon coating for ease in patient positioning. Water-soluble sonographic jelly could be used as a nonstaining aperture lubricant to aid in patient packing by hydraulic ram, if necessary. Small wiggling children might require a multinippled pacifier suspended in the gantry to reduce anxiety and motion artifacts.

Discussion

Anticipated savings in the cost of medical care are significant. Special "batch" rates could be offered to groups of patients with the same disease and/or same insurance carrier. For areas with certificate-of-need limitations on CT scanner purchases, this method provides an obvious solution. Multiinstitutional sharing of a CT scanning facility with the various patient slots (positions) assigned to different hospitals (e.g., hospital A patients at 3 o'clock position, hospital B patients at 9 o'clock position) is another possibility.

Among the advantages of the QUAC technique, air-tissue artifacts due to incomplete filling of the gantry aperture will be eliminated. Ideally, studies should be restricted to all male or female subjects, radially oriented with anterior surfaces outward, for patients' comfort and privacy. In view of the cost savings and other benefits, it is unlikely that patients will complain of used x-ray photons. Multiple simultaneous patient examinations recorded on the same film will provide some normal anatomic control, thus making abnormalities more apparent. Some examinations may be

*Reprinted from the American Journal of Roentgenology, ©1984; 142(4):845–846, with permission from Williams & Wilkins, Baltimore.

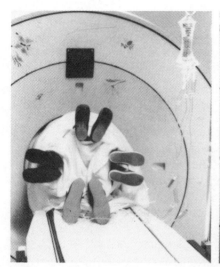 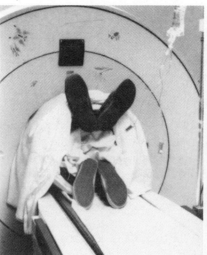 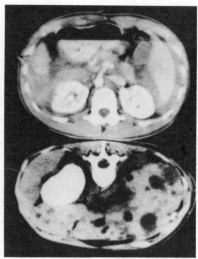

Figure 1. QUAC technique. A, *Four pediatric patients positioned in CT gantry aperture.* B, *Two adult patients positioned for simultaneous examination and* (C) *resulting image* (bottom, *liver cysts;* top, *ruptured spleen [unrelated to patient positioning within gantry]*).

difficult to combine, for example, pelvic CT with cranial CT. Otherwise, QUAC has much to offer the future practice of diagnostic radiology.

References

1. Evens RG, Jost RG. Computed tomography utilization and charges in 1981. Radiology 1982; 145:427–429.

2. Schoppe WD, Hessel SJ, Adams DF. Time requirements in performing body CT studies. J Comput Assist Tomogr 1981; 5:513–515.

3. Hughes GMK. National survey of computed tomography unit capacity. Radiology 1980; 135:699–703.

4. American College of Radiology. TEFRA and DRG's: section 108 revisited. ACR Bull 1983; Sep 7.

QUAC Proposal*

In perusing the April 1984 issue of *AJR*, I was chagrined to see that our more aggressive West Coast friends[1] once again have "scooped" their more conservative East Coast colleagues, who are still collecting cases. We agree that packing children in groups of four with their heels together and toes pointing outward (as shown in the authors' fig. 1A) is the only sensible way to perform computed tomographic (CT) scanning in a pediatric practice.

However, I do not think that figures 1B and 1C illustrate the optimal scanning position for adults. We have found that in selected cases, it is preferable to place one patient prone and the other supine, with the toes of each patient toward the toes of the other. This makes the examination considerably more enjoyable for the patients and can even lead to lasting relationships. I am surprised that the California-based authors did not think of this possibility.

It is reassuring to see that *AJR* is devoting some much-needed time and effort to improving the efficiency of medical care and lowering its cost.

Robert H. Freiberger
Hospital for Special Surgery

New York, NY

Reference

1. Reid MH, Dublin AB, QUAC: a modest proposal for optimal use of CT scanning equipment. AJR 1984; 142:845–846.

Reply

The Pauli exclusion principle prevents two electrons of a pair from facing in the same direction (i.e., spins must be opposite); the Reid-Dublin exclusion principle prevents two persons in a magnetic resonance scanner or computed tomographic scanner from facing in the same direction— except perhaps in San Francisco.

Michael H. Reid
University of California, Davis School of Medicine
Sacramento, CA

*Reprinted from the American Journal of Roentgenology, ©1984; 143(8):433, with permission from Williams & Wilkins, Baltimore.

Postmortem Medicine—
An Essential New New Subspecialty*

BERRILL YUSHOMERSKI YANKELOWITZ, M.D.

With increasing technical knowledge, medical care has necessarily become more and more subspecialised.[1-14] Both the local community and the government have tried to approach the problem of delivering this care to as broad a segment of the population as possible. Especially notable are the heavily funded programmes in geriatrics research, as all segments of society have come to recognise the increasing proportion of old people in the population. The time has now come for us to focus on the medically most underserved population in the world today—the deceased. The urgency of this is quite apparent. There are more people who have already died than are alive today, and their number is increasing at an alarming rate. Physicians have not focused on the problems of the dead. Aside from anatomy, it is not a subject taught in most medical schools; as a result, early sensitivity of the medical student to the needs of the dead is never formally developed. Postmortem medicine is not a mere extension or subspecialty of geriatric medicine, but a major specific and unique problem in health-care delivery. We have therefore undertaken a pilot project to determine how the medical profession might better serve the dead patient, and this is the subject of the present paper.

The University of East Dakota Medical Center's pilot project on postmortem medicine is a broad-based multidisciplinary undergraduate and postgraduate study programme designed to investigate all aspects of diagnosis and care for the dead patient. Early in their training our medical students are given a one-semester course in psychosocial problems of the deceased human. In addition to didactic sessions, students are taken on field trips to cemeteries and funeral parlours, because we feel that classroom sessions alone depersonalise the dead patient in the student's mind. The members of our psychiatric faculty have responded enthusiastically and like this subject because they get to do most of the talking during patient interviews. Psychoanalysts are especially happy because of the long, meaningful silences they get when treating a dead patient. In the second year of medical school we provide courses in pharmacology and physiology in the dead patient. We have found that the pharmacokinetics of drugs in the formalinised patients are quite different from those in the living. So far we provide only one clinical clerkship in cemetery medicine, but plan to offer a series of electives for interested students in funeral parlour physiology.

At this postgraduate level we have a pilot postmortem ward (separate from the morgue), which is staffed by two fellows who are supported by a National Institutes of Health (NIH) career development grant. The fellows are supervised by a senior attending physician, who is himself dead and therefore has an in-depth understanding of the specialty. The ward promotes active house-staff and nursing education and is a model for future programmes of similar type in the community. House staff who have just been on a ward with live patients have responded enthusiastically to the leisurely pace of the postmortem ward.

Research projects are going on, and we are fortunate to have received extensive Federal and local grant support for such studies as postmortem wound healing, the impact of embalming on social acceptability of the dead, management of the person who died before penicillin was available, and so on.

A series of new subspecialties is already appearing—postmortem endocrinology, postmortem podiatry, and postmortem neurosurgery to name a few. Some of our staff have developed a special interest in the long-dead patient, and we are considering a subsubspecialty of neanderthalogy.

In co-operation with the NIH and Rand Corporation, we have developed an extensive computerised programme of health-care services, delivery evaluation,

*Reprinted with permission from the British Medical Journal, ©1979; 2(Dec 22–29):1639–1640.

assessment of the dead patient with peer review panels, and HMO (Heaven's Medical Offices). Our social-professional interface is progressing nicely. We already have a board certifying examination, and memberships are now open for our National College of Postmortem Medicine. The women's auxiliary of the American Dead Society has actively supported our many community efforts.

We have made substantial inroads in a neglected area and it is our hope that other universities will benefit from the billions that our government now wants to spend in this exciting new subspecialty.

References

1. Parlov SM: Death as a Subspecialty. Sem Death 1979; 1:6.

2. Parlov SM, Puttersberg RK: The Mandate for Internists to Broaden Their Care for the Dead. Sem Death 1979; 1:100.

3. Puttersberg RK: Referral Patterns in Postmortem Medicine. Sem Death 1979; 1:120.

4. Puttersberg RK, Parlov SM: Health Care Delivery to the Dead. Rand J Financial Medicine 1972; 82:184.

5. Parlov SM, Yankelowitz BY: Management of the Dead Patient Embalmed Prior to 1842. Publications Unanimous 1648; 2:15.

6. Yankelowitz BY: Outcome Assessment and Proven Evaluation in Postmortem Care Delivery. Rand J Grant Med 1987; 8:43.

7. Yankelowitz BY: A Randomised Double-Blind Trial of Formaldehyde versus Placebo in Third Party Olfactory Detection of the Dead Patient. J Clin Invest Death 1979; 49:862.

8. Yankelowitz BY: A Longitudinal Study of 357 Dead Patients. Ethiop J Anat 1257 AD; 27:4.

9. Puttersberg RK. The Role of the Physician's Assistant in Caring for the Deceased—Letter. Ann Int Death Med 2027 AD; 53:60.

10. Parlov SM: Federal Regulation of Rehabilitation of the Patient Embalmed with Multiple Chemical Agents. Univ E Dak Newsletter 1979; (July 5):1.

Risks of
Curb-side Consults*

To the Editor: Near dusk on a recent afternoon, I had just returned from a four-mile jog. One of my neighbors, a state trooper, was walking by with his medium-sized poodle on a leash. He beckoned me to the curb, "Hey, Doc, will you take a look at this?" He pointed to a small lesion on his nose. I walked over to him and leaned over with my steaming glasses in the fading sun to offer an opinion. I felt a sudden, piercing pain in my medial right thigh. The poodle had bitten through my sweat pants and punctured my leg in five places.

The lesson here is to be wary of giving advice at the curb side. Beside giving the wrong advice, you may get into more trouble than you bargained for, especially at dusk, with a state trooper and his poodle.

William W. Stocker, M.D.

Hyannis, MA

*Reprinted with permission from The New England Journal of Medicine, ©1980; 302(19):1094.

Additional Readings

1. Barrett DS: Are orthopaedic surgeons gorillas? Br Med J 1988; 297(Dec 24–31):1638–1639.

Extrapolating from the fact that hand size correlates with body size, this study shows that orthopedic surgeons are only slightly bigger than their colleagues in general surgery. The author concludes that "The image of the orthopaedic surgeon as a man of massive bulk and strength with a low hairline who communicates with his colleagues in a series of grunts while proceeding along the hospital corridor in a succession of ape like bounds is unfair."

2. Bornemeier WC: Sphincter protecting hemorrhoidectomy. Amer J Proctol 1960; 11(1):48–52.

This is a serious article with an amusing introduction: "It (the sphincter ani) is like the goalie in hockey—always alert . . . It apparently can tell whether its owner is alone or with someone, whether standing up or sitting down, whether its owner has his pants on or off . . . a muscle like that is worth protecting."

3. Burton JL: Skins are simpler than you think. Bristol Med Chir J 1986; 101(1):15.

This article distills the practice of dermatology into a few easy to remember rules.

4. Dias JJ, Brenkel IJ, et al: Orthopaedic surgery: a health hazard. Br Med J 1988; 297(Dec 24–31):1637–1638.

The authors use a light touch to describe some of the dangers orthopedic surgeons face—both in and out of the operating room.

5. Gottschalk W: Dystocia on Mount Olympus. Obstet Gynecol 1959; 13(3):381–382.

The author presents the obstetric histories of the Olympian Gods. For example, "Athene, goddess of war, was delivered fully armed from her father's brow. . . The obstetrician in charge, far from being a physician (which

is probably just as well) was Hephaestus, god of fire." It's enough to make modern obstetricians quake in their booties.

6. Pry P: Surgery in the future. Boston Med & Surg J 1892; 127(16):395.

After observing that his cures by abdominal section had to be reopened at frequent intervals, a 19th century surgeon devised a technique whereby he could reinspect a patient's internal organs without the bother of parietal section: He simply closed the original incision with buttons and buttonholes. What is most interesting about this parody is that it anticipated by 90 years, the first implantation of a zipper into someone's abdominal wall (Leguit P: Zipper closure of the abdomen. Neth J Surg 1982; 34:40).

7. Reid MH, Dublin AB: Simultaneous anthropomorphic projections. AJR 1985; 144(4):861–862.

How to reduce radiology costs by overlapping body parts and x-raying them at the same time.

8. Rose I: Counterfellowshipmanship. Can Med Assoc J 1964; 90(Jun 20):1410–1413.

This article is a follow-up to Dr. Rose's satire, "Fellowshipmanship." Although this one isn't as funny as the original, it has some good lines for those of us who spend our time submitting consults rather than filling them out. The article was published under the auspices of "The National Society for the Prevention of Cruelty to General Practitioners."

9. Ryall RL, Marshall VR: Point of view: laws of urodynamics. Urology 1982; 20(1):106–107.

The authors bemoan all of the complicated formulas and biophysical jargon required to understand the idiosyncrasies of the urinary system. They present their own 7 laws of urodynamics. For example, "The patient with the best flow has the poorest aim."

MENTAL HEALTH
HUMOR

Psychotherapy, like the rest of medicine, is serious business. It also has its own brand of inconsistencies and absurdities that make it a good target for one's sense of humor. Unfortunately, mental health journals have not opened their pages to much wit and humor. As a result, most of the barbs hurled in this direction have come from the entertainment industry which provides a rather two dimensional and stereotyped view of the field. The following articles provide a much needed dose of humor from the professional's point of view, and I am grateful to two individuals for their existence: Robert Hoffman, M.D., without whom this chapter would be much smaller than it already is, and Glenn Ellenbogen, Ph.D., who saw the need for more mental health humor and, in 1984, created *The Journal of Polymorphous Perversity* (See Appendix).

The Varieties of Psychotherapeutic Experience*

ROBERT S. HOFFMAN, M.D.

1. Freudian

P: I could use a ham on rye, hold the mustard.

T: It's evident that a quantity of libidinal striving has been displaced to a regressive object with relative fixation on the anal-sadistic mode.

P: What do you suggest?

T: Perhaps a valve job and tune-up.

2. Rogerian

P: Shit! Do I feel shitty!

T: Sounds like you feel shitty.

P: Why are you parroting me?

T: You seem concerned about my parroting you.

P: What the hell is going on here?

T: You sound confused.

3. Existential

P: Sorry I'm late today.

T: Can you get more in touch with that sorrow?

P: I hope it didn't inconvenience you.

T: Let's focus on your capacity for choice rather than on my expectations.

P: But I didn't mean to be late.

T: I hear you, and I don't put it down. But where we need to be is the immanence of the I-Thou relationship (in Buber's sense) emanating from the here-and-now, and from there into a consciousness of the tension between be-ing and non-be-ing, and eventually into the transcendence of be-ing itself, through to a cosmic awareness of the oceanic I-dentity of Self and the space-time continuum.

P: Gotcha.

4. Behavioral

P: I feel depressed.

T: Okay. First, I want you to look at this list of depressing phrases, order them by ascending depression-potential and match them with these postcards. Then I want you to step over to these electrodes—don't worry—and put your head in this vise and your left foot in this clamp. Then, when I count to ten, I want you to . . .

5. Gestalt

P: I feel somehow that life just isn't worth living.

T: Don't give me that shit!

P: What do you mean? I'm really concerned that . . .

T: Real hell! You're trying to mind-screw me. Come off it.

P: You shmuck—what are you trying to do with me?

T: Attaboy! Play me—play the shmuck. I'll play you.

P: What's going on?

T: Not shmucky enough—try again, louder.

P: I've never met a therapist like this.

T: No good—you gotta stay in the here-and-now. Again.

P: (gets up to leave)

T: Okay, now we're getting somewhere. Stand up on that table and do it again.

P: (exits)

T: Good. Now I'll play the angry patient and walk out the door. "You shmuck—I'm leaving."

*Reprinted from the Journal of Irreproducible Results, ©1973; 19(4):76–77, with permission from Blackwell Scientific Publications. Edited from the original.

6. Confrontation

P: Hello.
T: Pretty anxious about the amenities, eh?
P: Not very.
T: Don't try to wiggle out of it.
P: I'm not. I just . . .
T: Trying to deny it?
P: Okay, you're right.
T: Don't agree just for agreement's sake.
P: As a matter of fact, I don't agree . . .
T: Sounds a bit hostile.
P: Have it your way. I'm hostile.
T: That's pretty dependent, that statement.
P: Okay, I'm EVERYTHING.
T: God, what modesty!

7. Primal

P: Can you help me stop cracking my knuckles, Doctor?
T: Okay. You're three years old—you're hungry—REALLY hungry—you want to suckle—you reach for your mother's bosom—what happens?—she pulls away—SHE PULLS AWAY!—SHE ISN'T GOING TO LET YOU HAVE IT—FEEL THAT!—WHAT DO YOU FEEL??—WHAT DO YOU WANT???—Get down on that mat there or you'll hurt yourself—YOU *WANT*, YOU REALLY WANT THAT MILK!—YOU WANT YOUR MOMMY!—YOU AREN'T GOING TO GET YOUR MONEY, I MEAN MOMMY!!—CRY OUT TO HER!—TELL HER YOU WANT HER!—CRY, YOU SONOFABITCH!!!!
P: But I'm allergic to milk products.

Developing Insight in Intensive-Extensive Psychodynamic Psychotherapy: A Case Study*

DON YUTZLER, Ph.D.

Although a voluminous, if not tedious, literature exists on the theoretical construct of insight and its conceptual and dynamic underpinnings, as well as its cognitive and affective precursors and concomitants, little in the way of hard clinical data, drawn from actual real-life therapy cases, has been cited as a means of illustrating the dynamics of insight and "the working through process." The author presents, here, an annotated transcript of therapy sessions with one of his more successful therapy patients in order to vividly illustrate the development of therapeutic insight.

This is the case of a 34 year old Caucasian male, who sought psychodynamic psychotherapy in order to gain insight into why he had left his ex-wife several years earlier. After a great deal of self-exploration, as well as another marriage and two children, the patient now wanted to embark on a formal journey of self-understanding.

The treatment began with 8 sessions of therapy, during which rapport and a strong "working alliance" were established. The following crucial interchange occurs in the 9th session:

THERAPIST: "So, tell me about your ex-wife."
PATIENT: "She was a short woman."

As is evident, this purely descriptive reply reflects no true insight. Note also the therapist's technique which, although highly directive, remains remarkably free of any countertransferential cathexes.

By the 14th visit, the therapist assessed that the patient was ready to tolerate more intensive, affectively charged material and so begins to probe more daringly:

THERAPIST: "So, tell me about your ex-wife."
PATIENT: "As I told you, she was a short woman."

*Copyright 1986, Wry-Bred Press, Inc. Reprinted by permission of the copyright holder from the Journal of Polymorphous Perversity 1986; 3(1)14–15.

THERAPIST: "Um-hmm. Tell me more."
PATIENT: "Well, she weighed about 180 pounds."

In this lively interchange, we immediately note the gains in self-understanding. Although to the naive observer this patient seems rather superficial, the therapist begins to speculate that perhaps the patient is only superficial on the surface.

Again, to the casual listener, the juxtaposition of these descriptive concepts could immediately bring to mind an interpretative intervention; i.e., the woman was obese. But this patient clearly is not yet ready to draw such a conclusion himself and it would be a serious error if the therapist were to precipitously and wantonly blurt out such an anatomical observation. A premature insight could be extremely detrimental to the course of therapy, perhaps shortening it a great deal, perhaps even rendering any further sessions altogether unnecessary. Wisely, the therapist waits.

The next stage of therapy is focused on strengthening the patient's defenses to prepare him to handle the truth. Although the therapist thinks the patient is ready, he has erred, as the following dialogue in the 26th meeting reveals:

THERAPIST: "12 sessions ago, you described your ex-wife as a short woman weighing 180 pounds. Have you given any further thought to these two ideas?"
PATIENT: "No."
THERAPIST: "Why not?"
PATIENT: "I don't know."
THERAPIST: "Would you like to know?"
PATIENT: "I don't know. Do you think it's important?"
THERAPIST: "Important? I didn't say it was important. Do you think it is?"
PATIENT: "I asked you first."

Here, it is evident that the therapist has pushed too hard, and the patient is decompensating. The patient shows this by missing the next 2 appointments, thus requiring 4 more to explore resistance and billing issues.

A breakthrough occurs in the 33rd session when the patient refers to his ex-wife as a "tubster." The therapist, unfamiliar with this slang expression, asks for clarification:

THERAPIST: "What?"
PATIENT: "Tubster."
THERAPIST: "No, I mean what do you mean?"
PATIENT: "She was fat."

Here, the patient is obviously in touch with deeper levels of emotion, for he could have chosen a less pejorative term, e.g. "pleasingly plump," "rotund," or "the wide ride." In "fat," we have hit a nerve. But it was still too early to press for further insight. What remained, of course, was a fuller understanding of the many rolls of the ex-wife's fat in their marriage and its demise.

Finally, in the 40th session, the patient arrives at a marvelous insight:

THERAPIST: "So, why did you leave your wife?"
PATIENT: "I just couldn't stand that short, stupid, fat woman any longer!"

So this was it. He had left her because she lacked height and depth, while being overly wide. Notice the exclamation point at the end of the patient's statement, clearly signifying his angry yet liberated tone. Here, we have full simultaneous cognitive and affective insight.

The author is pleased to report that the treatment was successfully concluded in only 12 more sessions, as termination issues were worked through to satisfy the therapist's needs for closure and further income to cover malpractice insurance.

A Proof of the Beneficial Effects of Psychotherapy, with an Evaluation of Two Competing Models*

JOHN ELLARD, A.M., FRACP, FRCPSYCH, FRANZCP

There have been many attempts to estimate the effects of psychotherapy and to demonstrate that it is a useful form of treatment.[1-3] Some of the obstacles which stand in the way of achieving valid results are the difficulty in defining the psychotherapeutic processes involved, the measures of outcome to be used and the attributes of those thought to be qualified as therapists.

In recent years a number of reports have drawn attention to a psychotherapeutic process which not only benefits the patient's state of mind, but also prolongs his or her life. The evidence is unequivocal, and these studies suggest that it is time for further research to take place. I refer to the beneficial effects of pet animals in old persons' homes and institutions generally.[4,5] The secondary issue is that until now studies of psychotherapy have been concerned either with humans or computers[6] as therapists; none has evaluated the result of therapy by members of other species. It is true that there is a report of monkeys as therapists,[7] but they were treating other monkeys, so it may be argued that the results obtained there do not apply to the therapy of human beings.

The purpose of the study reported here is two-fold:

1. To evaluate the effects of psychotherapy when the therapist is an animal other than *Homo sapiens*.

2. To compare the results achieved by two different psychotherapeutic techniques.

The first type of therapy is predominantly verbal, the therapist responding to the patient's communications with certain predetermined phrases, but nevertheless maintaining a neutral affective response to the patient's behaviour.

The second type of therapy is non-verbal, comprising essentially non-possessively warm responses to the patient's behaviour. The warmth is not endless and uncritical; should the patient behave negatively (for example, by kicking the therapist) then the therapist's affective response would be of a kind to discourage repetition of such behaviour.

The Population

On the basis that psychotherapy is good for everyone, the patients were recruited from those seeking employment at the Commonwealth Employment Service agency nearest to the clinic. This was necessary because the available undergraduates have obtained a Supreme Court injunction which stated that they could not be compelled to be the subject of experiments in order to pass their examinations.

Each patient was paid $15 for each completed day of involvement in the study. Payment was by cheque.

Ethical Considerations

Informed Consent

The patients were told that they would be paid to receive therapy which would certainly enrich their lives and make them live longer. Their personal attractiveness would increase dramatically, as would their capacity for experiencing sexual pleasure. It would be possible for the short in stature to gain as much as 2 cm in height. There were no known adverse effects of the projected treatment.

Thus informed, each patient signed the consent form.

Approval

The author thought it best to conduct the study in the long vacation so as not to add to the workload of the Ethics Committee. However, he has evidence which will establish that one member of the Committee is moonlighting in the armaments industry, another is

*Reprinted with permission of the Australian and New Zealand Journal of Psychiatry, ©1988; 22(2):210-214.

being dried out in a private clinic under an assumed name, and that the third, widely believed to be studying elsewhere, is holidaying with his secretary. It is not anticipated that the Ethics Committee will offer public criticism of the project.

The Therapy

Verbal Therapy

The therapists were adult members of the species *Eolophus roseicapilla*, a pink and grey Australian cockatoo, commonly known as the galah. Each was trained to repeat the following six phrases.

- "Tell me some more about that."
- "It must've been a difficult time for you."
- "Do you remember feeling like that when you were a child?"
- "You look sad, just now."
- "I guess people come and go all our lives."
- "It's important to be able to cry when you feel like it."

The patients lay on a couch, their feet pointing to the north, with the therapist on a perch 1.5 m high, and 1 m to the west of the patient's feet. The distances were measured using a laser theodolite.

Each of the ten therapeutic sessions lasted twenty minutes, during which time the therapists uttered the therapeutic phrases randomly. The patients understood that if they did not listen attentively to the therapists' observations they would not be paid. The therapists maintained their affective distance by not changing their facial expressions, by becoming preoccupied with eating and drinking from time to time, and occasionally by defaecating on the floor, while looking as if nothing had happened.

If was recognized that the therapists' neutral stance made them powerful transference figures, but analysis of this reaction was outside the present study.

Non-verbal Therapy

The therapists were Labrador retrievers, carefully selected from the author's collection of some three and a half thousand Labradors. During the study the author suddenly remembered that as a small boy he had been in love with a little girl who resembled a Labrador, but subsequent to this realisation his interest in Labradors did not depart. This is worth recording, for when Descartes realised that his adult fascination for women with squints was due to a similar experience with a little girl who squinted, he lost that proclivity.

This part of the project drew heavily upon Bartz and Volger's magisterial study[8] on the use of hounds as therapists, for it was their realisation that hounds have "natural abilities of unconditional positive regard, warmth, compassion and the ability to openly express emotions" that inspired the present author in his development of the second part of this survey.

Bartz and Volger's reported experiences were very useful in devising the details of therapy. It may be observed that Labradors are very large dogs, with very short hair. This gives them an appearance of nakedness, introducing a variable into the study which is difficult to control. Anecdotes from patients who had encountered naked human therapists persuaded the author that this was a situation to be avoided.

Accordingly each Labrador was neatly dressed in a plain white T-shirt and jeans, the latter specially constructed so that their tails could protrude. This procedure removed some of the problems reported by Bartz and Volger; for example, the therapists were less inclined to urinate on the floor or to attempt to have intercourse with the patients' legs. They were also prevented from licking their genitals while in a reflective mood. As a measure of the success of this procedure, patients who had extensive experience of therapy from human therapists reported that the human therapists were more inclined to do these things than were the Labradors in this study.

In therapy, the Labrador sat on a chair in the same spatial relationship to the patient as that which had been occupied by the verbal therapists. They expressed their feelings for the patient by wagging their tails, by putting their heads to one side and looking wistful, and by whining and shifting about. Occasionally they jumped down and licked the patients' faces impulsively, and sometimes they offered to shake hands.

Measures of Outcome

Before the patients entered therapy they completed a number of measures (Table). A prorated IQ was obtained by asking the first ten words of the vocabulary test of the WAIS. They were also asked their favourite colour, and to think of a number.

The same measures were completed on the day after the last psychotherapeutic session, so permitting

Table. Measures completed by patients prior to therapy

The Minnesota Multiphasic Personality Inventory (MMPI)
Inglis' Paired Association Learning Scale (IPALT)
The Hospital Anxiety and Depression Scale

The Hamilton Depression Rating Scale

The Zung Self-Rating Depression Rating Scale
The Comprehensive Psychopathological Rating Scale (CPRS)
The Mill Hill Vocabulary Test
The Spectrum of Suicidal Behaviour Scale
The General Health Questionnaire (Conventional and Revised)
The General Psychopathology (recent and past) Scale
Michigan Alcohol Screening Test (MAST)
The Continuous Performance Test (CPTC and CPTO)
A Child's Concept of Death Scale

The Millon Clinical Multiaxial Inventory (MCMI)
The Bentler Medical Psychological Functioning Inventory
The Parental Bonding Instrument (PBI)
The Draw-a-Person Test
The Occupational Attitude Survey and Interest Schedule (OASIS)
The Miller-Yoder Language Comprehension Test (MY)
The Computer Attitude, Literacy and Interest Profile (CALIP)

The Abbreviated Mental Test Scale (AMTS)

The Edinburgh Postnatal Depression Scale
The Anxiety and Depression Scale of Bedford and Foulds
The Montgomery and Asberg Depression Rating Scale (MADRS)
Folstein and Luria's Depression Scale
The Visual Analogue Mood Scale (VAMS)

The SET Test
The Spectrum of Assaultive Behaviour Scale
The Precipitating Events Scale

Draw a Slow Line Test (DALS)
The Personal Feelings Scale
The Ego-Defence Scale
Andreason's Scale for the Assessment of Thought, Language & Communication
The Personality Diagnostic Questionnaire
The Delusions–Symptoms–States Inventory (DSSI)

The Life-Event Inventory of Tennant and Andrews
The Seashore Test of Musical Ability
The Uzgiris and Hunt Scale of Infant Psychological Development (UHSIPD)
The Diagnostic Test of Arithmetic Strategies (DTAS)

---

the benefits of therapy to become fully established before they were assessed. Those patients whose attention seemed to be flagging were reminded that they would not be paid until all protocols were completed.

Statistical Analysis

The large array of data collected was entered into a series of multiplexed Cray computers. It was felt that this would discourage replication. After the usual Bayesian transformation they were confined within a region R enclosed by S, d being a volume element of R. The divergence theorem of Gauss states that under these conditions the following formula is true.

$$\iint_{S} f \cdot \delta\sigma = \iiint_{R} (V \cdot f) \, \delta\tau$$

The Vector V x v (that is, the curl of v) was calculated according to the formula:

$$V \times v = \begin{vmatrix} i & j & k \\ \dfrac{\partial}{\partial x} & \dfrac{\partial}{\partial y} & \dfrac{\partial}{\partial z} \\ v_1 & v_2 & v_3 \end{vmatrix}$$

$$= \left(\frac{\partial v3}{\partial y} - \frac{\partial v2}{\partial z} \right) i + \left(\frac{\partial v1}{\partial z} - \frac{\partial v3}{\partial x} \right) j + \left(\frac{\partial v2}{\partial x} - \frac{\partial v1}{\partial y} \right) k$$

It is recognised that under these conditions the curl is a pseudo-vector. The pseudo-vectors so obtained were rotated several times in a virtual barrel, and the factors which emerged and appealed to the author were retained. The final results were recorded after an adjustment using Cnut's Arbitrary Correction Coefficient (CACC). This correction disposes of the inaccuracy imported into most research by conducting it as if the universe were four-dimensional, whereas it is eleven-dimensional.[9] It can be very useful.

It had been intended to use a two-tailed Student's test, but no suitable student was available. Unfortunately the study was performed before the author had read Seigert *et al*'s paper[10] which distinguished between the GHQ30 and the GHQ30, and Boyle's paper[11] on the conjoint dR-factoring of the 8 SQ/DES-IV multivariate mood-state scales.

Result

Non-verbal affectively laden therapy was shown to be superior to verbal therapy provided by affectively neutral therapists.

The final score was: dogs 198 (31 goals, 12 behinds), cockatoos 101 (14 goals, 17 behinds).

Discussion

There is little to discuss. Whoever thought that a man's best friend was his cockatoo? The economic consequences of this study are important. The time spent in training the Labrador therapists (approximately seven hours) is significantly shorter than that required to become a Fellow of the Royal Australian and New Zealand College of Psychiatrists, or a fully accredited psychoanalyst. The author is seeking an item number for this form of therapy from Medicare.

References

1. Frank JD. Therapeutic components of psychotherapy: a 25-year progress report of research. Journal of Nervous and Mental Disease 1974; 159:325–342.

2. Rachman SJ, Wilson GT. The effects of psychological therapy. 2nd ed. Oxford: Pergamon Press 1980.

3. Bloch S, Bond G, Qualls B, Yalom I, Zimmerman E. Outcome in psychotherapy evaluated by independent judges. British Journal of Psychiatry 1977; 131:410–414.

4. Rynearson EK. Humans and pets and attachment. British Journal of Psychiatry 1978; 133:550–555.

5. Friedmann E, Katcher AH, Thomas SA, Lynch JJ, Messent PR. Social interaction and blood pressure. Influence of animal companions. Journal of Nervous Mental Diseases 1983; 171: 461–465.

6. Carr AG, Ghosh A. Response of phobic patients to direct computer assessment. British Journal of Psychiatry 1983; 142: 60–65.

7. Suomi SJ, Harlow HF. Social rehabilitation of isolate-reared monkeys. Developmental Psychology 1972; 6:487.

8. Bartz WR, Vogler RE. A proposal for eliminating the chronic shortage of mental health service providers: hounds as humanists. In: Ellenbogen GC, ed. Oral sadism and the vegetarian personality. New York: Brunner/Mazel, Inc. 1987:28–35.

9. Freedman DZ, van Nieuwenhuizen P. The hidden dimensions of spacetime. Scientific American 1985; 252:62–69.

10. Seigert RJ, McCormick IA, Taylor AJW, Walkey FH. An examination of reported factor structures of the General Health Questionnaire and the identification of a stable replicable structure. Australian Journal of Psychology 1987; 39:89–100.

11. Boyle GJ. A conjoint dR-factoring of the 8 SQ/DES-IV multivariate mood-state scales. Australian Journal of Psychology 1987; 39:79–87.

The Itemized Statement in Clinical Psychiatry

A new Concept in Billing*

ROBERT S. HOFFMAN, M.D.

Due to the rapidly escalating costs of health care delivery, there has been increasing pressure on physicians to document and justify their charges for professional services. This has created a number of serious problems, particularly in the field of psychiatry. Chief among these is the breach of confidentiality that arises when sensitive clinical information is provided to third-party insurance carriers, e.g. the patient's diagnosis or related details about his/her psychiatric disorder. Even when full disclosure of such information is made, insurance carriers frequently deny benefits because the description of the treatment appears imprecise or inadequate. There also has been some criticism of the standard hourly fee-for-service, the argument being that psychiatrists, like other medical specialists, should be required to adjust their fees depending upon the particular treatment offered.

In view of these considerations, a method is required which will bring psychiatric billing in line with accepted medical practice. The procedure illustrated below, which we have successfully employed in our clinic for the past two years, achieves this goal. It requires only a modest investment in time and effort: the tape-recording of all psychotherapy sessions, transcription of tapes, tabulation of therapeutic interventions, and establishment of a relative value scale for the commonly used maneuvers. This can easily be managed by two full-time medical billing personnel per psychiatrist. The method, in our hands, has been found to increase collections from third-party carriers by 65%

and to raise a typical psychiatrist's annual net income almost to the level of a municipal street sweeper or plumber's assistant.

Below is a specimen monthly statement illustrating these principles:

CALVIN L. SKOLNIK, M.D., Inc.
A Psychiatry Corporation

Jan. 5, 1978

Mr. Sheldon Rosenberg
492 West Maple Dr.
East Orange, N.J.

Dear Mr. Rosenberg:

In response to the request by your insurer, Great Lake Casualty and Surety Co., for more precise documentation of professional services rendered, I have prepared the enclosed itemization for the month of December. I trust that this will clarify the situation sufficiently for your benefit payments to be resumed.

Until next Tuesday at 11:00, I remain

Cordially,

Calvin L. Skolnik, M.D.

---

*Reprinted from the Journal of Irreproducible Results, ©1980; 26(3):7–8, with permission from Blackwell Scientific Publications.

Itemized Charges	No.	Charges ($)	
clarifications	140 @	.25	35.00
restatements	157 @	.25	39.25
broad-focus questions	17 @	.35	5.95
narrow-focus questions	42 @	.30	12.60
reflections of dominant emotional theme	86 @	.30	30.10
resolutions of inconsistencies	38 @	.35	17.10
pointings out of nonverbal communications	22 @	.40	8.80
encouragements to say more	187 @	.15	28.05
sympathetic nods with furrowed brow	371 @	.10	37.10
acknowledgments of information reception (Uh-huhs, Um-hmmm, etc.)	517 @	.08	41.36
interpretations of unconscious defense configurations	24 @	.30	7.20
absolution for evil deeds	16 @	.50	8.00
pieces of advice	2 @	.75	1.50
expressions of personal feelings	6 @	.50	3.00
personal reminiscences	2 @	.65	1.30
misc. responses (sighs, grunts, belches, etc.)	35 @	.20	6.00
listening to remarks disparaging therapist's appearance, personal habits, or technique	7 @	1.75	12.25
listening to sarcastic remarks about psychiatry	12 @	1.00	12.00
listening to psychiatrist jokes	3 @	.80	2.40
telephone calls to therapist	3 @	.15	.45
telephone call to therapist at especially inopportune moment	1 @	10.50	10.50
Kleenix tissues	22 @	.005	.11
ashtray	1 @	3.50	3.50
filling and repainting of ashtray-size dent in wall	1 @	27.50	27.50
shampooing of soft drink stain on carpet	1 @	15.00	15.00
letter of excuse from work	1 @	2.50	2.50
surcharges for unusually boring or difficult sessions	2 @	35.00	70.00

Itemized Credits	No.		Credit
unusually interesting anecdotes	4 @	.45	1.80
good jokes	3 @	.50	1.50
item of gossip about another patient which was found useful in her therapy	1 @	3.50	3.50
apology for sarcastic remark	1 @	1.00	1.00
use of case history at American Psychiatric Association convention	1		10.00
chicken salad sandwich on whole wheat w/mayo	½ @	1.75	.86
bummed cigarettes (1.00/pack)	7		.35
damaged Librium tablet returned unused	1		.10

Subtotal: charges $438.52

Subtotal: credits $19.11

Total: PLEASE REMIT— $419.41

Prenatal Psychoanalysis: A New Approach to Primary Prevention in Psychiatry*

ROBERT S. HOFFMAN, M.D.

Although it is widely appreciated that the emergence of psychoneurotic symptoms in adult life results from unconscious conflicts deriving from early childhood experiences, little effort has been directed toward primary prevention in this area. A possible approach to early intervention was evaluated by offering intensive psychoanalysis to third trimester fetuses during the two weeks prior to their delivery. Long-term followup was obtained on 46% of the sample (N = 110) at age thirty, via interview and psychometric data. The primary criterion for adequate adult adjustment was an annual gross income exceeding $36,000.

Factor analysis of the data revealed six therapeutic factors to be correlated with good outcome:

(1) Appropriate timing of interpretations, i.e. between contractions.

(2) Analysis conducted with the fetus in the horizontal position. This can be achieved by first determining the alignment of the fetus in the uterus via sonography and then positioning the mother so that the fetus lies flat.

(3) Thorough working-through of fetal feelings of anticipatory anxiety related to labor and imminent delivery.

(4) Development of a full-blown transference neurosis wherein the fetus's behavior toward the analyst reflects earlier experiences with fellow germ cells in the prezygotic stage.

(5) High forceps extraction, which appeared to enhance the effect of deep interpretations by pressing them into the fetal skull at the time of delivery.

(6) The necessity that the fetus himself pay for the analytic sessions. Although this was impractical to arrange prior to delivery, it was found equally effective to inform the fetus that he would be billed at the age of 18.

In addition to the above therapeutic maneuvers, it was found that certain specific aspects of the fetal situation affected the subsequent course of personality development:

(1) In several patients, inadequate materno-fetal circulation had a pronounced negative effect, a finding consistent with Melanie Klein's concept of "good and bad placenta."

(2) Witnessing of the primal scene by the fetus was judged to be highly traumatic, no doubt due to close proximity to the action. This, of course, was predicted by Freud in his classic paper, "Kinderpee-pinshtuppe" (1903), in which he noted that such experiences can eventuate in hysterical blindness, tunnel phobias, or plantar warts. Whether these effects are related to heightened Oedipal conflicts or to rhythmic compression of the fetal brain is still unclear.

(3) Two sets of twins were followed in the study, and twinship was found to engender a certain degree of sibling rivalry. One twin garroted his brother with the umbilical cord. In the other pair, rivalry appeared to be less of a problem: since the mother had a bicornuate uterus, each twin had his own room.

These data suggest that psychoanalysis need not be delayed until neurotic symptoms emerge in adulthood, since efforts at early intervention *in utero* can be highly rewarding. Further research would be necessary to confirm these preliminary findings as well as to explore possible extensions of the technique. We are currently evaluating the effect of psychoanalytic therapy upon spermatogonia and primordial ovarian follicles prior to conception.

*Reprinted from the Journal of Irreproducible Results, ©1981; 27(1):5, with permission from Blackwell Scientific Publications. Originally appeared in Throwaway J Psychoanal 46:4, Dec. 1978.

A Brief Report of a Psychodiagnostic System for Mental Health Clinic Patients:

Diagnosis by Parking*

JOHN B. PITTENGER, Ph.D.

In a recent issue of the *Journal of Polymorphous Perversity,* Schofield (1984) suggested that clients of mental health clinics park by diagnosis. Spaces in the parking lot would be marked with symbols indicating various diagnoses, thus allowing clients to park in a space appropriate to his/her problems as he/she perceives them. The author presents, here, a proposal to augment the diagnostic system through *observation of the parking behavior* of clients.

The therapist, or perhaps a full-time parking diagnostician, would observe the parking pattern of the client and note the problem indicated by the parking behavior. By inclusion of this aspect of adaptation to everyday life, we may be able to improve the accuracy of the diagnosis. Figure 1 illustrates a number of parking patterns and the diagnostic categories they indicate.

References

Shofield LJ Jr. A brief report of a psychodiagnostic system for mental health clinic patients: Parking by diagnosis. Journal of Polymorphous Perversity 1984; 1(2):9.

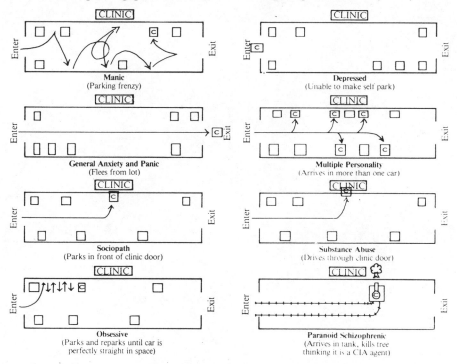

Figure 1. Psychodiagnostic Parking Patterns.

Additional Readings

1. Ellenbogen GC (ed): Oral Sadism and the Vegetarian Personality. New York, Brunner/Mazel, 1986.

A collection of readings from the first few years of the Journal of Polymorphous Perversity.

2. Ellenbogen GC (ed): The Primal Whimper. New York, Guilford Press, 1989.

A second collection of amusing articles from J.P.P.

3. Hillman J, Boer C (eds): Freud's Own Cookbook. New York, Brunner/Mazel, 1987.

This is a funny book that parodies the analytic theories of Freud and some of his contemporaries. Written in Freud's "own hand," the book contains analysis, commentary, and a number of delicious recipes: Birth Trauma Cake, Slips of the Tongue in Madeira Sauce, Erogenous Scones, and Fettucine Libido, to name just a few.

4. Holt RR: Researchmanship or how to write a dissertation in clinical psychology without really trying. Am Psychologist 1959; 14(3):151.

In this brief satire, the author discusses eight techniques to help PhD candidates sail through their dissertations. It includes advice on how to survey the literature, how to be sure your dissertation will be publishable and how, in the name of science, to manipulate your subjects.

INFORMED CONSENT & OTHER COMPLICATIONS OF HEALTH CARE

The articles in this chapter and the one that follows poke fun at some of the frustrations endemic in medicine. Although the division of articles is somewhat arbitrary, the ones in this chapter seemed to fit better under the subtitle, "Complications of Health Care." It also made sense to group them with the two parodies on Informed Consent. Considering the range of subject matter and the dates of publication, it is surprising how up-to-date the articles appear. George King's article, the "Human Nature Chart," is particularly revealing in the durability of its satire. Although it is listed as a 1965 publication, the article originally appeared in *Medical Economics* in the early 1930's. I used the 1965 citation because that issue is more likely to be available for anyone who wants to review the journal itself.

Slowly he would cruise the neighborhood, waiting for that occasional careless child who confused him with another vendor.

WILDLIFE PRESERVES. Copyright 1989. Universal Press Syndicate. Reprinted with permission. All rights reserved.

"Now, Mrs. Blare,
About the Complications . . ."*

WILLIAM P. IRVIN, M.D.

After his lawyer left, Dr. Tom Jones sat at his desk, staring moodily out the window. He was thinking of what he'd just heard about informed consent: "I guess you have to warn patients about almost everything that might go wrong," he told himself. "I sure wouldn't like to get hit with a $100,000 verdict, like that radiologist

*Reprinted with permission from Medical Economics, ©1971; 48(Apr 12):183–190, Medical Economics Company, Inc., Oradell, N.J. 07649.

who gave local X-ray treatments without telling the patient about possible burns."

His reverie was cut short by the entrance of his nurse. "Mrs. Blare is here, Doctor."

"Oh yes, she's to be admitted to the hospital tomorrow for surgery, isn't she? Send her in."

Mrs. Blare entered, sat down, and lit a cigarette. "Well, here I am, Doctor. My husband was a little upset until I told him you said it was just a fibroid tumor, just a simple hysterectomy, and there really wasn't much to it."

Dr. Jones winced. What his lawyer had told him made him sorry he'd used those words. "Now, Mrs. Blare, I didn't exactly mean it that way. You see . . ."

"Doctor, what is it? Do I have cancer?"

"No, still fibroids, Mrs. Blare. But a hysterectomy—well, frankly, there are some things that can go wrong. Not often, of course. But I should tell you of the possibilities."

"Oh, I'm not worried, Doctor. But if it'll make you feel better, go ahead and tell me."

"Well, after you're admitted to the hospital, they'll shave you. And occasionally they may nick the skin a little. . . . No, I realize that's not so bad. . . . Yes, I realize you're not the type to get upset over little things. . . . Well, then they'll draw your water. Sometimes this can cause a little inflammation of the bladder. . . . That's right—like you had with your last pregnancy. . . . Well, I know it took four months, but usually we can cure it much faster. We'd use some of the newer drugs because they don't cause as many reactions. . . . A reaction? Well, you break out in a rash and itch and . . . That's right—like your cousin, John, after he got penicillin. . . . He died? Oh, I didn't know. Mrs. Blare, you're shaking ashes all over my rug.

"Next they'll draw some blood from your arm for tests. . . . Yes, I know you've had it done before. But sometimes you can get a virus infection that causes a little liver reaction. . . . Your friend's husband died, too? Well, most people get better. Of course, it takes years sometimes, and—well, anyway, it doesn't happen often. Mrs. Blare, you look pale. Here, take this pill. That's better.

"Now at bedtime, they'll give you some drugs to help you sleep. . . . Yes, I guess you could get a drug reaction from them, but usually . . . No, I don't mean that would be your second drug reaction, I mean you probably wouldn't have any reaction. . . . Yes, I know what I said about the bladder.

"You'll also get a little enema at bedtime. . . . Mrs. Blare, what happened to your cousin in Omaha has nothing to do with this case. They won't push a hole in your intestine. . . . Of course, I don't guarantee it. . . . Peritonitis? Well, yes, a hole in the intestine can cause it, but nobody will punch a hole in your intestine. . . . No, I was not aware that your brother is a lawyer.

"Well, let's see. Early the next day they'll take you to the operating room, which brings us to the anesthetic. Occasionally, it can cause a little problem. . . . Well, the heart might stop working. . . . Oh, yes, we can start it again. Usually. If we can get it going, it usually keeps on working O.K. Of course, if the brain has been damaged, the patient might not be too bright after surgery. . . . Yes, an idiot, you might say—but really, that doesn't happen often.

"Next we open the abdomen and remove the uterus. Of course, once in a while—not very often, you understand—but just sometimes . . . Mrs. Blare, just because your grandmother said you were born under an unlucky star . . . Now stop shaking. Here, take another pill. . . . No, it won't cause a drug reaction—I don't think. You mustn't worry so, Mrs. Blare.

"Now, in removing the uterus, we might—on very rare occasions, you understand—get into the bowel. . . . I mean, we might cut a small hole in the bowel. Sort of like the enema thing, yes. . . . Well, we just sew it up. . . . Yes, peritonitis is possible.

"If all goes well, and we haven't nicked the ureter . . . Oh, the tube that goes to the bladder. . . . Well, it might cause a fistula and—let's talk about that later. . . . Yes, your insurance would cover it if it should happen.

"Now, the uterus is out, and the incision is closed. . . . No, we won't sew the bowel up too tight. I mean, we won't touch the bowel. . . . Yes, I know what I said before. . . . No, I'm not contradicting myself. Now, now, please relax. . . . After the surgery you'll be given some fluids through a needle in your vein. . . . Well, yes, I guess so. That old virus and the liver again. . . . Yes, you mentioned that he died.

"If the wound doesn't break open we'll . . . Well, all your intestines could spill out. . . . Oh, we'd put them back. . . . No, that wouldn't cause idiocy.

"There's only one more thing. Of course, it doesn't happen often. We call it a Staph infection. . . . Oh, you've read about it in the papers? . . . They all died? But that was in a nursery. . . . Well, yes, grown-ups can die from it, but we have drugs, and . . . Well, a drug reaction isn't usually as bad as a Staph infection.

"To sum it all up, Mrs. Blare, a hysterectomy really isn't so simple. Now if you'll just sign this paper that says I've informed you of these little complica—Mrs. Blare! We're not through! Where are you going? *Come back, Mrs. Blare!*"

Proposed Informed-Consent Form for Hernia Patient*

PRESTON J. BURNHAM, M.D.

I, ..., being about to be subjected to a surgical operation said to be for repair of what my doctor thinks is a hernia (rupture or loss of belly stuff—intestines—out of the belly through a hole in the muscles), do hereby give said doctor permission to cut into me and do duly swear that I am giving my informed consent, based upon the following information:

Operative procedure is as follows: The doctor first cuts through the skin by a four-inch gash in the lower abdomen. He then slashes through the other things—fascia (a tough layer over the muscles) and layers of muscle—until he sees the cord (tube that brings the sperm from testicle to outside) with all its arteries and veins. The doctor then tears the hernia (thin sac of bowels and things) from the cord and ties off the sac with a string. He then pushes the testicle back into the scrotum and sews everything together, trying not to sew up the big arteries and veins that nourish the leg.

Possible complications are as follows:

1) Larger artery may be cut and I may bleed to death.

2) Large vein may be cut and I may bleed to death.

3) Tube from testicle may be cut. I will then be sterile on that side.

4) Artery or veins to testicles may be cut—same result.

5) Opening around cord in muscles may be made too tight.

6) Clot may develop in these veins which will loosen when I get out of bed and hit my lungs, killing me.

7) Clot may develop in one or both legs which may cripple me, lead to loss of one or both legs, go to my lungs, or make my veins no good for life.

8) I may develop a horrible infection that may kill me.

9) The hernia may come back again after it has been operated on.

10) I may die from general anesthesia.

11) I may be paralyzed if spinal anesthesia is used.

12) If ether is used, it could explode inside me.

13) I may slip in hospital bathroom.

14) I may be run over going to the hospital.

15) The hospital may burn down.

I understand: the anatomy of the body, the pathology of the development of hernia, the surgical technique that will be used to repair the hernia, the physiology of wound healing, the dietetic chemistry of the foods that I must eat to cause healing, the chemistry of body repair, and the course which my physician will take in treating any of the complications that can occur as a sequela of repairing an otherwise simple hernia.

_____
Patient

_____
Lawyer for Patient

_____
Lawyer for Doctor

_____
Lawyer for Hospital

_____
Lawyer for Anesthesiologist

_____
Mother-in-Law

_____
Notary Public

_____
Date

_____
Place

*Reprinted from Science, ©1966; 152(Apr 22):448–449, with permission from the American Association for the Advancement of Science. Edited from the original.

The Professional Patient*

IAN ROSE, M.B., B.S.(LOND.)

The concept of the professional patient is new to most people. In this context we have reference to the patient who, by virtue of long study and diligent effort, has brought his attitude towards his status and his doctor to new heights of self-expression. Until only a few years ago the patient was eternal, and the unwilling, amateur. Only the doctor was professional. With the publication in Canada of the report of the Royal Commission on Health Services the day of equality draws closer and we feel it is time to issue formal instruction, a "Manual of Basic Instruction for Candidates Seeking the Professional Patient Status," to the servile multitude of patients in this country.

It must be understood at the outset that professionalism is essentially a state of mind. The patient must realize at all times that he is the essence of medicine. Where would the physician or surgeon be but for him? Harvey, Lister, Pasteur and all the other greats of medicine would have lived in vain but for the patient.

He must also remember that the patient-doctor relationship is a constant battle. The patient must learn not to give an inch. Yet his approach must be subtle; he must never appear antagonistic or uncooperative, even when actively opposing and undermining the doctor.

As we shall see later, the first rule is never openly to refuse a doctor's order. It is always possible to thwart the doctor without open revolt. Thus, when the patient is told to go into the examining room and take his things off, he should not object, but merely enter the room and hang his hat upon the peg. This has been classed as Phase I of the examination revolt.

Phase II occurs when the physician returns, finds the patient still fully dressed, instructs him in peremptory tones to strip, and then again leaves him. The patient should then remove his jacket and open his shirt. The original description of this revolt, by Petrikov in his "Médecin en bas", contains 16 phases through which the patient moves before he has reduced his physician to a state of servile impotence; and only then does he allow himself to be examined in the nude.

The Greeting

The doctor's first impression of the patient frequently determines who will have the upper hand during the rest of the examination. Many opening gambits are described, most of which are satisfactory. They all have, however, one facet in common: the patient must take the initiative. If the doctor is allowed to ignore the patient and complete the notes he is making or whatever he may be doing when the patient enters the consulting room, the inestimable advantage of a winning greeting is lost. A few of the well-established patient-openers will now be described.

The first is described by Throgmorton Willerston in his *Patient's Manifesto* of 1959. He entered the office of Lord Meterbrook and, finding himself ignored while the doctor continued to make diligent notes, Willerston unhesitatingly stepped up to the desk. He spread his left hand wide across the notes on the desk and, leaning on it, he reached across and proffered his right with a most polite, "How do you do?"

The author of "Lie Down Fighting," Silas K. Morton, better known as "The Butcher," is most renowned for his greeting, which consisted of a 200-lb. slap on the shoulder that sends the doctor sprawling across his notes; this is accompanied by a resounding "Hi ya, doc!" This, he says, was usually effective in gaining the physician's attention.

Before leaving the matter of the greeting, a word of warning must be entered against measures such as fainting or having an epileptic convulsion on entering the consulting room. Although they may effectively gain the doctor's attention, they do so in his own field. Such maneuvers give the fundamental initiative to the doctor and for that reason are to be avoided.

*Reprinted with permission from the Canadian Medical Association Journal, ©1965; 92(Apr 24):923–926. Edited from the original.

The History

Once the initial greeting is over, the lead should be passed to the doctor. Rule IV states clearly that the history must never be given; the physician must be made to extract it.

When the physician is clearly ready to take the history, the professional patient falls silent and waits with a pleasant and confident look on his face.

The first response to the doctor taking the history is of importance. It must undermine his confidence and make him realize that he is dealing with a nimble mind. As the doctor has certain standard openings, the patient should use standard replies or counters. A selection of these follows:

Doctor: Well, what seems to be trouble?
Patient: That's what I am here to find out.
Doctor: And how are you today?
Patient: I am hoping you will be able to tell me at the end of the examination.

The really experienced physician will often open with: "What are you complaining of?", and sit back with a complacent smile on his face because he feels that there is no effective counter to this approach. Segway Mathieson disproved this on many occasions and in his paper, "The Conquest of Dr. Tinglefoot, or To the Far Corners of Medicine in an Open Boat," concludes that the best counter-move was to reply quietly: "I am not complaining of anything except, perhaps, your phraseology, which is ugly, unworthy of a noble profession such as medicine, and ends in a preposition!"

Contrary to what many people expect, the trained professional patient will lead the doctor through the main complaint and paramount symptoms without confusion, because this lulls the physician into a false sense of security and he is less wary of the pitfalls that lie before him. However, exceptions can be made to this general rule in special circumstances; for instance, when a doctor shows himself to be insistent on the exact time of origin of a symptom the special process of "time derouting" is appropriate. This process is best explained by an illustration. The following example is taken from Fanny Timberflossetts' book, "Thoughts of a Picaresque Patient—The Naked Truth."

On being pressed for the date of origin of a symptom such as constipation, diarrhea or anything else, she would hesitate and appear to think for a moment.

"It was just after Fred had his accident," she would say, smiling sweetly at the physician. When he did not look satisfied, she would hurriedly add, "Yes, I am sure it was about two months after his accident."

"And when did your husband have his accident?"

"Oh my husband hasn't had any accident."

"Then who is Fred?"

"Fred, he's my eldest boy."

"All right" (the doctor is now controlling himself with difficulty), "when did Fred have his accident?"

"Which accident?" Then, noticing the flushed face of the doctor, she would add, "He's had two bad ones, and was on Compensation for a long time with them."

Fanny says that this is generally a turning point in the conversation. More excitable doctors will have an explosion of temper at this point, while in the more phlegmatic such an outburst may be delayed further. The latter will say that they are interested in the accident that occurred just before onset of diarrhea. Fanny would then continue: "Oh, that one. That was when he twisted his back on the uneven path leading to the restroom at the construction site where he was working. He was in hospital for two months and had to have traction and . . ."

Fanny says that she has never yet been able to finish her account of Fred's second accident, although she committed a 200-word description of it to memory. It may be thought by many that, at this point, the doctor would give up and pursue a different symptom, but generally doctors show a remarkable perseverance and will return to the direct attack on the symptom after an interval in which they either light a cigarette or attempt to tear the phone book in half, depending on their temperament.

The questioning of the doctor is now very direct. He says: "When did the diarrhea begin?" Or alternatively, "When was the last time you felt perfectly well and had no diarrhea?"

In either case Fanny's response to renewed questioning had no reference to Fred's illness but she would start out on a completely new tack.

"Oh, you want to know when the diarrhea started?"

"Yes."

"Oh well, that's easy. It started about five or six days before the headache."

"And when did the headache begin?"

"I've just told you. About five or six days after the diarrhea."

Owing to limitation of space we cannot quote this dialogue at greater length. However, the general tenor of time derouting can be easily discerned from the foregoing. So long as the doctor returns to the same questions, the question can be easily evaded by associating the temporal origin of a symptom with something in the patient's private life rather than with a calendar. Eventually the doctor will give up if no other reason than that set out in Rule V: *The doctor has less time than you do.*

Past and Family History

A great deal of time can be successfully wasted with the past history and the family history. The patient should carefully prepare beforehand and learn by heart the full list of all the illnesses he has ever had, together with their complications, their dates of origin, and their duration. These must include all childhood illnesses, all attacks of flu, colds and accidents, however trivial. These should be given to the doctor at dictation speed. If there is one important illness among them, such as rheumatic fever, tuberculosis, typhoid, poliomyelitis and so on, this provides a good opportunity to practise one of the variants of time derouting.

Similarly, the family history should be learned by heart and include all brothers, sisters, aunts, uncles and first cousins. It is most probable that the doctor will interrupt the process, but the parental history should be taken back three generations on both the maternal and paternal sides. Such preparation is the first sign of professionalism in the patient.

The Physical Examination

We have previously alluded to the wonderful vistas that open up for the patient when he is told to disrobe for the examination. This matter will not be discussed further at this point; the reader should refer to Petrikov's paper. The postgraduate student is referred to a little known book, Miss Lee's "Gypsy, or Button by Button" from which he, or she, can gain a great deal of unexpected help.

Head and Neck. The tactics to be used during this examination are sufficiently obvious that they need not be described in detail. Such measures as choking on the spatula and coughing in the doctor's face; turning the head to the left when the left ear is being examined and to the right for the right ear, causing the eyes to wander and the eyelids to close for a funduscopic examination—are all part of the rather obvious gambits of this phase.

In a similar way we may dispense with a detailed description of examination of the limbs and lymphatic system. A high degree of ticklishness underlies an elementary but highly effective gambit.

We will now leave these matters to the patient's native ingenuity and pass to more important fields.

The Chest. The student of professional patient practices will find this a most rewarding field for diligent study. When the doctor places his stethoscope anywhere near the sternum (breast bone) or underneath the fifth rib, the patient should breathe in and out deeply and noisily. When the doctor is attempting to listen to any other part of the chest, the breath should be held. Breaths should be taken hurriedly while the doctor is moving the bell of his stethoscope from one place to another.

Occasionally the doctor will notice the absence of breath sounds and will instruct the patient to breathe. When this occurs the patient should inspired as slowly as possible, hold his breath for at least 30 seconds, and then exhale equally slowly.

Rarely, a persistent physician may not instruct the patient to breathe but merely wait patiently for cyanosis and the inevitable breath. When it is impossible to hold the breath any longer, victory may still be obtained by covering a few quick gasps of life-giving oxygen by a fit of paroxysmal coughing.

It will be noticed that we have not advised the ploy of talking while the doctor is trying to listen. This is too obvious and we feel that it raises the doctor's suspicions. The processes we have described are sufficiently subtle to be effective with most physicians.

The Abdominal Examination. The abdominal examination can be made frustrating and almost impossible by three simple maneuvers. (1) By complaining of the coldness of the doctor's hands; this causes delay while he tries to warm them. (2) By squirming and laughing because he is tickling. (3) By raising the head each time his hand touches the skin of the abdomen—this effectively tenses the abdominal muscles, making it impossible for him to feel any of the internal organs.

C.N.S. The examination of the central nervous system is a highly specialized subject and will not be referred to in this elementary text. Those interested are referred to the paper "Physicians, Jerks, and Neurosurgeons", by Stetler and Merryweather, published in the April 1964 issue of the *Journal of the Canadian Professional Patient.*

General Considerations

In addition to the general training of the professional patient, it is desirable for him to have up his sleeve, as it were, a number of statements that he can use to arrest the progress of the doctor, if the latter seems to be getting the upper hand. Since Silus K. Merryweather published his exciting "Heel! Healers, Heel!", these phrases—expressing the quintessence of patient professionalism—have been known as "doctor-stoppers." Quite frankly we regret this, since we do not feel it is in keeping with the dignity of our calling—and indeed Merryweather agrees with us. He has on a number of occasions tried to popularize some other phrase of higher literary merit such as physician-paralyzer or healer-halter; but it seems that doctor-stopper has caught the public imagination and nothing can be done about it. The following are some of the more classic examples:

"Doctor, I don't want you to examine me. I just want you to refer me to a chiropractor."

"Can I have the treatment they are using in Patagonia? Oh, haven't you heard of it? It was in last month's *Reader's Digest.*"

"You tell me the symptoms of Tsutsugamushi fever and I'll tell you if I've got it."

"I hate to call you out at such an hour in the morning but we're leaving to go the Grey Cup game tomorrow and I know how difficult it is to get into your office in the mornings."

"Thank you for coming, Doctor. I usually have Dr. X but I didn't want to disturb him at this time of night."

Conclusion

In conclusion, certain general rules may be advanced for the guidance of practising or would-be professional patients.

1. Never go to the doctor's office if a house call will do.

2. Never call the doctor during the day if a night call will do.

3. Never openly oppose the doctor; the art of professionalism must be more subtle.

4. Make the doctor extract the history. Remember, you're paying him.

5. Take your time. The doctor is probably in more of a hurry than you are.

6. The doctor needs you more than you need him.

The foregoing article is intended to be of an introductory nature only, and the serious student is urged to join the local chapter of the Society of Professional Patients of Canada where group classes and practical demonstrations are arranged monthly. For those unable to attend, the Society has a correspondence course entitled "New Horizons for the Patient in Six Easy Lessons", obtainable from the secretary. Please enclose 50 cents for handling and the top of any unpaid doctor's account.

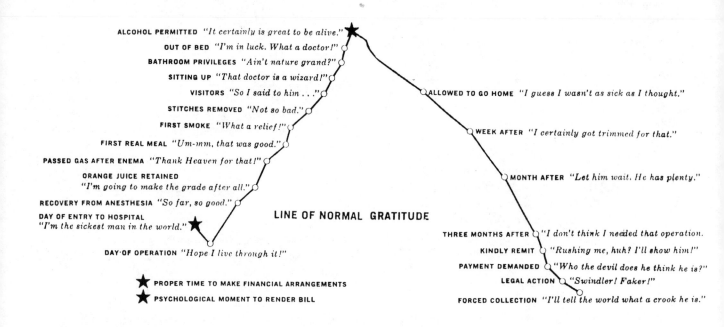

ALCOHOL PERMITTED *"It certainly is great to be alive."*
OUT OF BED *"I'm in luck. What a doctor!"*
BATHROOM PRIVILEGES *"Ain't nature grand?"*
SITTING UP *"That doctor is a wizard!"*
VISITORS *"So I said to him . . ."*
STITCHES REMOVED *"Not so bad."*
FIRST SMOKE *"What a relief!"*
FIRST REAL MEAL *"Um-mm, that was good."*
PASSED GAS AFTER ENEMA *"Thank Heaven for that!"*
ORANGE JUICE RETAINED *"I'm going to make the grade after all."*
RECOVERY FROM ANESTHESIA *"So far, so good."*
DAY OF ENTRY TO HOSPITAL *"I'm the sickest man in the world."*
DAY OF OPERATION *"Hope I live through it!"*

ALLOWED TO GO HOME *"I guess I wasn't as sick as I thought."*
WEEK AFTER *"I certainly got trimmed for that."*
MONTH AFTER *"Let him wait. He has plenty."*
THREE MONTHS AFTER *"I don't think I needed that operation."*
KINDLY REMIT *"Rushing me, huh? I'll show him!"*
PAYMENT DEMANDED *"Who the devil does he think he is?"*
LEGAL ACTION *"Swindler! Faker!"*
FORCED COLLECTION *"I'll tell the world what a crook he is."*

LINE OF NORMAL GRATITUDE

★ PROPER TIME TO MAKE FINANCIAL ARRANGEMENTS
★ PSYCHOLOGICAL MOMENT TO RENDER BILL

Human Nature Chart:
That's Gratitude!*

GEORGE S. KING, M.D.

Above is a chart that shows how a patient feels, at each stage of his sickness and convalescence, about his doctor and the doctor's fee. The chart first appeared in the May, 1934, issue of *Medical Economics.* We published it again in 1956. And we still get requests for copies.

So does the chart's creator, Dr. George S. King, a still-active 86-year-old G.P. of Bay Shore, N.Y. Over the years, he estimates, nearly 1,000 doctors have asked him for copies. He has sent reprints all over the world. Twice his own framed copy has been stolen from his office wall.

The chart has been reprinted in consumer magazines, newspapers and a textbook on business procedures. A medical school handed out copies of the chart along with diplomas. It has been distributed by the New York County medical society and the Australian Medical Association to all their members.

Why such widespread and continuing interest in a chart that was first published more than 31 years ago? "The world changes, and medicine changes," answers Dr. King, "but human nature remains the same."

*Reprinted with permission from Medical Economics, ©1965; 42(Nov):102–103, Medical Economics Company, Inc., Oradell, N.J. 07649.

The Last of the Detail Men*

HOMER B. MARTIN, M.D.

In the summer of 1960, fate assigned me a leading role in the revolution of the drug industry. I was the director of a relatively new firm at the time, and our only product had been a nutrient used in the treatment of hypocholesterolemia. However, because business had been bad, we changed the name to Slurp^R, an adipose enhancer for the underweight. In fact, we were using the very same preparation, only the bottles and labels were different.

Faced with the dilemma of promoting an agent that no reputable physician would prescribe, our company decided to review the whole process of drug promotion in order to gain a fresh approach. Also, since the government insisted that we put on our label that Slurp^R contained sodium chloride (actually that was all it contained), we knew we had to do something. With these crucial factors in mind, I eagerly awaited the results of a survey sent to 72,474 doctors.

Criticism of Detailing

The results of our survey were computer tabulated without delay. It became evident early on that we were dealing with a most fractious group and that physicians were distressed by drug promotion as currently practiced. The results showed that:

- 99% thought detailing was too time-consuming,

- 93% became choleric when asked if they had used products shown at the previous visit,

- 91% resented having detail men bring more than two supervisors per visit,

- 86% thought no more than 10 new drugs should be detailed per visit, and

- 82% agreed it would be acceptable to use the same charts and statistics all the time and only change the names of the drugs as an economy move.

Despite the compliments that a grateful drug industry paid me personally, it did not take a genius to see that the human being had outlived his usefulness in this line of work.

The Roboburp

In 1961, the nation enjoyed unparalleled scientific progress; therefore, we turned to science for an answer. Dr. Franz Finkel, our research chief, was summoned from his laboratory in Las Vegas to head up the experts working to replace the detail man. Leading authorities on motivational sales techniques, computer science, and transistor engineering secluded themselves in a special lab at one of our subsidiary companies—a distillery in Kentucky. Two years later they staggered forth with Roboburp, the first mechanical detail man.

Although complicated in design, Roboburp is actually quite simple to operate. Its computer is programmed to know the locations of doctors in the area as well as office hours, and schedules, etc. Roboburp can then be directed to a physician's office with infallible regularity. A tape located within Roboburp cheerfully greets the receptionist as he rolls, collision-free, into the office. He then waits patiently beneath the universal magazine rack until summoned by the doctor. During this waiting period, Roboburp uses his thermocouples to determine the number of warm bodies (patients) present. He automatically subtracts one-third for children since they take less time for the physician to see. Where couples are concerned, he triples the time element because each one not only describes his own illness, but also reminds his partner about forgotten complaints. This information is then applied to the famous Franz Finkel formula to determine how much time the doctor is likely to spend with Roboburp:

$$\text{Interview time} = \frac{\text{Doctor's average appointment (in minutes)}}{\text{Number of patients waiting} \times 3}$$

*Reprinted from JAMA, ©1961; 177(1):A206–210, with permission from the American Medical Association. Edited from the original.

Thus, if a doctor has 15 minute appointments and five warm bodies are present, the detail interview will last only one minute. To compensate for unexpectedly short interview periods, Roboburp is equipped with a clutch that allows the tape to be played at three times its regular speed.

Method of Detailing

On confronting the doctor, Roboburp extrudes a card listing his serial number and company. If it is a first visit to the office, Roboburp reassures the doctor that he has not interfered with office procedures, nor prescribed anything for patients in the waiting room. At appropriate intervals, graphs and samples are ejected from slots, and the tape pauses until the doctor has accepted them. If the sound of material dropping into the wastebasket is picked up by Roboburp's sensors, a loud alarm sounds and the lottery ticket usually presented at the end of the interview is withheld.

Incidental Problems

Needless to say, drug sales are at an all time high, which proves the human element is definitely passé.

In all fairness, however, we must confess a few problems. In the first place, the schedule must be carefully supervised. Doctors who neglect to make accurate vacation plans end up complaining if Roboburp breaks down their front door. There is also the rare doctor who actually asks a question or, more commonly, the greedy one who wants a larger sample. To solve these problems, we installed a button for additional information and a larger bin for samples. As expected, however, it is the human element which proved the most troublesome. For example, one unreliable mechanic ran out of calling cards and loaded his Roboburp with pawn tickets. This error went undetected for 3,129 physician visits. The mechanic was castigated, of course, and promoted according to our contract with the union.

Personally, things could not be more promising for the company which made it all possible—Frantic Pharmaceuticals. Our research division has just come up with a sensational new product. As many of you already know, it is called Shrink^R, a new medication for those who are overweight. An ethically promoted pharmaceutical, it tastes very much like sodium chloride. Roboburp will have the details for you at his next visit.

Dial-A-Lawyer*

DALE ORTON, M.D.

*On first thought, a 24-hour-a-day legal question answering service
seems a great idea. On second thought . . .*

DOCTOR: Hello? Is this 1-800-LAWYERS?

LAWYER: Yes, it is. Please give me your Visa number and expiration date or your Federal BNDD number if you are a physician, osteopath, or veterinarian.

Thank you. How may we help you paddle up life's legal rivers?

DOCTOR: First of all, I think this 24-hour-a-day legal question answering service is a great idea. We doctors are always being second-guessed, but now we can have that legal advice right from the beginning.

You see, I'm the doctor on call tonight in the emergency room, and I've got this drunk here who was punched in the nose. He won't let me examine him.

LAWYER: Was he the fighter or the fightee?

DOCTOR: He's not sure.

LAWYER: What?

DOCTOR: He drank a fifth of Old Grand Dad before arriving.

LAWYER: Did he sign a permission-to-treat form?

DOCTOR: Yes, he did.

LAWYER: Then I see no problem. You'll just have to treat him.

DOCTOR: He did sign the chart permission form, but I doubt that Screw You is his legal name.

LAWYER: So do I. This could be a problem. Why don't you ask him if he wants to be treated? A verbal permission is better than nothing.

DOCTOR: I did, but he wanted to talk about my mother's nationality and sexual preferences instead.

LAWYER: Your patient has come to your emergency room, and you have an obligation to treat him.

DOCTOR: Easy enough for you to say, but this fellow wants to tear my head off. By the way, let's say this guy punches me, too. Can I sue him?

LAWYER: Well, we lawyers are an argumentative lot, and that question could go either way, especially if a 40-percent contingency fee were at stake. I think the real question here involves that venerable legal tenet called The Law of the Deep Pockets. Are you familiar with it?

DOCTOR: No, but I'm afraid to ask.

LAWYER: To put it in a nutshell—at our dollar-a-minute telephone charge, I'm sure that's what you want—if you have insurance, you can and you will be sued.

DOCTOR: Even if not guilty?

LAWYER: Yes.

DOCTOR: How about the patient?

LAWYER: Does he have insurance?

DOCTOR: Not unless it's on the Harley-Davidson sitting out in the parking lot.

LAWYER: That brings us to the other cornerstone of modern legal thought, which is, by the way, the converse of The Law of the Deep Pockets. Plainly stated: A Bum is Judgment Proof.

DOCTOR: So if I don't treat him, I get sued, but if he beats me up, that's too bad.

LAWYER: So to speak.

DOCTOR: Wait a minute. I think my problems are over. The patient just took a swing at the investigating police officer. His nightstick accidently struck the patient on the head, and he's out cold. I'll call the neurosurgeon in. Besides, the city must have an excellent liability policy.

LAWYER: Isn't that called "turfing" in medical parlance?

DOCTOR: Yes, it is. But I'm asking the questions here. While you're on the line, how about a quickie?

LAWYER: Lawyers don't do quickies, not at $75 an hour.

DOCTOR: I have another patient here, a cute little four-year-old named Sally. She fell off her Hot Wheels and bumped her forehead. She didn't lose consciousness and looks entirely normal to me right now.

*Reprinted with permission from MD, ©1986; 30(1):37–44.

LAWYER: What's the problem?

DOCTOR: Her mother watched "Half-Hour Magazine" last week. Some guy said that the only way to really diagnose head injury is with a CT scan. If I order the test, the girl would receive an unneeded dose of radiation, and it would be expensive.

LAWYER: What are the chances that there could be something wrong on the scan?

DOCTOR: Oh, I'd guess about one in 500.

LAWYER: Are you a betting man.

DOCTOR: Not usually.

LAWYER: Do you want to see your whole medical career go down the drain in case you're wrong?

DOCTOR: No, but . . .

LAWYER: Tell you what, go back and explain to the mother what you've just told me. I'll do some quick research on the issue and put you on hold. Besides, there is a wife-beater on the other line who's frantic and needs my advice.

DOCTOR: Hello? I talked with the mother and she said no go. She wants the CT scan and mumbled something about paying all those insurance premiums, but when you need the coverage, they always try pinching pennies.

LAWYER: Let's see. *Roe vs. Wade . . . Miranda . . . Escobedo.* Ah, here it is. An interesting case on the West Coast. Just last year a teenager fell down and hit her head. She also didn't lose consciousness. The physician who first saw her didn't find any physical signs of closed head injury and refused any further tests. The girl complained of headaches for the next week and finally she managed to convince another doctor to perform a CT scan on her.

DOCTOR: What did they find?

LAWYER: Nothing. Unfortunately, they sued the first doctor anyway and collected ipso facto because he caused her the pain and suffering of *not* knowing that there was anything wrong. What did your four-year-old's mother say?

DOCTOR: First of all, she took out a note pad and copied my name off my name tag. Then she asked me if that was my legal name. Right now she's calling her lawyer.

LAWYER: Did you inform her of our service?

DOCTOR: No.

LAWYER: Just kidding. I rest my case. Look on the bright side. This country already spends $30 billion a year on preventive medicine. So what's another $600? Fire up the CT scanner.

DOCTOR: I will. First I need to get permission. I'll have to call 1-800-BUREAUCRAT, the clearinghouse for hospital admissions and tests not covered under 1-800-FEDERAL, the clearinghouse for Medicare and Medicaid patients.

LAWYER: Just mention our discussion. If they refuse, inform the mother that she can sue them, too.

DOCTOR: Well, it's been interesting.

LAWYER: And your bill is only $24.95. Now isn't that a small price to pay to sleep well at night?

DOCTOR: It certainly is.

LAWYER: Don't forget to tell your colleagues about our new program—Rent-A-Lawyer. For the next month, you can take advantage of our introductory offer. We'll give you an attorney who will follow you on rounds and advise you on any legal pitfalls right on the spot. He even brings his own lab coat. At just $495 a day, this is really a bargain.

Have a nice day.

"This Is Corporate Medicine. Please Hold . . . Please Hold . . ."*

KENNETH L. TOPPELL, M.D.

A physician imagines what might happen if corporate medicine were carried to its logical extreme. You can laugh . . . for now.

Woolworth J. Smith, M.D., reached for the phone as soon as Mrs. Way nodded. Tired, short of breath, and in pain, she'd given in and agreed to enter the hospital. Her physician was concerned, but confident that a few days of inpatient care would relieve her symptoms and allow her to resume her active life. Now all he had to do was get her admission approved.

Smith was pleasantly surprised to hear the phone ring only once. Usually his secretary, Pat Wordwhiz, handled details such as these, but today she had jury duty, so the doctor was on his own.

"CorpuCare Practitioner Services and Support," a Voice answered. "Your well-being is our problem; your problems are our well-being."

"Yes, um, I'm Dr. Smith, and I'd like to admit Mrs. C. N. Way. She's. . . ."

The Voice broke in: "Is Mrs. Way a member of our Plan?"

"Yes, of course. Her number is 11–426–72." Smith smiled with satisfaction, thinking, "They never expect physicians to have that information."

The Voice responded: "Is that her authorization number?"

"No. That's her membership number. I'm trying to admit her to the hospital," Smith said.

"She must have an active authorization before she can be admitted." The Voice continued, "I'll transfer you to Authorization."

The phone clicked a few times, and an electronic message intoned: "Please wait. All of our operators are busy, but you will be serviced in a moment."

"Serviced?" Smith thought.

The sound of music, as if transmitted through cloth wrapped in plastic, drifted through the phone. It was a full orchestral treatment of "Yellow Submarine."

Abruptly a higher-pitched, nasal Voice cut in. "Authorization."

Smith identified himself and repeated his goal, "I'm trying to admit Mrs. C. N. Way, member No. 11-426–72."

"What is your patient's name?" the Voice asked.

Puzzled, Smith tried again. "She is Mrs. C. N. Way. Her membership number is 11–426–72."

"Thank you. Please hold." The muffled holding music was now playing "Don't Fence Me In," full orchestra. Smith smiled benignly at Mrs. Way, who was now leaning a bit to the right in her chair. The telephone symphony had swung into "Muskrat Ramble" before the new Voice cut back in. "The beneficiary's authorization number is 74-A-Arnold-B-Box-26."

Mildly annoyed, Smith hung up the phone, and hurried around his desk to straighten up the tilting Mrs. Way. She had chronic forniculation. This was her first full-blown attack since Smith had made the diagnosis some months earlier.

Regatta Lovely, Smith's laboratory assistant, came to take Mrs. Way to the hospital. The patient was calm, relieved to know that her discomfort would soon be ended.

As Regatta and her charge were leaving, Pat returned, released from the jury box once the plaintiff's lawyer learned she worked for a physician. She was the most efficient secretary Smith had ever employed, and until today she'd shielded him from CorpuCare's admissions process. He told her of his phone call, and she smiled knowingly.

Smith returned to the preparation of his evening lecture, "The Role of Body Language in the Treatment of Chronic Forniculation." He was a fornicular specialist, renowned in his field. It seemed that only a few

*Reprinted with permission from Medical Economics, ©1987; 64(June 8):171–175, Medical Economics Company, Inc., Oradell, N.J. 17649.

moments had passed when he heard a knock on his door. "Come in," he called, and Pat and Regatta entered his office. Smith was surprised to see Mrs. Way, propped up against the wall.

"Dr. Smith, the hospital won't admit Mrs. Way," Regatta announced. "The business office said she hasn't received preadmission clearance."

"I spoke to CorpuCare myself," Smith said, indignant. "What are they talking about?" He reached for the phone again.

"CorpuCare Practitioner Services and Support. Your well-being is our problem; your problems are our well-being." It was the same Voice, at least.

"This is Dr. Woolworth Smith again. I just called to arrange to admit Mrs. C. N. Way, member No. 11-426-72. The hospital says she hasn't been cleared. What's going on?"

"Is that her authorization number?" said the Voice.

"No, that's her membership number. Her authoriz . . . ."

"I'll transfer you to Authorization, Doctor."

"Wait!" Smith sputtered helplessly as the phone clicked and the syrupy sounds of "Girls Just Want to Have Fun," full symphonic arrangement, came through. As the orchestra swung into "On the Road Again," he was tapping his fingers impatiently on his desk.

"Authorization." It was the same nasal Voice. "How may we help you?"

"You can't," Smith began to explain. "I have an authorization number for my patient. I am trying to get her admitted."

"You need to speak to Someone Else, Doctor. This is Authorization. I'll transfer your call."

The lush notes of "Monster Mash" made Smith's eyes cross. He looked out to see Pat lifting Mrs. Way's head from a tub of ivy as Regatta wiped the potting soil from her once-smart coiffure.

Someone Else came on the line. "Practitioner-Provider Relations. How may we help you?"

"This is Dr. Woolworth Smith. I have been trying to admit a patient to the hospital." Hearing the angry edge to his voice, Pat was worried.

"Is the patient a beneficiary?" Someone Else asked.

"Beneficiary, hell! She's a member of the plan. She has been authorized. And she is sick."

"There is no need for profanity, Doctor." Someone Else sounded a bit prissy. "What is her membership number?"

"11-426-72."

"What is her authorization number?"

"74-AB-26."

"Is that B-box or V-vehicle?"

Smith paused and forced himself to swallow before he answered, "B-box."

"Thank you. Please hold." Before Smith could react, the phone had clicked and the telephone orchestra was playing "Itsy Bitsy Teenie Weenie Yellow Polkadot Bikini."

Pat could feel the tension in the room. Smith was holding the phone by the mouthpiece, leaning forward at his desk. His knuckles were white, and there was a line of sweat glistening on his upper lip. In the waiting room, Regatta was trying to keep Mrs. Way from forniculating in the wheelchair.

Someone Else came back on the line, saying, "Now then, how may I help you?"

"First, do not put me on hold. Next, tell me how to get my patient into the hospital." Smith was trying to regain his composure; surely he could reason with the Voices.

"Certainly. All the beneficiary needs is a preadmission clearance."

"But I was given an authorization number to admit Mrs. Way," Smith's voice was rising slightly.

"An authorization doesn't mean anything," Someone Else chuckled. "That's just the number you use when you call for preadmission clearance. What is the nature of your patient's problem?"

"Acute exacerbation of chronic forniculation," Smith answered smoothly, back on his own turf at last.

"And who gave the second opinion?" Someone Else was obviously filling in blanks on the preadmission clearance form.

"I didn't get a second opinion. There's not time. Mrs. Way is acutely ill," Smith's voice was much louder. Through the door, he could see Regatta and Pat lifting the twitching Mrs. Way back into the wheelchair.

"We have found that many admissions can be avoided if another physician sees the patient. Often these problems can be handled on an outpatient basis," Someone Else was reciting. "We recommend that Dr. Woolworth Smith review all forniculation cases. Why don't you call him?"

As Smith screamed, "I *am* Woolworth Smith!" Someone Else hung up.

Pat heard the scream and sensed what was needed. She grabbed the damp washcloth off the now comatose Mrs. Way's forehead and forced it into Smith's mouth.

She gently guided him onto his couch. Then she went for decaffeinated coffee.

When she returned, Smith was back at his desk.

"Who's the medical director of that damned plan?" he was back in control—angry, but controlled.

"R.I.P. King," Pat replied immediately, and provided the telephone number from memory. She'd run this maze often.

Smith dialed King's office.

"CorpuCare, Medical Director King's office." It was a recording. "Dr. King will return your call after 11 p.m. if you leave your name, number, and a brief message after you hear the tone. . . . ."

Smith didn't hang up the telephone. He dropped it on his desktop as he rose with enormous dignity, removed his white coat, slipped calmly into his sports jacket, straightened his necktie, and stepped over to open the window of his 12th-floor office.

Pat dived for his ankles as he got the window fully open. Regatta helped her to wrap the struggling, howling Smith in the straightjacket he kept on hand for the most acute fornicular episodes. Then Pat picked up the phone and dialed. It rang just once.

"CorpuCare Practitioner Services and Support," the Voice answered. "Your well-being is our problem; your problems are our well-being."

The following article demonstrates how humor and satire can effectively be used to address a serious topic in health care. As such, it provides a good lesson on how to add punch to one's editorial style. —*H.B.*

The Biblical Basis for the Rising Cesarean Section Rate:

A Historical, Hysterical, Hysteretic Account of the Rising Cesarean Section Rate and a Proposal to Classify Under a Single Term All Indications for Cesarean Section*

BARRY S. SCHIFRIN, M.D.

The incidence of cesarean section is increasing. In many hospitals, as many as one fourth of all babies are delivered abdominally. So ubiquitous is this awareness that such diverse groups as the National Institutes of Health, the Editorial Board of Better Homes and Gardens, and a counter-revolutionary group called "These Bodies" have come to suspect that contemporary obstetrics is practiced more by incision than decision. Indeed, a recent survey showed that the most common form of greeting among obstetrical personnel is "what's your section rate?"[1]

There is universal agreement that a cesarean section rate of 25 per cent is unacceptable. It is less certain, however, whether that number is too high or too low. Despite all the commentary, no one has defined what the cesarean rate should be—what we should aspire to. Indeed, everyone seems to know the section rate at their own hospital, but few know their own experience. Even fewer know the age-adjusted perinatal survival rate. Whither this paradox? The hospital section rate has no known relationship to the quality of care, while the perinatal outcome according to gestational age at birth would seem to define the quality of care.

Despite the commotion over cesarean section rates, is this all really new? Hardly. The incidence of cesarean section has risen inexorably since the first operation many centuries ago. Heretofore, only the prohibitive risk of death from infection or hemorrhage daunted the most intrepid accoucheur, and stemmed, to some extent, the inevitable tide.

There is a little known sideline of those bygone days. In a randomized study (the first in obstetrics) it was clearly demonstrated that mothers who delivered in the fields as a result of goring by a bull (so-called taurectomy) had far more salutary outcomes than women delivering by cesarean section in the hospital.

Does not the Bible command that "every generation discover the rising cesarean section rate" (St. Elsewhere 26.3)? Does it not also mandate that this information "be trumpeted from hilltops, and by pamphlets and by television with great alarems and excursions" (*ibid.* 28.4). Indeed, all the breast-beating (now recorded), that accompanied the rise from 3 to 5 per cent appears as contemporary today as it did 25 or 2500 years ago. It is likely that it will also seem fresh to our children and our children's children.

At the current rate of increase, the cesarean section rate will exceed 100 per cent in the year 2007. (If you divide the total number of babies born by the total number of cesarean sections the answer is greater than 100 per cent.)

To stem the tide, the NIH convened a Consensus Development Conference. After much deliberation this panel concluded that the predominant cause of

*Reprinted from the Journal of Perinatology, ©1986; 6(3):99–100, with permission from Appleton & Lange, Inc.

primary cesarean section is "dystocia"—a Greek term coined over 2000 years ago. We use the Greek word to describe difficulties during labor for obvious reasons—it is Greek to us.[2] In truth, the term is so general as to impart no specific meaning. The term does convey more "culture" than "failure to progress" or "CPD" or "FTP" which are modern Greek. Why use the Greek word at all? Well, it seems that there is no common terminology to describe the problems of labor. Several hundred have been collected from an old Chinese parchment.[3] While such designations would suffice if each term were specific, there appears to be sufficient confusion about the definitions of these acronyms, acrostics, and poetic phrases to challenge the workers of Babel for preeminence in interactive dyslexia. Pointedly, the NIH Committee recognized the problem but failed to recommend the adoption of any new terminology. Although not a soothsayer, I predict that when the next generation reviews the problem, they will make no more sense out of it than did their forebears.

The concentration on individual causes of the rising cesarean section rate does not give a full accounting of actual practice; it only documents certain "acceptable" indications, missing, for example, "obstetrician distress." Missing also from these discussions is the widespread use of fractional arithmetic in defining indications for cesarean section. In truth, few if any cesarean sections are ever done for a single reason. More often, parts of indications are used. By this I mean that instead of preeclampsia, dysfunctional labor, fetal distress, or advanced maternal age, we invoke some hypertension, some fetal distress, some advanced age, etc., as indications (plural) for operative delivery. If, for example, a blood pressure reading of 200/100 (MAP = 133) is 100 per cent indication for cesarean section, then a blood pressure of 140/90 (MAP = 107) can only be an 80 per cent indication. We are also confronting euphemistic changes in the designation of the operative procedure itself. Anatomically oriented folks refer to it as "vaginal bypass" (Twins are "double bypass"), environmentalists refer to it as "perineal preservation."

Enough of these succedanea. I believe that it is possible, even desireable, to define a single, accurate, comprehensive, indisputable, seminal indication for cesarean section that would sweep all others before it, rid all confusion, eliminate all discrepancies, and banish all misunderstandings. And that indication is—"THREATENED VAGINAL DELIVERY."

References

1. Logian, Theo: Angels on pinheads—a quantitative analysis. Biblical Convivialities 9:26, 1938.

2. Juste, Le Mot: When in doubt—Greek. Living Semantics 7:10, 1980.

3. Wu, Dum Luc: Excavations of Shanghai Winter Gardens. Corner of Wilshire and Hauser, 1964.

Additional Readings

1. Bennett HJ, Weissman M: Agenesis of the corporate callosum: a new clinical entity. N Engl J Med 1987; 316(19):1220.

This is a satirical case report about a new corporate malady. It involved a health maintenance organization, Moneycare Corporation of America, and a community hospital (St. Avarice).

2. Kamholtz T: When you're the patient. Med Economics 1957; 34(Oct):148–149.

The author presents some amusing thoughts about what happens when doctors are on the other side of the stethoscope.

3. Markle GB: What if everybody had to get informed consent? Med Economics 1976; 53(Apr 5): 148–152.

The author ponders what might happen if nonprofessionals were required to tell customers about the risks associated with their services. For example, the likelihood of crashing into the City National Bank during a flight, of choking to death during a steak dinner, of contracting salmonella after eating a chicken dish, or of making it out of the hair cutter's with your carotid arteries intact.

4. Morgan KR: What to tell third parties who use and abuse you. Med Economics 1974; 51(Aug 5):130–135.

The author, who is tired of dealing with myopic insurance companies, presents some of the pungent letters he has written over the years on his patients' behalf.

5. Rochelson B, Stone ML: The designated defendant. Obstet Gynceol 1987; 70(4):662–663.

In this clever satire, the authors propose that elderly physicians (85+ years of age) be used as the attendings of record at teaching hospitals. That way, in the ten or more years it would take for a malpractice case to get to court, that should be the worst of his problems.

THE PHYSICIAN AT WORK

There are a number of safeguards built into medical practice that are designed to prevent boredom. Besides having to deal with lab personnel, answering services, hospital administrators, and upset families (our patients'), we also have to contend with specialists, partners, busy schedules, and upset families (our own). With so much to do, it's a wonder more of us don't quit and go into law.

Although I did not actively look for jokes during my research, I did run into a number of funny ones along the way. Therefore, to kick off the chapter, I am including the following joke from Patricia Thomas' article, "The Anatomy of Coping: Medicine's Funny Bone" (see appendix).

> A doctor dies and goes to heaven, where he finds a long line at St. Peter's gate. As is his custom, the doctor rushes to the front, but St. Peter tells him to go wait in line like everyone else. Muttering and looking at his watch, the doctor stands at the end of the line.
>
> Moments later, a white-haired man wearing a white coat and carrying a stethoscope and black bag rushes to the front of the line, waves to St. Peter, and is immediately admitted through the pearly gates.
>
> "Hey!" the doctor says angrily. "How come you let him through without waiting?"
>
> "Oh," says St. Peter, "that's God. Sometimes he likes to play doctor."

The Trouble With Treating Your Relatives*

RALPH T. STREETER, M.D.

You probably owe your relatives a lot for the way they helped you get started in practice. But do you owe them the care of their pets and other oddities?

Every movie fan knows that a small boy with an injured puppy is every young doctor's first patient. Every experienced physician knows that this boy is a relative of the young doctor he goes to. And in *my* experience, the aunt who sent her boy and his dog over to me thought treatment of an injured paw was about the limit of my ability.

Doting aunts are quick to spread the word of your skill as a physician. But they themselves won't follow your advice, even if you simply suggest that they take two aspirins for a headache.

While still in medical school, I was often asked my medical opinion by members of the family. I realized that this was in the nature of chaffing a young fellow who had graduated from high school eight years ago and had yet to earn his first dollar. It was later, while I was serving my internship, that I became seriously initiated into that vast subspecialty of every doctor: relative practice.

Father-in-Law's Rx

My father-in-law developed a mild case of conjunctivitis during the course of a week-end visit to my home. I was delighted to be of some help to him. I presented myself at the corner drugstore, borrowed a prescription pad, and wrote a beautiful prescription for benzalkonium chloride (refined) 1:5,000 in normal saline with gtt i epinephrine hydrochloride 1:1,000 to the ounce.

My father-in-law thanked me. My mother-in-law thanked me. But after they left, I found the unopened bottle on the top shelf of a bookcase.

A few days later, my mother-in-law phoned. "We're so proud of you," she said. "The Lincoln Life nurse said it was conjunctivitis, just as you did. She gave Walter some eye drops, and they're clearing his eyes nicely."

There's no way to avoid this segment of practice. If you're an orphan, there are always plenty of friends to fill your kinless vacuum.

I don't mean casual acquaintances, whose questions can usually be stopped by suggesting an appointment. The friends I speak of are those old and dear ones who consider themselves part of the family.

All such friends and relatives can be divided into three categories. There are the ones with pets, the ones with absurd ailments, and the ones who belong to *other* physicians. (As a matter of fact, *all* of them are regular patients of other doctors. But we'll go into that later.)

To begin with, let's look at category #1:

Their Pets Are Sick

There was the friend who called me at 2 a.m. one winter morning to assist in the delivery of a litter of pups. A week before, the bitch had defecated in the room we call my study. This apparently gave my friend the idea that he ought to call *me* rather than disturb the veterinarian.

That tops anything my relatives have ever done. In fact, it tops anything I've ever heard, except for the colleague who was called out of a staff meeting to prescribe an abortifacient for a neighbor's cat. At least *I* wasn't asked to do anything questionable.

Relatives with pets have to be handled with just as much tact as the old maid in your private practice with a positive serology. A faltering diagnosis on a helpless animal can ruin you.

*Reprinted with permission from Medical Economics, ©1957; 34(Dec):141–147; Medical Economics Company, Inc., Oradell, N.J. 07649.

I almost lost an old and trusted friend when I failed to recognize an advanced case of Bumblefoot in an owl he'd acquired. It's doubtful if his wife's obstetrician would have recognized it either. Still, I came off better than another of his M.D. friends who prescribed streptomycin for the owl. As soon as the needle was withdrawn, the bird fell over dead.

It took a lot of persuasion and the better part of a bottle of brandy to re-establish my friend's faith in medicine. He seriously questioned whether doctors who couldn't treat an owl were any better equipped to treat humans.

It's just such a challenge that made a competent orthopedist of my acquaintance put a modification of a Peterson nail in a parrot's femur. Or that pushed a certain psychiatrist into an attempt to resolve the frank homosexuality of a French poodle. Or that caused a full professor of pathology whom I know to make a section of a piece of steak, in order to convince his mother that the butcher wasn't selling horse meat.

The Queer-Ailment Ones

Category #2 consists of relations who ask you to treat vague complaints of bizarre etiology, without recognizable pathology. These ailments, you've probably noticed, occur only on those portions of the body that can be shown without taking off anything (except, rarely, a shoe). And the suffering relative always points out that the problem is too trifling to bother his regular doctor—the difference between you and a "regular doctor" being that *he* sends a statement.

You Know the Type

I have a light-headed second cousin with recurring ganglia on her wrist. With each occurrence, she admits that the lump appears only when she wears her wrist watch. My recurring answer is that the cause might be pressure from the band. She smiles vaguely and says something like: "It's a very good watch, Ralph dear." And so she goes on thinking of me as Betsy's boy, the one who took so long to get through school.

There is in every family a brother-in-law with athlete's foot. My brother-in-law's last athletic experience was touch football at Yale ten years ago; but his dermatomycosis pedis is refractory to all the sample medications that pile up in the mailbox. Every time I

see him, he says: "I've still got that itch on the bottom of my foot."

He says it in an injured way. He's indicating that a better, more responsible doctor would have cleared it up by now.

The easy way out would be to suggest that such individuals see their own physician. But only a narrow, begrudging doctor would refuse a few words of advice to an uncle or an old friend—especially if he's a hydraulics engineer and only last week advised you on the best way to drain your new patio. The main difference is that *you* followed *his* advice.

Cured—by Someone Else

Some of these relative ills can be helped, of course—but never by you.

The tic in my older brother's left eye failed to respond to all the ophthalmology, psychiatry, and neurology I knew. But it has been completely cured at the neighborhood health bar with a daily pint of carrot juice and eight ounces of sunflower seeds. Naturally, he tells me about it every chance he gets.

Our cook acts the same way. Long ago, I urged treatment for her goiter, and I made appointments for her with qualified men. She didn't keep them, but the goiter disappeared. She says a practitioner of black magic conjured it away by laying on the hand of a recently demised seventh son of a seventh son.

The only person in our household who doesn't chuckle when she tells the story is me.

They Have Other Doctors

Finally, we come to category #3: the friends and relatives who are already being treated by their own physicians. If you can handle them, you're probably qualified to get Hungary back from Khrushchev. They present their signs and symptoms in detail, and all they want is for you to tell them what the doctor's doing wrong.

Naturally, you take a firm stand. "I think yours is a very interesting case, and Dr. Blank is doing exactly the right thing," you say firmly.

But this doesn't help, since everybody's aware of medical ethics. "But what do you *really* think?" asks the persistent sister-in-law (females outnumber males about four to one on this). "Don't you think it's taking too long to get results? Don't all those X-rays show that Dr. Blank doesn't know what's wrong?"

You repeat your first statement with increased firmness. The following day, she calls your wife and asks *her* opinion of your opinion. She explains that the serious expression on your face the evening before suggested that hers is a far advanced and hopeless case. (A smile, however, would have convinced her that Dr. Blank is an utter incompetent. And on her next appointment she'd probably have implied as much to him.)

'Check Me, Daddy'

In the relative practice of medicine, nobody can cause you more self-doubt, nobody can frustrate and harass you more, than your own wife and children. The only time the married physician really envies his bachelor colleagues is when he's nursing a bruised ego as the result of making an effort to play the role of family doctor (as opposed to doctor in the family).

My 4-year-old son has never awakened me at dawn with a cheery "Good morning," as I'm told lawyers' children do. Mine comes stumbling in with the demand: "Check me, Daddy." Only a hand on his forehead, with assurance that he's in excellent health, gives him the strength to continue through the day.

So far he's too young to doubt my word. But he'll learn. The doctor's immediate family are never silly enough to believe Daddy really knows medicine.

During my senior obstetrical clerkship days, I expressed the opinion that my wife and I were shortly to become parents of twins. She expressed the opinion that I needed more practice on the maneuvers of Leopold. Six weeks later the obstetrician and X-ray confirmed my diagnosis. She was as surprised as if she were hearing it for the first time.

Doctor's Best Friend

Occasionally, though, you *will* find gratitude in the immediate family. One of the most grateful patients I've ever had was our dog, Genevieve. During my residency, she kept giving birth to litters of tremendous size and variety. All canine preventive measures failed; so we decided to make a permanent change. Since the veterinarian's fee was almost the same as my monthly salary, my wife took the familiar attitude that anyone who can treat people can certainly treat cocker spaniels.

A fellow gynecology resident, an anesthesia resident, and I planned the operative procedure. We were a little handicapped because none of us could read German, and the only appropriate book in the medical library was entitled "Der Hund." But all things considered, the operation went very well.

During the immediate postoperative period, I carefully examined the incision and probed the abdomen morning and night. That was four years ago. For four years now, every time I come home Genevieve lolls foolishly on her back with all four legs extended. I say, "Nice incision, Genny." And she gets up and romps gratefully away.

I should like something of the same brand of respect from my children. But their mother is teaching *them* to be brighter than Genevieve.

And now I see my nephew and his dog coming up the walk. Browny has the mange. I must get back to my subspecialty again. How's it with yours?

Please Get My Patient Off the Referral Merry-Go-Round*

JOHN R. EGERTON, M.D.

Exasperated at what's happening with some of his patients, a primary-care physician airs his feelings in this tongue-in-cheek letter to a fictitious specialist who exemplifies what's wrong.

Dear Dr. Meddler:

I'm writing to you about my patient, Mr. Ivor Payne, whom I referred to your care several months ago with a possible diagnosis of X disease. Since I considered you an expert Xologist, I felt you would give the best advice on the management of Mr. Payne's condition. Although I have not heard from you, I gather that you have seen my patient because I have received a letter from Dr. Nervroot indicating you had referred Mr. Payne to him for a neurological consultation about his headaches.

I was pleased to read that the CT scan, EEG, and complete blood chemistries were within normal limits and that Dr. Nervroot agrees with my long-standing diagnosis of tension headaches. These have been bothering Mr. Payne more than usual lately and perhaps are related to his impending divorce. But it is nice to know that despite his edginess, there is nothing neurologically wrong.

I was also interested to hear from Dr. Waterworks, to whom you referred my patient for a urological opinion of his nocturia. It's very reassuring to learn that a second blood test proved again that Mr. Payne's chemistries were normal and that his urine culture, I.V.P, and cystoscopy were all negative.

But may I venture to suggest that my patient's problems may be related to his lifelong habit of drinking a six-pack of beer before retiring? He claims that it helps him relax, and he probably feels that need more than ever now that the divorce is imminent.

The unexpected news about the orthopedic consultation you obtained came to me from either Dr. Stick or Dr. Stone—I can't decipher the signature. I was delighted to have it confirmed that Mr. Payne's lower back pain is due to nothing more serious than chronic strain. He has had this problem, incidentally, every spring because of an overzealous approach to his garden. I'm pleased to learn that the back X-rays show no abnormality and all that is required is for him to do a series of exercises and take some pills.

I disagree, however, with the orthopod's choice of medication. When Mr. Payne took this particular drug last year, he found that it didn't help as much as his usual anti-inflammatory.

So Mr. Payne's poison-ivy sensitivity has been acting up again! He never can seem to avoid it when he gets down to yard work. Dr. Coverall wrote me after his dermatology consultation to confirm this diagnosis and to recommend treatment. I'm not sure who requested this consultation; I note that copies of the report were sent both to you and to the orthopedic clinic.

I've also received a copy of a second letter from Dr. Nervroot responding to another consultation request, this time from Dr. Stick or Dr. Stone concerning the question of whether the pain in my patient's legs was of neurological origin. It seems that no neurological abnormality was found. This dovetails with my own findings.

Happily, not all the information concerning my patient is coming to me secondhand. Yesterday I was surprised to meet Mr. Payne wandering slowly around the medical floor of the hospital, dressed in pajamas. I took the liberty of asking him how he had ended up as a hospital patient. Imagine how surprised I was to find he was being treated by the psychiatric service.

* Reprinted with permission from Medical Economics, ©1983; 60(Nov 14):313–315; Medical Economics Company, Inc., Oradell, N.J. 07649.

We had quite a long, if disjointed, chat, and I was pleased to learn that he hasn't yet been diagnosed as having any specific psychiatric illness but is merely being observed and medicated. He certainly seemed medicated, since he could hardly stay awake during our conversation. I was puzzled as to why Mr. Payne had been referred to a psychiatrist and by whom. But it all fell into place when he informed me that he had become confused and morose following his surgery.

Naturally, I was reluctant to pry into the nature of the surgical procedure but, since he *is* my patient, curiosity got the better of my good manners. Mr. Payne then told me that he'd been persuaded by Dr. Cuttemup to do something about his gallstone. It wasn't clear who had referred him to the surgeon. In any event, it so happens that Mr. Payne's gallstone had been his asymptomatic and non-troublesome companion for more than two decades. Long ago he and I discussed the pros and cons of removing it or of leaving well enough alone. He was adamant that he would not be subjected to what he considered unnecessary surgery.

I presume that Dr. Cuttemup must have given him some very attractive reasons for having his gallbladder removed. Fortunately, Mr. Payne seems to have recovered from the surgery with no problem apart from the symptoms for which he is now being treated by the psychiatrist.

But to get to the crux of the matter—and I shall phrase this as delicately as possible—will you please tell me whether or not he has X disease? Now that my patient has been tested, checked, X-rayed, bled, bled again, and separated from his gallbladder, may I beg of you to send me a report of your findings?

I would ask Mr. Payne himself whether he has been diagnosed as having X disease but he seems incapable of concentrating on such abstractions.

I hope I'm not being overly possessive, but as Mr. Payne's primary-care physician I have some lingering interest in getting the facts about his condition before he is passed on to the next referral.

I remain your obedient servant.

John Egerton

Your Most
Mysterious Colleague*

THEODORE KAMHOLTZ, M.D.

You've never met him, yet you hear about him all the time. He's the least rational, most inscrutable physician you know of.

He's your patient's Former Doctor.

Let's say you're taking a history on a new patient. She's fair, fat, and forty. She has cholelithiasis. She sticks to a diet ninety-nine days out of a hundred. Every hundredth day, she just can't resist potato pancakes with gravy, and she's rewarded with a 3 A.M. seizure of biliary colic.

So far, no surprises. But suddenly the cogs slip. "My former physician"—says the patient—"gave me some medicine and then massaged the stone right out."

"Massaged?" you ask warily.

"Oh, yes." And she shows you some calculi removed in just that way. As a matter of fact, the Former Doctor had a way with renal calculi, too. He had a medicine that dissolved them.

One characteristic, then, of the Former Doctor is that his medicine appears to be entirely different from yours. It's not that he's a charlatan. It's just that a few details get garbled when the patient relays them from doctor to doctor.

You recall one of your own patients who thanked you profusely for curing his cough and palpitations during fluoroscopy. That form of therapy really

*Reprinted with permission from Medical Economics, ©1958; 35(Apr 14):122–128; Medical Economics Company, Inc., Oradell, N.J. 07649.

impressed him. You shudder to think how it will sound when he describes it to the next doctor who sees him.

Meanwhile, you still have a sneaking suspicion that your colleague's psychotherapy is more flamboyant than yours. This is particularly true after a patient tells you that his previous physician uses gold and silver hypodermic needles.

Another thing that impresses you about the Former Doctor is that he has a pharmacopoeia substantially different from yours. One day, a patient asks if the medication his last doctor prescribed could cause numbness in the ears. You've never heard of the drug in question, so you look it up. Two hours in the medical library produce only one small reference to it—and that in an untranslated Swedish journal published more than twenty years ago.

Shot Therapy

Another patient wants an injection of the stuff his former physician gave him. It cured his psoriasis overnight. He went to bed in misery and awoke the next morning unblemished. The scales are beginning to come back now, and . . .

Sometimes you wish that his Former Doctor would just hang onto his patients. (It probably comes to you as a second thought that he wishes the same thing.)

A woman with a kidney condition tells you her previous physician put her on a diet of almond, celery, potatoes, and apricot brandy. Should she continue it? You can't detect one iota of logic in it. Yet can you unhesitatingly condemn? After all, they laughed at Pasteur . . .

You suggest that she return to the other fellow for management of her case. But she can't. She never paid his bills.

Most of the time, you're grateful that you don't actually know your predecessor on the case. Occasionally, however, you do get to know him. Then you discover that the irrational Former Doctor doesn't really exist.

"I saw a patient of yours the other day—Egbert Blank," you may say to your colleague in the hospital staff room. Then you add hesitantly: "He says you cured his tuberculosis with shoe supports."

Your colleague laughs. Then he tells the story:

Egbert had been coming home tired and aching all over. Even his feet had hurt him. When his great aunt died of tuberculosis, he became convinced he had it, too. He began to lose weight and to have night sweats. No amount of X-rays, examinations, or assurances helped.

Your colleague found a local foot condition, prescribed supports, and told him that as long as he was going to die of tuberculosis (which the patient believed and the doctor doubted), he might as well die with happy feet.

"I gather it worked," your colleague says. "What's his trouble now?"

"Nothing much," you reply. "Just syphilophobia."

For each case handled by the mysterious Former Doctor that finally is clarified, a dozen cases remain tantalizingly unbelievable. His office, seen through your patients' eyes, varies from alchemist shop to temple; his prescriptions are incantations.

They'll Talk About You

But, aware of your own patient's misunderstandings, you hesitate to criticize, no matter how wild the story. After all, a patient of yours may tell *his* next doctor that his wife's menses became regular after *he* took a tonic—forgetting all about the intensive course of estrogen therapy she was given. If so, your only hope is that he also forgets your name.

Short Course in Euphemism*

PHILIP A. KILBOURNE, M.D.

After a few years of practice, most of us get pretty slick at interpreting "patientese." We soon learn, for example, that "Spare no expense" or "Money is no object" can mean "I have no intention of paying you anyway."

All well and good. But how about the other side of the coin? The list that follows is a mere neophyte's armamentarium of some reliable clichés of consulting-room technique. The column on the left represents the actual spoken words; the column on the right, the thought behind them.

If some of you younger men in the front row still haven't caught the knack of it, maybe you'd better see me after class for further coaching. But perhaps it will help if you simply keep this point in mind: Your diploma only starts you in practice; it's your diplomacy that keeps you there.

When you say:	You may mean:
"Just get this prescription filled and come back in about two days."	"Darned if I know what you've got. I'll need a couple of days to read up on the symptoms."
"Who's your regular physician?"	"How many doctors did you shop before you got down to me?"
"When a child like yours presents a behavior problem, it often helps to look for environmental causes."	"There's nothing wrong with your kid that a new set of parents wouldn't cure."
"Let me just check the current cost of this drug."	"I'm looking up the dose in PDR."
"I'm sure that if Dr. Smith had not been so terribly overworked he'd have arrived at the same diagnosis as I did."	"That cloth-head couldn't diagnose his way out of a wet paper bag."
"Yes, you went to the only man in the country who could have performed that operation."	"Old Krankheit's the only man in the country who still *does* that operation."
"I happen to have a limited stock of that drug right here, so we can get you started on it now."	"The detail man just left."
"Your baby certainly looks like his father."	"No teeth, no hair, and the same pot belly."

*Reprinted with permission from Medical Economics, ©1963; 40(Feb 25):90–91; Medical Economics Company, Inc., Oradell, N.J. 07649.

I'm 100 Per Cent Publicly Owned!*

MYRON C. GREENGOLD, M.D.

Corporate practice? This M.D. has carried it one wild step further. Here's the sly account of how he became the first solo OBG man in his state to incorporate and how he went public.

Now that the first flush of enthusiasm for Keogh-type retirement plans is ebbing, many doctors are looking around for more promising ways to beat taxes. For my money, you can't beat incorporation. Sure, I know the Internal Revenue Service recently proposed regulations aimed at squelching doctors' efforts to incorporate. Matter of fact, I was the first solo OBG man to incorporate in my state, and it just may be that those I.R.S. regulations were aimed at me. I think you'll be interested in my story.

I'd always wanted to be a corporation, and as soon as our state Legislature passed its enabling act, I jumped right in. Quicker than it takes to say "Internal Revenue Service," I set up generous retirement, disability, sickness and accident plans for me. I put me under Social Security. I sold me my home, cars and summer cottage and then rented them back; Uncle Sam helped pick up the tab for maintenance, repairs, and depreciation. The corporation bought and leased back my appliances and office furnishings. Pretty soon, I didn't even own the shirt on my back. There I was without a cent to my name, and I was sitting pretty!

I don't mean to imply I didn't have a qualm, public-imagewise. As I took down the old shingle and hung the new one with "Inc." after my name, I had some doubts.

How would the patients take it? I needn't have worried. The response was terrific. Far from questioning my new mode of practice, they wanted in! It's surprising how many patients have always wanted to be doctors. Through my new corporation, I could give them a chance to realize a lifelong dream. I felt I had no choice. I went public!

My first stock issue was a smashing success. To eliminate middleman costs, I underwrote the issue myself. (My aide sold it over-the-counter while I was tied up in delivery.) I'd figured I was worth about half a million, so I planned to sell just 250,000 shares at $1 and keep the controlling interest myself.

It didn't work out quite that way. I found myself selling at a 25-cent premium the first day. In two weeks, I was up to 4¼, was listed on the Cow Counties Stock Exchange and, with the options I exercised, had disposed of over 700,000 shares. I guess the stock was getting a little edematous by then, but all my patients were clamoring for shares. I hated to disappoint any of them.

How does it feel to be a 100 per cent publicly owned OBG man? Well, I don't know how I ever practiced any other way. The rich bond between doctor and stockholder cannot be equaled by any other form of practice. When one of my owners gets a little cystocele or prolapse, she doesn't have to think twice about which doctor can do her the most good.

Most of the doctors in my area have followed my example and gone public, so my patients generally carry a sprinkling of pediatricians, dermatologists and orthodontists in their portfolios. I've installed in my waiting room a stock ticker and an up-to-the-minute board on most of the local medical issues around. A young chap who's taking premeds at night at our local college chalks the board—wonderful experience for the lad—and patients can follow the market for hours when I'm held up. They don't mind the wait a bit.

One of the nice features about public-stock practice shows up in the troublesome area of Christmas gifts. You know how hard it is to remember which

*Reprinted with permission from Medical Economics, ©1964; 45 (May 18):94–99; Medical Economics Company, Inc., Oradell, N.J. 07649.

pediatrician drinks Scotch, which G.P. drinks bourbon and which oddball doesn't drink. Well, nowadays, I send all my referrers the same gift: shares in me. It's a gift that keeps on giving, and it's a little remembrance that keeps on reminding. Colleagues who have a little block of me generally feel freer about requesting a consultation. Even if they never see the patient again, they still have their interest in her without having to assist or any of that malarkey.

To give you an idea of the financial flexibility of corporate practice, I need only tell you about something that happened last Christmas. The incident actually started the June before, when I got a pathology report of "normal sigmoid mucosa" on some uterine curettings I'd sent to the lab. I knew then I'd have a hard time with the patient's family. She'd been bellyaching to them about gas and bloat and pain ever since she'd come out of the anesthetic, and I just didn't like the fishy look they gave me when I explained what had happened. Anyway, I did the bowel repair, she recovered, and I heard no more about it until just before Christmas.

Then, right after I turned the bill over to the collectors, what did the family do but find themselves a shyster lawyer and file suit for malpractice? To make matters worse, I'd been so tied up in June with our annual meeting and other stockholders' business that I'd neglected to sign my progress notes on the second admission. My lawyer told me our defense was hopeless. We settled.

On Dec. 23, when the news finally got out, I was selling at 7½. By the 27th, I bottomed out at 1¼. I'd seen this coming, of course. As I've said, I knew the family were troublemakers, so I'd been selling all summer and fall. By the 20th of December, I was short 88,000 shares at 7½, and in the next two weeks I closed at 1¼ and 2. What's more, I kept right on buying,

running the stock up to 9½ on the strength of a good fourth-quarter report featuring 12 successful New Year's Eve inductions and two elective sections. I'm now ahead $515,000 on the short sales (short-term capital-gains income, but spread over two years) plus $370,000 in paper profits, which I'm holding for long-term capital gains. The corporation has a nice $120,000 tax loss carry-forward on our out-of-court settlement, and I'm out smelling like a rose.

Well, that should give you some idea of what going public can do for you. I'm not saying it's all peaches and cream, mind you. Our little proxy fight last year gave me a turn, and there are little problems with the S.E.C. that you probably don't run into in a closed corporation. But I feel I've grown, and I've barely scratched the surface.

I've got a little securities-analysis service going now. I limit myself to local medical issues; being on the tissue committee of my community hospital helps me spot special situations for my clients and my own trading account. My corporate diversification program is just getting into high gear: Baffin Island Land Development and Philanthropic Finance are wholly owned subsidiaries, and I'm moving into a franchise shoeshine-box operation I'd rather not identify right now. I'm giving up all my OB work on the first of the year, and I've cut way back on gynecology, doing just enough to keep my hand in.

If you'd like to know how corporate methods can be applied to your practice, send for my free booklet, "You Can Be a Blue Chip!" There's absolutely no cost or obligation, and no salesman will call. Or, if you prefer, your management consultant may be able to turn out a corporate setup for you. But tell him to think big.

The author, in point of sober fact, is a California G.P. in solo—and completely noncorporate—practice.

Clinical Algorithms*

R. G. NEVILLE, MRCGP, DRCOG

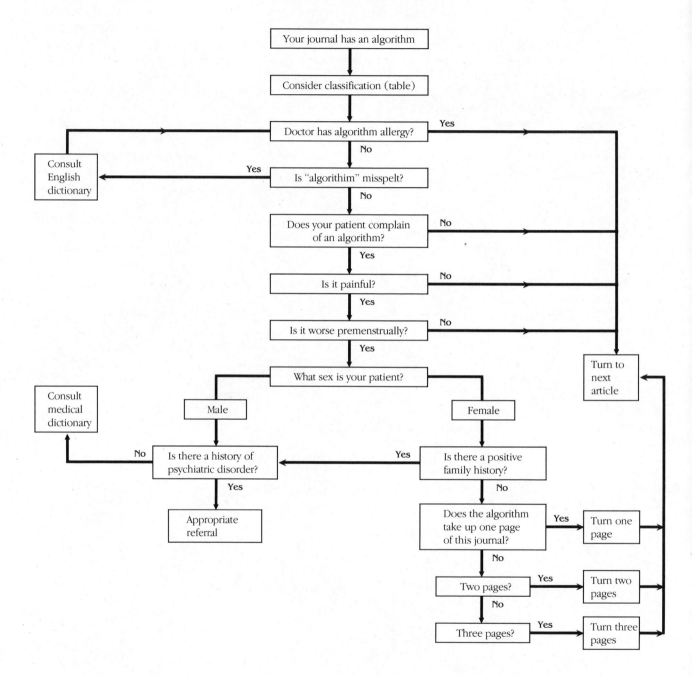

*Reprinted with permission from the British Medical Journal, ©1985;
291(Dec 21–28):1819.

The Index of Arrival*

THEODORE KAMHOLTZ, M.D.

In medicine, doctors start at the bottom of the ladder and climb up rung by tedious rung. The pursuit of the apex is so demanding that they rarely survey their position. Will you get the appropriate signal once you've reached the top? Or will you overshoot your mark like the comic hero in a cartoon movie? Perhaps you should take stock of your position and determine your own index of arrival.

There is a little old lady who can tell when you've arrived. She works behind the counter in the hospital cafeteria. She looks gossamer frail, but has the soul of a meat grinder. When you first enter the hospital, she serves your soup half in the bowl and half on the tray. One day when you order chicken salad, she indicates that she recognizes you. She knows you are up and coming so she gives you sliced corned beef instead. But when you reach the top, she no longer tries to please you but to do good by you. She casts an appraising look at your belt size, ladles out a 32 calorie portion of cottage cheese and says, "Here you are, Curly." You've arrived!

The elevator operator is an expert at rating the status of doctors. When you first come to the hospital, your capital epiphyses have just fused. He takes one look at you and says, "Where's your pass, Sonny?" He begins to think you're a regular guy when he lets you see the photograph of him kissing a starlet good-bye after her 12th suicide attempt. You're promoted when he starts to plumb your professional judgment. "Say Doc, are you going to operate on the guy in Three North whose wife tried to knit him to death?" But when he stops the elevator between floors to show you the largest scrotal hernia in the hospital—you've arrived!

The x-ray technician has a keen sense about the relative status of doctors. If he takes your requisition slip, asks blandly what idiot filled that out, and tosses it in the waste basket—you are gauche. When he acquiesces to your request for taking the skull and foot on the same film, he believes you are headed in the right direction. But when he tells you the radiologist has read the GI series as negative, but that if he were you he'd look twice at that ulcer niche high on the lesser curvature—You've arrived!

The operating room squad has great facility in recognizing which side of the bread is buttered. When you first arrive you not only get little time in the O.R., but are also assigned scrub nurses with PMS and interns who have lost the toss of the coin. As your prestige mounts, they give you 15 minutes prime time, the chief resident, and all the instruments you need. But when you've been working all morning over a hot belly and the circulating nurse goes out of her way to scratch your back and give you a soggy paper cup filled with hot, undrinkable coffee—You've arrived!

Hospital administrators indicate the status of doctors by the quality of their introductions. At your first staff meeting, he introduces you as Dr. David Clown when your name is really Dr. Robert Brown. You have moved up a notch when he introduces you to the ladies auxiliary as Dr. Brown, our eminent neurosurgeon, even though you're board certified in hematology. But when he introduces you at an annual dinner as "Dr. Robert Brown, a man who needs no introduction" and then launches into a 15 minute one—You've arrived!

In the final analysis, however, it is your colleagues who determine your true status as a doctor. If they refer you patients who live out of town and require home visits at night, your meteor has not yet left the ground. If they refer only their headache patients, but at least the ones who will pay, your star is in its ascendancy. If they refer all their cases to you, the dull and the interesting, the penniless and the wealthy, your star is bright. But if they refer only relatives (not the paying kind) they are indicating that you possess not only the highest medical skill, but the highest ethical standards as well—You've arrived!

*Reprinted from JAMA, ©1963; 186(6):A206–207, with permission from the American Medical Association. Edited from the original.

Additional Readings

1. Bluestone N: Professional courtesy. New Physician 1979; 28(11):6,26,28.

After the author refers her mother to a group of colleagues for a minor ailment, a lively bit of correspondence ensues regarding the etiquette of professional courtesy.

2. Cohn A: See this tic? I owe it to "Alternative Therapists." Med Economics 1988; 65(Nov):205–214.

In this amusing satire, the author relates some of his experiences with chiropractors, homeopathists, foot reflexologists and other practitioners from the opposite side of the tracks. Dr. Cohn also writes under the pseudonym Oscar London (see below).

3. Felson B: My most unforgettable patient. Seminar Roentgen 1976; 11(2):77–79.

A radiologist tells the story of how he ended up x-raying a cow in his hospital. Getting the films done was a little tricky, and the cow retaliated with some emissions of her own.

4. Guttman G: Things they never warned me about in medical school. Med Economics 1985; 62(Dec 23):59.

In this brief article, the author presents 15 bits of wisdom he has learned as a practicing pediatrician. For example, "Never trust a naked baby," and "The only way to keep a child from ingesting a drug is to prescribe it for him."

5. London, Oscar: Kill as Few Patients as Possible (and fifty-six other essays on how to be the world's best doctor). Berkeley, Ten Speed Press, 1987.

A collection of essays on medical practice that are witty, amusing, and provocative.

6. Matz R: Principles of medicine. NY State J Med 1977; 77(1):99–101.

7. Matz R: More principles of medicine. NY State J Med 1977; 77(12):1984–1985.

The author presents 144 rules and laws of medicine. Most ring true and some are funny. For example, the Principles of Intensive Care: (1) air goes in and out (2) blood goes round and round (3) oxygen is good.

8. Rose I: Robert's rules of parliamentary procedure: III. the phenomenon of records. Can Med Assoc J 1963; 89(Aug 17):308–309.

This article satirizes a physician's least favorite task—dealing with medical records.

9. Schiedermayer DL: The Hippocratic oath—corporate version. N Engl J Med 1986; 314(1):62.

A brief satire that updates the original. For example, "I will not use the knife unless I am a surgeon, but I will try to learn some form of endoscopy."

10. Shaw BA: If doctors bargained like car dealers. Med Economics 1987; 64(Sept 7):139–143.

The shoe is on the other foot!

ODDS & ENDS

When I began my research, I had no preconceived ideas about the type of humor I would find. As the collection grew certain categories began to emerge, however, and the resulting chapters more or less fell into place. As you might expect, not all of the articles fit neatly into these chapters, so this one was created to handle the rest. Although the following selections defy organization into a single whole, they do add a dimension to the rest of the book. For example, the article by S. N. Gaño, "A Gloss Attributed to the Hippocratic School," is not only one of the funniest I found, but it was also published in a rather obscure journal: *The Leech* is the Journal of the Cardiff Medical Student's Club of the Welsh National School of Medicine.

A Gloss Attributed to the Hippocratic School*

S. N. GAÑO

This article was received from America. S. N. Gano is the pen-name of a well-known New York M.D.—*Editor.*

It is well known to students of ancient medicine that the Greek authors are very incompletely represented in English translation. Similar neglect has befallen the Hippocratic writings. The text which is given herewith has suffered the neglect of centuries. While thorough palaeographic and critical analysis must be reserved for the future, quite obviously the text is a gloss or series of notes on various familiar Hippocratic writings, and was probably prepared by a student or member of the Hippocratic group. The stylistic traits bear strong evidence of genuineness, and the reader cannot fail to be impressed by the conciseness, clarity, and sagacity which are displayed in almost every paragraph.

Prognostics

- Absence of respiration is a bad sign.
- It is unfavourable for the patient to be purple, especially if he is also cold. The physician should not promise a cure in such cases.
- Appetite is better without hellebore.[†]
- Haemorrhoids are not improved by horseback riding or by riding on an ass.
- When bloodletting is followed repeatedly by sweating and convulsions, the patient will not have a crisis on the fortieth day.
- Drowsiness and the itch are incompatible.

Epidemics

- Plutocrates the moneylender, who dwelt by the Wall, went to Potos during the Olympic Games. The itch appeared on the third day, followed by burning and discharge. Returned home to his wife; unfavourable crisis. Leeches were applied. Death on the twentieth day.
- On the island of Tenebros, in the spring of the year, several maidens were attacked by swelling of the abdomen and absence of the menstrual discharges. Giddiness; face flushed. A voyage to Asia was recommended. Complete crisis at the end of the ninth month.

Aphorisms

- Patients who always wake up on the wrong side should be treated by purges.
- To have the mouth constantly open is usual in persons entrusted with affairs of state. Usually nothing comes out.
- Fevers of eighty days where no cause is apparent produce alienation of mind in the physician.
- In cases of severe pain in the side of the chest, with profuse expectoration of blood and shortness of breath, it is best to observe carefully whether there is a knife between the ribs.
- Fevers, haemorrhages, and convulsions are bad; wine is good, in spring, summer or winter.
- Maidens, after the age of puberty, are subject to deep respiration at night, especially if the warm winds are blowing.
- Life is short and the art long; patients are inscrutable; their ignorance is impenetrable and their relatives are impossible.
- When swarthy parents have a blonde child and a blonde serving-maid, the physician should suspect a displacement of humors.

*Reprinted from the Leech, ©1958; 4(8):17–19; with permission from the author. Edited from the original.
[†] poisonous herb

• Logorrhoea* can be treated by placing a reed firmly beneath the tongue. In severe cases bandaging is helpful.

• When the spleen is found on the right side, the patient should consider changing physicians.

In the Surgery

• The surgeon requires a steady hand and a calm disposition. It is also essential to have a patient.

• In young women abduction is commoner than in the aged, and produces greater results.

• Great delay in resolution of the humors is more common among the rich than among the poor.

Fractures and Articulations

• Dislocation of the neck, which has been produced by a rope, cannot be treated with barley water.

• If the thumb is placed on the nose while the other fingers are alternately flexed and extended, fracture of the jaw may follow.

• Those who have recently fractured both thighs or dislocated one knee should not take part in the Olympic Games.

Ancient Medicine

• In patients who are filled with nothing but crude humors, removal of all the blood relieves the symptoms.

• The physician who understands the humors of women and the aged will not live on gruel.

• In those who have hiccup and talk at random and cannot hold the head erect, the pneuma may have become mixed with undiluted wine. In such cases the crisis follows on the next day.

• Where symptoms are severe and protracted it is good (for the physician) if the patient's relatives are few, and best if they be absent altogether.

• The physician should not thoughtlessly condemn ancient medicine merely because it was ineffective. The Art is eternal.

*Excessive and often incoherent talkativeness.

A Mercifully Brief History of Medicine*

RICHARD ARMOUR, PhD, LittD

Medicine began with the dawn of history. In fact it began shortly before dawn, at about 3:00 A.M., when the first Stone Age doctor was routed from his bed by a patient who thought he was dying. Transportation being none too good (this being before the invention of the wheel), by the time the doctor arrived the patient was well.

Ancient

During the Stone Age the most common complaints were gallstones, kidney stones, and stumbling over stones. Surgery was in its infancy, largely because of the difficulty of making an incision with a sharpened stone and of performing a suture with a stone needle. When a surgeon decided not to operate, everyone breathed a sigh of relief, especially the surgeon and, if he was still alive, the patient.

Having no stethoscope, the Stone Age doctor was forced to place his ear directly against the patient's chest. This was not easy, if the patient was male, because of the thick growth of hair which not only muffled sounds but in some instances pierced the doctor's eardrum. A small flat stone served excellently as a tongue depressor. Only rarely was it swallowed by a patient who might have thought it was a throat lozenge. Accidental swallowing of small flat stones, with dramatic improvement of sore throats, led to the invention of the placebo. Not until near the end of the Stone Age were chocolate-covered stones available for children and others who had trouble getting the plain ones down.

The doctor's little black bag was at first a little brown bag, since it was made out of tree bark. A doctor with a friendly bedside manner often made a joke of this as he entered the sickroom. "My bark is worse than my bite," he would say, thereupon laughing so uproariously that it was hard to believe he had used the same witticism as an icebreaker at six previous calls that day.

Despite this difference between the color of the bag used in those early days and the one used today, a precedent was set that has not been deviated from since. Before leaving to make his calls, the doctor carefully filled his bag with every possible medical item, omitting only such things as he later discovered he needed desperately.

Since everyone lived in caves during the Stone Age, the Stone Age hospital was also a cave. Attendants worked ceaselessly to keep the dirt off the dirt floors. Nurses hurried about, wearing a sterilized bearskin and, in the interest of quiet in the corridors, no shoes. In the operating room, the anesthetist stood by with a large club in his hand, ready to anesthetize the patient if he should show signs of returning to consciousness.

Great strides in medicine were made in ancient Greece. The greatest strides were perhaps made by Hippocrates, who nervously walked up and down the hall. The reason he paced about in this way was that he was the father of medicine and was pretty jumpy, especially when near the delivery room. Before Hippocrates, medicine was in the hands of priests, which may be why there is confusion today between two kinds of doctors, the DD and the MD. The priests thought diseases were caused by demons and angry gods, which still sounds pretty plausible. But Hippocrates thought sickness could be traced to natural causes, such as bad diet, lack of fresh air, too much carousing around, and falling off the top of the Parthenon. Ever since Hippocrates, graduating medical students take the Hippocratic oath, which starts out, "I swear." After they have been in practice for a few years they learn how right Hippocrates was, and how much there is to swear about.

It was in the time of Hippocrates also that doctors learned to write prescriptions illegibly. Patients taking

*Reprinted from JAMA, ©1965; 192(2):129–131; with permission from the American Medical Association.

prescriptions to their apothecary to be filled would try to read them but soon gave up, saying, "That's Greek to me." They were Greek to everybody, but fortunately the Greek apothecary could read Greek, even when written by a physician.

Roman medicine made a great contribution in the field of sanitary engineering and public health. The Romans drained swamps, built aqueducts, constructed sewers, and killed off enough people in surrounding countries to keep cities from becoming overcrowded. Perhaps the most famous doctor in Rome was Galen, who started his career by attending gladiators. His studies of anatomy were furthered by an unlimited supply of corpses. However, he preferred to dissect apes. Galen wrote many books about the four humors, and was so obsessed with the idea that many thought him a better humorist than scientist.

Medieval

Medicine took an unexpected turn in the Middle Ages, when it became affiliated with astrology. No one would swallow a pill without first checking to see whether the stars were in a favorable position, and on a cloudy night this could be difficult. The horoscope was more important than the microscope, perhaps because it could be used with both eyes. Moreover, a good deal of dependence was put on magic, of which there were two kinds: black magic and white magic. Black magic was powerful stuff, sold under the counter, and you had to know a magician to get it.

Blood letting was a popular cure in the Middle Ages. The idea was to get rid of impurities in the blood by opening a vein or (if in a hurry) an artery and letting the patient bleed to death. Much of the blood letting was accomplished by barbers, some of whom were very accomplished. There was also considerable therapeutic blood letting in tournaments, when knights with lances, tilting full tilt, could lance a good deal more than a boil.

Knights in full armor were something of a problem when they came into a doctor's office for an examination. For one thing, they were noisy, clanking around in the waiting room trying to find an illuminated manuscript they hadn't already read. For another, it was hopeless to try to feel a pulse through a metal sleeve and rather silly to ask a grown man to stick out his tongue through a visor. But getting a knight to disrobe was no fun either, since he couldn't do it by

himself, and a nurse usually wasn't strong enough to lift some of the larger pieces of metal. This meant the doctor had to lend a hand, when his waiting room was filling up and there were house calls to make.

Now and then a knight would step on the scales with his armor on, and the hand would go around twice and a few pounds left over, which was confusing and none too good for the springs.

Often a knight who had been fighting a fire-breathing dragon would come in with third-degree burns. What pained him was not so much the burns as their being on his back, thus giving people the impression that he was running away, which was correct. Or a fire-breathing dragon might come in and ask for something for his breath, which many found offensive.

It was during the Middle Ages that great universities such as Montpellier in France and Oxford in England began to develop their own medical schools. Henceforth medical students could be recognized as the ones who were still studying for several years after everyone else had graduated. They could also be recognized by their drawn, or sometimes overdrawn, look. At the medical school of Salerno, in Sicily, the famous woman doctor Trotula (no relation to Spatula) was supposed to have flourished. However, there is some skepticism about her having existed, much less flourished. If she did exist, along about 1150, she was Middle Aged.

Modern

Medicine developed rapidly in the Renaissance, when doctors had wider horizons. The study of anatomy was advanced by an Italian, Vesalius, who is not to be confused with Vesuvius, even though he occasionally blew his top. Vesalius was especially annoyed by the writings of Galen, which he thought full of errors about the human body. Galen, for example, believed that the pus which forms in wounds was a good thing. But Vesalius was less than enthusiastic. The pro and anti groups, or the pus and minus factions, stirred up a good deal of controversy, but Vesalius won out with his famous slogan, "Pus must go!" For this, Vesalius will be remembered, and thanked, by pusterity.

The greatest family in Italy in the Renaissance was the Medici family, though it is not quite clear whether Medicine was named after the Medici or the Medici were named after Medicine. Mostly the Medici were patrons of artists and writers rather than doctors, which may explain why they died out in 1743, surrounded by books and paintings but in bad shape physically.

During the Elizabethan period, an English physician by the name of Harvey (his last name, not his first name) discovered the circulation of the blood. Without even the aid of a microscope, he found that blood goes around and around. This is very economical, since a little blood goes a long way, and people should be a lot more grateful than they are.

Probably the greatest development in the 18th century was Edward Jenner's discovery of a method of vaccinating against smallpox. It is said that if Jenner's method of vaccination were adopted everywhere, smallpox would disappear entirely from the face of the earth and pock marks would disappear from the faces of people. Jenner's description of his work, *Inquiry into the Causes and Effects of the Variolae Vaccinae*, could have had a catchier title, such as *A Pox on Pox*, but it was widely read in medical circles anyhow. Jenner's name is gratefully remembered, except by small boys with sore arms.

During the modern era the progress of medicine has been rapid. In England, Joseph Lister made operations safer by getting surgeons to wash their hands. The practice spread to the US, where it was hailed by the manufacturers of soap. In France, Louis Pasteur discovered how to keep food from spoiling and thereby made it necessary to eat leftovers. He also made it possible to survive the bite of a mad dog, though he was so interested in saving human lives that he never stopped to inquire what the dog was mad about. In Austria, Sigmund Freud discovered the id, ego, superego, and libido, all of which had been going unnoticed in the subconscious for years. Thanks to Freud, boys discovered it was normal to want to kill their fathers and marry their mothers. Also people no longer had to listen to friends tell in great detail about their dreams, now that there were psychiatrists who were paid to do it.

Of recent years there have been marvelous developments in medicine. For instance Sir Alexander Fleming, the discoverer of penicillin, proved that you should never throw out something just because it is moldy; it may be more valuable than you think. Salk and Sabin have practically eliminated poliomyelitis, at least in those who are not too busy to drop in for the vaccine. Those who have taken it become so enthusiastic that they come back for it year after year, and are known as boosters.

With x-rays, wonder drugs, gray ladies, and self-sealing return envelopes for the paying of overdue accounts, medicine has come a long way since the Stone Age. Unlike the doctor awakened at the dawn of history by a patient suffering from a psychosomatic ailment, the modern doctor rouses himself only long enough to prescribe two aspirin and then goes back to his dream of being awarded the Nobel Prize for discovering a cure for the common cold. Or, still better, he leaves the whole thing to his answering service.

Jenner and the Ad-Man*

What would have happened if Dr. Edward Jenner had called in a press agent-promoter to help him put across his smallpox vaccine discovery?

Well, Dr. Jenner, I'm Joe Blowhard—the XYZ agency has assigned me to work up something with you on this new discovery of yours...yes, yes, I know, we'll stick to the facts, but don't forget, we have to get people stuck on them, too—ha, ha. Now, let's see... you say this protects against smallpox...hmmm ...maybe our best approach would be with the cosmetic angle...you know, "preserve your beautiful complexion, avoid disfiguring scars—get vaccinated the Jenner way"—how does that sound to you?...Oh, sure, I know people die from smallpox, but that sort of fright approach won't appeal like something that shows a woman how to be more beautiful....We've got quotes from Helen of Troy on that. And if there had been any live wires in the Garden of Eden, I'll bet we could have worked up something from Eve on it, too.

Treatment or Application?

Now, Ed, just how do you go about this—er—treatment—or application, whatever you call it?...You *scratch the skin?* Isn't that a bit rough? We want people to get the idea you are helping them, not harming them....Oh, sure, the help comes later, I know, but you have to allow for the shallow thinking of the average individual. Isn't there some other way... drinking the vaccine, say...or maybe just rubbing it in?...OK, Ed, if we have to do it that way, that's the way we'll do it...maybe we can hop it up a little—give it some schmalz—by calling it something like glorified scarification.

Next, Ed, just what is this vaccine? Something mysterious about it...comes from an isolated peak of the Andes...the tombs of the Pharaohs...a cauldron deep in the African jungle?...Ed, I guess I must have misunderstood you...I thought you said "cow"...oh, you did say cow...hmm...not very inspirational, is it? Well, a cow is a MOTHER, after all, so maybe we can

work the angle of how the young cows...it's calves? I'll make a note...how the Mother cow protects her young by producing this vaccine...oh, cows don't get smallpox? It's what? Cowpox?...Well, Ed, I guess I lost me on that last turn. Let's not get away from the central theme. Ed...none of this scatter-gun approach, you know...loses all its punch.

Let's try again...oh, it's the dairymaid? Well, that's better...chance for a lot of good buildup—got a couple of good models in mind already. Let's see...in her tender, loving care of her cow...yes, it fits right in, for who else would give a whoop for a cow, except perhaps a bull—ha, ha—the dairymaid is miraculously protected against this blight on fair womanhood by getting cowpox (whatever that is...we'll gloss it over), and now, as a result of your amazing break-through ...conquest of another of Nature's mysteries...this boon is available to all! Sounds great, doesn't it?

Now, what about some color? Can't we get a cow in on this act...you know, all fluffed up, with a pink ribbon on her tail? We can put her up in a hotel...say the Savoy...and make with the idea she's really people...folks lap up that sort of whimsy, you know....Oh, I'll take care of the details...I'll find somebody to milk her, and all that sort of thing.... Yes, Ed, better start in production on the vaccine...no, better not bring a cow with the rash or whatever it...we could have a photogenic problem, and a cow's face isn't exactly...what's that? It's on the *udder?* Oh, oh...uh....Well, Ed, that rocks the boat a little, you know...maybe a bit too sexy, I'm afraid.

Tell you what, Ed, let me dream over this stuff for a day or so...something will click, I know...but it takes some thinking-through right now....OK, Ed, but don't release any of this info to anyone for the present—it's red-hot....Sure, the scientists can wait just like everyone else.

Fine, Ed, and it has been real great talking to you.

CONTRECOUP

*Reprinted from JAMA, ©1961; 175(2):A234–236; with permission from the American Medical Association.

Transcription errors and medical malapropisms are everyday occurrences in health care. Whether it's reading that a lesion was "two sontameters long" or that a patient was admitted with a "cerebral conclusion," it's amusing to see how medical reports can get turned on their ears. As much as doctors like to think that support staff and patients are the ones responsible for all of these goofs, the article by Dorothy Reid (p. 218) shows that this is not always the case—*H.B.*

Serendipitous Neologisms*

ARLAN L. ROSENBLOOM, M.D.

From time to time an inadvertent witticism shatters the repetitive jargon in the communications among physicians. These nuggets of fortuitous humor arise either from erroneous translations of mumbled dictation or from conjectural interpretations of medical cryptography. Though blunders, they are welcome, since they often imply wildly improbable definitions. I have called them "serendipitous neologisms" (SN) because of their unpremeditated origin.

Notations

Over a two year period, I screened all my professional correspondence for errors, including letters, x-ray reports, medical records, and similar papers. Among several thousand misinterpretations encountered, a handful met the following criteria for SN:

1) The error *did not* result in a well-recognized word or phrase with an established meaning or connotation.

2) The error *did* result in the formation of a word or phrase not previously a part of the language (American).

3) The new word or phrase suggested a meaning whose only value was humorous (sic).

Twenty-one discrete instances of SN are listed in Table 1.

Table 1.   Twenty-one SN

What Was Intended	What Was Written	Connotation
1. ulcerative colitis	all-sorts-of colitis	every bowel complaint possible
2. ultimate short stature	alternate short stature	every other patient is below the 3rd percentile
3. karyotype	carrier-type	mailman
4. chromosomal deletion	chromosomal delusion	inherited form of psychosis
5. consult	conslut	disreputable girl friend
6. double-blind study	double-lined study	insulated library
7. femoral vein	efemeral vein	one difficult to find
8. erythroblastosis fetalis	erythroblastosis vitalis	greasy kid stuff
9. phallic	fallic	sex-linked tendency to stumble
10. phospholipids	forceful lipids	the predominant fats
11. growth hormone	gross hormone	the one responsible for obesity
12. hirsute	hair suit	worn with a hair shirt
13. inborn error of metabolism	inborn era of metabolism	the current subspecialty fad
14. intersex	inner sex	mental masturbation
15. labia minora	lybia minor	prehistoric country in North Africa
16. myocardial infarct	myocardial infart	coronary air embolus
17. auto analyzer	otto analyzer	German psychiatrist
18. pregnanetriol	pregnant trial	pithy legal case
19. prepubertal	prepubital	sedative for children
20. siblings	siklings	unhealthy brothers and sisters
21. slightly ectatic ascending aorta	slightly ecstatic ascending aorta	a lukewarm affair of the heart

*Reprinted from Clinical Pediatrics, ©1972; 11(9):496–497; with permission from J.B. Lippincott/Harper & Row. Edited from the original.

"That's What You Dictated, Doctor!"*

DOROTHY REID

All the following gems are quotations from the dictation of staff physicians at Memorial Mission Hospital in Asheville, N.C., where I supervise the transcription unit. I don't intend this to be critical of our fine staff. It just shows how things sometimes come out no matter who happens to be doing the dictating.

The left leg became numb at times and she walked it off.

Patient has chest pain if she lies on her left side for over a year.

Father died in his 90s of female trouble in his prostate and kidneys.

Both the patient and the nurse herself reported passing flatus.

Skin: Somewhat pale but present.

On the second day the knee was better, and on the third day it had completely disappeared.

The pelvic examination will be done later on the floor.

Patient stated that if she would lie down, within two or three minutes something would come across her abdomen and knock her up.

By the time she was admitted to the hospital her rapid heart had stopped and she was feeling much better.

Patient has bilateral varicosities below the legs.

If he squeezes the back of his neck for 4 or 5 years it comes and goes.

Patient was seen in consultation by Dr. Blank who felt we should sit tight on the abdomen, and I agreed.

Speculum was inserted between the eyes.

Dr. Blank is watching his prostate.

Discharge status: Alive but without permission.

Coming from Detroit, Mich., this man has no children.

At the time of onset of pregnancy the mother was undergoing bronchoscopy.

She was treated with Mycostatin oral suppositories.

Healthy appearing decrepit 69 year old white female, mentally alert but forgetful.

When you pin him down, he has some slowing of the stream.

*Reprinted with permission from Medical Economics, ©1973; 50(Oct 15):143; Medical Economics Company, Inc., Oradell, N.J. 07649.

What If the Patients Billed Us?*

HOWARD J. BENNETT, M.D.

After many years in practice, I've become accustomed to a certain amount of give and take with patients. Compromising about which lab tests are necessary or when to seek a second opinion are part of day-to-day medical care. I've even mellowed in those situations when patients need to exercise some control in their lives—even if the research they quote comes from the Journal of Community Advice or from Grandparent's Quarterly.

But I never thought I'd see the day when I might have to compromise on the most fundamental aspect of the doctor-patient relationship—namely, who bills whom. Given the current climate of patients' attitudes toward health care (not to mention its practitioners), I can now imagine certain scenarios in which that, too, comes into question.

Case 1: Be Late, Be Billed

It's 1 p.m. on a Friday. Following a rough night on call, Dr. Donald Krauss has just worked through his fifth lunchtime this week. He's finishing up with his last patient when the child's mother hands him a bill for $165.

"This is my fee for Jacob's visit today," Mrs. Wright says.

"Pardon me?" asks a bewildered Dr. Krauss.

"It's a late fee. You know, for being late."

"But you never objected to my being late before," says Dr. Krauss.

"Well, no, but I was never a member of P.A.I.D. before."

"What's P.A.I.D.?"

"Patients Against Inconsiderate Doctors. It's a new consumer group."

"Catchy name," says Dr. Krauss.

"Our motto is 'A doctor's time is just like mine.'"

"I see," Dr. Krauss says. "So you're billing me for the 50 minutes I kept you cooped up in the waiting room."

"Exactly," Mrs. Wright says. "And, as you'll recall from that rather long social history I provided at Jacob's first visit, I work as a lobbyist for a prestigious firm downtown."

"I remember," Dr. Krauss says.

"My consulting fee is $200 an hour," Mrs. Wright adds.

Not bad, Dr. Krauss thinks to himself, wondering if it is too late in life for a career change. If not as a lobbyist, then perhaps as a professional patient. "Will a check suffice?" he asks.

"That will be fine," Mrs. Wright says. "Just remember to put your Social Security number on the back."

Case 2: The Costly Pinworm

It's 8 a.m. on a dreary Thursday, and Dr. Evan Cameron has just finished his morning telephone hour. He leans back to relax with his second cup of coffee when the phone rings.

"This is Dr. Cameron."

"Yes, this is Roberta Barnes. I'm Chester Barnes' mother."

"Hello, Mrs. Barnes, how can I help you?"

"I wanted to talk to you about Chester's last visit. If you check his chart, you'll notice that we were in about a month ago."

"Well, ummm, I don't actually have his chart in front of me at the moment."

"Oh, that's okay. I realize that you're busy, and I want to let you know that I didn't mind having to wait an hour to see you last month."

"Thank you for being so understanding, Mrs. Barnes."

*Reprinted with permission from Medical Economics, ©1990; 67(July 9):83–87. Copyright by Medical Economics Company, Inc., Oradell, N.J. 07649.

"After all, Chester is a resourceful child. He busied himself with your toys, while I spent the time writing a letter to my ex-husband."

"It's always good to keep busy."

"Dr. Cameron, have you ever seen what some children actually do with the toys they find in your waiting room?"

"I try not to."

"Well, about three days after the visit, Chester came down with a terrible case of pinworms. And I am certain that he picked up the infection at your office."

"I see," says Dr. Cameron. "Is he still having trouble?"

"No, he's okay now. But the night he got sick was awful. He began scratching at 3 a.m. and had the whole house up by 4."

"I'm sorry to hear that."

"I knew you would be, Dr. Cameron, since you've always been a sensitive doctor."

"Thank you, Mrs. Barnes. I try my best."

"I want you to know that I have discussed this issue extensively with Chester's therapist. Although she reassured me that pinworms will not cause an anal personality disorder, I've come to the conclusion that the only way we can put this episode behind us is to have you pay the emergency room fee. Including X-rays, the bill came to $287. I will be glad to do my share and pick up the cost of the medication."

A loud thud is heard from the upper end of Mrs. Barnes' receiver.

"Hello? Dr. Cameron? Are you there?"

Case 3: Paying for Pox

It's 5 p.m. on a Friday, and Dr. Agnes Ryan is getting ready to leave for a well-deserved vacation. After she finishes with her last patient, she stops to read the mail before heading out to meet her husband. The first thing she picks up is a registered letter that her receptionist signed for earlier in the day.

Dear Dr. Ryan:

This is to inform you that your patient, Emily Stone, returned to nursery school before all of her 463 chicken pox lesions had completely crusted over. Based on interviews with the girl's parents, it is apparent that this breach in the school's health policy was a direct result of improper patient education on your part.

The consequences of this omission can hardly be overstated: Every child in our school and three staff members (one of whom was about to get married) came down with chicken pox over the past six weeks.

Enclosed you will find an itemized bill for all of the physician, lab, and hospital fees that accrued as a result of this epidemic. Also included is the cost of cleaning calamine lotion out of the school's two Oriental rugs, and the cost of replacing our pet hamsters (Ying and Yang) who died mysteriously during this time. The total bill comes to $28,417.

We accept all major credit cards.
Sincerely,
Bernice Johnson, Director
The Get Ahead Nursery School

Of course, it is doubtful that any of these cases would *really* take place. But if they did, would we be ready to rise to the challenge?

Would existing malpractice insurance pay these new costs? Or would we need a new breed of coverage? In addition to Blue Cross insurance for patients, would there be Double Cross coverage for doctors? And would competition among carriers lead to the development of prepaid patient payment organizations (PPPOs)?

I can hardly wait to find out.

Additional Readings

1. Armour, Richard: It All Started with Hippocrates.* New York, McGraw-Hill, 1966.

The author takes you on a hilarious romp through the history of medicine, from the Stone Age to the present (the present being 1966 of course). The book is an expansion of the article Dr. Armour has in this chapter.

2. Cranefield PF: Diagnosis and treatment of book collecting. JAMA 1964; 188(3):274–275.

This article pokes fun at book collecting by discussing it as though it is a disease. For example, although the history and physical exam are usually nonspecific, an elevated CBC (complete book count) and RBC (rare book count) make the diagnosis highly probable.

3. Escobar GJ: The genius of Friedrich Siegenthaler, M.D. Perspect Biol Med 1985; 29(autumn):37–40.

This article contends that Dr. Siegenthaler is the real author of the works attributed to William Shakespeare. Dr. Escobar proves his point with some compelling analytic skills: "Macbeth, an allegory describing a chief resident's meteoric rise to the top, is replete with overt and symbolic references to the surgical world."

4. Gaño SN: Computers and a paradox for librarians. Bull Med Libr Assoc 1963; 51(4):499–500.

An essay satirizing the arrival of computers in the medical library. The main problem are the doctors who, according to the author, "Read less and less, but write more and more."

5. Newman TB, Browner WS: The epidemiology of life and death: a critical commentary. Am J Public Health 1988; 78(2):161–162.

Using a style that satirizes epidemiologic writing, the authors present their analysis on the State of the Art in life and death research. For example, death is defined as ". . . the ultimate state of the final common pathway that emerges subsequent to a terminal morbid event culminating in the eventual biocessation of animate bioprocesses."

6. Reyes MG, Teramura K: Ultrastructural study of the faces of diseases. Mt Sinai J Med (NY) 1984; 51(6):714–715.

Some interesting faces were found in the electron-micrographs of biopsy specimens.

7. Slay RD: The exploding toilet and other emergency room folklore. J Emer Med 1986; 4(5):411–414.

The exploding toilet is one of many patient related stories that get told and retold in emergency rooms across the country. The author presents a few of these improbable case histories and discusses why they are so intriguing to emergency room personnel.

8. Terry JS: A proposal for new careers in health care. Perspect Biol Med 1984; 28(autumn):35–39.

A satire which creates job descriptions for roles already operational (informally, that is) in many health care settings. Some examples are "Turf Monitor," "Nihilism Therapist," and "Liaison Jargonist and Director of Initials Management."

---

*This book is no longer in print, but should be available through interlibrary loan.

APPENDIX

Additional Journals of Interest

The Journal of Irreproducible Results (JIR): First published in 1955, JIR is the "Official Organ of the Society for Basic Irreproducible Research." It is published six times a year and features humor and satire from many disciplines: physics, mathematics, astronomy, medicine, education, and others. Blackwell Scientific Publications, Inc., Three Cambridge Center, Suite 208, Cambridge, MA 02142 (617)225-0401.

Examples of medical articles include the following:

1. Eastern J, Drucker L, et al: The inheritance pattern of death. JIR 1982; 28(1):22–23.

While attempting to stay awake during a boring departmental meeting, the authors accidently discovered "a classic Mendelian autosomal recessive pattern for the phenotype of death." The implications of this finding are discussed, including their recommendation to avoid marrying someone who has already shown evidence for expression of the gene.

2. Laerum OD: Rare diseases. JIR 1972; 19(3):61–63.

The author begins his article by reminding us that rare diseases are uncommon in medical practice. He then goes on to categorize them according to their various subgroups. For example, "Diseases which have not yet occurred, but will be discovered some time in the future—sooner or later," and "Diseases which have not yet occurred and will never occur in the future either." It is not necessary for the clinician to know anything about this latter group.

Note: For more information about JIR as well as some other humorous publications in the scientific literature, see the following reference: Garfield E: Humor in scientific journals and journals of scientific humor. Curr Contents 1976; (Dec 20):5–11.

The Journal of Polymorphous Perversity (JPP): First published in 1984, JPP features humor and satire in the fields of psychology, psychiatry, social sciences, education, and related disciplines. It is published twice a year. Wry-Bred Press, Inc. P.O. Box 1454, Madison Square Station, New York, N.Y. 10159 (212) 689-5473.

Examples of articles with broad interest include the following:

1. Smoller JW: The etiology and treatment of childhood. JPP 1985; 2(2):3–7.

The author describes the causes of this highly prevalent disorder and its clinical features (congenital onset, emotional lability, legume anorexia, etc.). Despite widespread treatment facilities (public schools) and its 95% remission rate, childhood remains one of the most costly disorders facing health care professionals today.

2. Polloway EA: The influence of tenure on the productivity of faculty in higher education. JPP 1986; 3(2):7.

This article is similar to one I heard about on writer's block a few years ago: It's a blank page!

Humor (International Journal of Humor Research): First published in 1988, this journal presents a forum for serious research on humor as an important human faculty. It is published four times a year and features articles from many disciplines: anthropology, history, linguistics, literature, medicine, philosophy, psychology, and others. Walter de Gruyter, Inc., 200 Saw Mill River Road, Hawthorne, N.Y. 10532 (914)747-0110.

Examples of some of the articles that have appeared in **Humor** include the following:

1. Fry WF, Savin WM: Mirthful laughter and blood pressure. Humor 1988; 1(1):49–62.

2. Mundorf N, Bhatia A, et al: Gender differences in humor appreciation. Humor 1988; 1(3)231–243.

3. Ziv A: Humor's role in married life. Humor 1988; 1(3):223–229.

Additional Books of Interest

1. Ellenbogen, Glenn C (ed): The Directory of Humor Magazines & Humor Organizations in America (and Canada). New York, Wry-Bred Press, 1989.

This reference book provides information on humor magazines and organizations, including those that study humor as well as publish it. The book is broad in scope and contains material on both trade and professional organizations. The publications are cross referenced under 43 subject headings, including medicine, nursing, psychiatry, psychology, and the social sciences.

2. Fishbein, Morris: Tonics & Sedatives.* Philadelphia, J.B. Lippincott, 1949.

A collection of anecdotes, jokes, poems, and other humorous items from *JAMA*'s Tonics & Sedatives column, selected by one of the journal's former editors.

3. Garden, Graeme: The Best Medicine. New York, St. Martin's Press, 1984.

A collection of jokes, cartoons, anecdotes, and amusing stories.

4. Hawkins, Clifford (ed): Alimentary, My Dear Doctor: Medical Anecdotes and Humour. Oxford, Radcliffe Medical Press, 1988.

This is an amusing collection of short and long anecdotes that has an interesting story behind it. The collection is the result of a competition on humor sponsored by the publisher. All of the contributors are members of The General Practitioners Writers Association (GPWA) which is based in Great Britain. As the title suggests, each of the pieces lands on some niche within the GI tract. For example, "The general practitioner's association with the bowels begins with the digestion of large amounts of information at medical school. Quite often the intellectual nutrition is in a high fibre form; much of it is unabsorbed and goes straight through."

Note: At the time my anthology went to press, there was no American distributor for this book. The address for the publisher is 15 Kings Meadow, Ferry Hinksey Road, Oxford OX2 0DP, England. For more information about the GPWA, write to 102A High Street, Henly-in-Arden, West Midlands B95 5BY, England.

5. Mould, Richard F: Mould's Medical Anecdotes. Bristol, England, Adam Hilger; Philadelphia, Taylor & Francis, 1984.

The items collected in this book range from brief notations to short articles. Although some of the material is funny, most of it can be described as amusing curiosities of medicine. For example, "Head Shrinking," "Foreign Bodies," and "Internal Combustion," to name a few.

6. Ricks, Anne E: The Official M.D. Handbook. New York, New American Library, 1983.

A ribald look at medicine that begins with getting into medical school, winds its way through internship and residency, and ends up with a chapter on "Doctorspeak." Along the way, the book also lampoons specialists, all types of medical practice, and much more.

7. Scherr, George H (ed): Selected Papers from the Journal of Irreproducible Results, 3rd ed. Cambridge, MA, Blackwell Scientific Publications, 1986.

This is the third collection of the best articles from JIR.

8. Thomas, George and Schreiner, Lee: That's Incurable: The Doctor's Guide to Common Complaints, Rare Diseases, and The Meaning of Life.* New York, Penguin Books, 1984.

This is one of the funniest medical books to ever hit the stands. The authors counsel the reader on everything from "Ten Diseases You Were Better Off Not Knowing About" to "How to Get into the Hospital." (For a small taste of what the book is like, see the excerpt, "A Hypochondriac's Handbook" which was published in Esquire, March 1984, pp 81–88.)

---

*These books are no longer in print, but should be available through interlibrary loan.

Selected References on Humor & Medicine

Humor & The Physician

1. Aring CD: A sense of humor. JAMA 1971; 215(13):2099.

2. Blair W: What's funny about doctors. Perspect Biol Med 1977; 21(autumn):89–98.

3. Coser RL: Laughter among colleagues: a study of the social functions of humor among the staff of a mental hospital. Psychiatry 1960; 23(1):81–95.

4. Cushner FD, Friedman RJ: Humor and the physician. South Med J 1989; 82(1):51–52.

5. Editorial: The "sense" of humor—art and science. JAMA 1970; 212(10):1697–1698.

6. Elliot-Binns CP: Laughter and medicine. J Royal Coll Gen Pract 1985; 35(8):364–365.

7. Felson B: Humor and medicine. Semin Roentgen 1987; 22(3):141–143.

8. Jarcho S: Some hoaxes in the medical literature. Bull Hist Med 1959; 33(4):342–347.

Note: Dr. Jarcho also wrote under the pseudonym, S. N. Gaño. He has an article in the chapter "Odds & Ends" and a couple of "Additional Readings" in the book.

9. Liechty RD. Humor and the surgeon. Arch Surg 1987; 122(5):519–522.

10. Lindsey D, Benjamin J: Humor in the emergency room. In Mindess H, and Turek J (eds): The Study of Humor.* Los Angeles, Antioch College, 1979, pp 73–76.

11. Mandell HN: Frivolity in medicine: Is there a place for it? Postgrad Med 1988; 83(8):24–28.

12. Rakel RE: Humor and humanism. Houston Med 1989; 5(1):7–9.

13. Reece RL: Humor in scientific medical writing. Minn Med 1968; 51(4):563–566.

14. Roland CG: Thoughts about medical writing: can it be funny and medical? Anesth Analg 1971; 50(2):229–230.

15. Scarlett EP: Some hoaxes in medical history and literature. Arch Int Med 1964; 113(2):291–296.

16. Segal D: Playing doctor seriously: graduation follies at an American medical school. Int J Health Serv 1984; 14(3):379–396.

17. Stevens H: Humor plus humility equals humaneness. JAMA 1964: 190(13):88–91.

18. Thomas P: The anatomy of coping: medicine's funny bone. Med World News 1986; 27(13):42–66.

Note: See p. 112 for additional references of interest on William Osler's sense of humor.

Humor & Health

1. Black DW: Laughter. JAMA 1984; 252(21):2995–2998.

2. Blumenfeld, Ester and Alpern, Lynne: The Smile Connection: How to Use Humor in Dealing with People.* Englewood Cliffs, N.J., Prentice-Hall, 1986.

3. Carlyon W, Carlyon P: Humor as a health education tool. In Lazes PM, Kaplan LH, and Gordon KA (eds): The Handbook of Health Education. Rockville, MD, Aspen, 1987, pp 111–121.

4. Coser RL: Some social functions of laughter: a study of humor in a hospital setting. Human Relations 1959; 12(2):171–182.

5. Cousins N: Anatomy of An Illness (As Perceived by the Patient). New York, W.W. Norton, 1979.

6. Davis MS: Variations in patients' compliance with doctors' advice: an empirical analysis of patterns of communication. Am J Public Health 1968; 58(2):274–288.

7. Dillon KM, Minchoff B: Positive emotional states and enhancement of the immune system. Int J Psych Med 1985–86; 15(1):13–17.

8. Fry WF: Humor, physiology, and the aging process. In Nahemow L, and McClusky-Fawcett KA (eds): Humor and Aging. Orlando, FL, Academic Press, 1986, pp 81–98.

9. Klein, Allen: The Healing Power of Humor. Los Angeles, Jeremy P. Tarcher, Inc., 1989.

10. Lefcourt, Herbert M, and Martin, Rod A: Humor and Life Stress: Antidote to Adversity. New York, Springer-Verlag, 1986.

11. Leiber DB: Laughter and humor in critical care. Dimens Crit Care Nurs 1986; 5(3):162–170.

12. Ljungdahl L: Laugh if this is a joke. JAMA 1989; 261(4):558.

13. Martin RA, Dobbin JP: Sense of humor, hassles, and immunoglobulin A: evidence for a stress-moderating effect of humor. Int J Psych Med 1988; 18(2):93–105.

14. Moody, Raymond A: Laugh After Laugh: The Healing Power of Humor,* Jacksonville, FL, Headwaters Press, 1978.

15. Nezu AM, Nezu CM, et al: Sense of humor as a moderator of the relation between stressful events and psychological distress: a prospective analysis. J Pers Soc Psychol 1988; 54(3):520–525.

16. Powell BS: Laughter and healing: the use of humor in hospitals treating children. J Assoc Care Child Hosp 1974:; 3(2):10–16.

17. Robinson VM: Humor is serious business. Dimens Crit Care Nurs 1986; 5(3):132–133.

18. Robinson, Vera M: Humor and the Health Professions. Thorofare, NJ, Charles B. Slack Co., 1977. (*Note:* Second edition is currently in press.)

19. Robinson VM: Humor and health. In McGhee, PE and Goldstein JH (eds): Handbook of Humor Research, Vol 2. New York, Springer-Verlag, 1983, pp 109–128.

20. Rodning CB: Humor and healing: a creative process. Pharos 1988; 51(3):38–40.

21. Silberman IN: Humor and health: an epidemiological study. Amer Behav Scientist 1987; 30(3):100–112.

22. Williams H: Humor and healing: therapeutic effects in geriatrics. Gerontion 1986; 1(3):14–17.

*These books are no longer in print, but should be available through interlibrary loan.